GRAVE CONCERNS

THE FOLLIES AND FOLKLORE OF ROBIN HOOD'S FINAL RESTING PLACE

KAI ROBERTS

Edited by Corinna Downes
Typeset by Jonathan Downes,
Cover and Layout by Le chat d'orange for CFZ Communications
Using Microsoft Word 2000, Microsoft , Publisher 2000, Adobe Photoshop CS.

First published in Great Britain by CFZ Press

CFZ Press
Myrtle Cottage
Woolsery
Bideford
North Devon
EX39 5QR

ISBN: 978-1-905723-83-6

CONTENTS

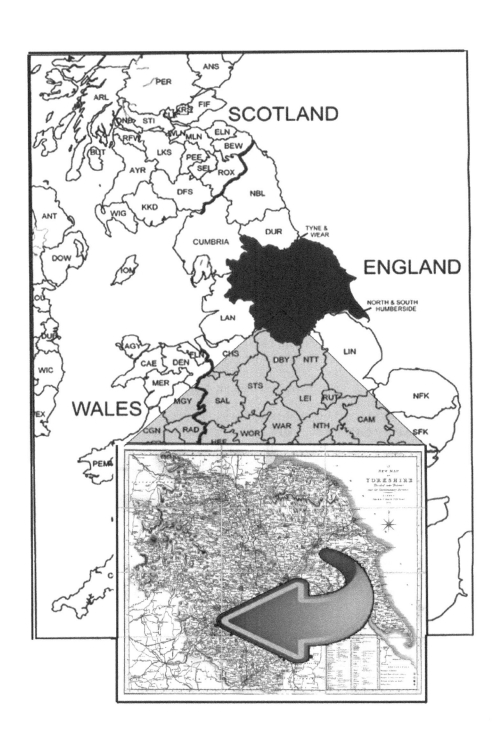

INTRODUCTION

In the modern era, the narrative of Robin Hood's death is increasingly one of the least familiar aspects of the outlaw's legend. Whilst the icon of Robin himself still shines brightly in the psyche of this nation and many others, his story has always been adapted to reflect the dominant concerns and modes of transmission of the era. Today, the legend is primarily communicated through film and television, and with the escalating mania for durable franchises, few production companies are interested in portraying the death of such a bankable hero. Only one film – 1976's *Robin and Marian* – has ever tackled this aspect of the legend, but despite Sean Connery and Audrey Hepburn in the title roles, it remains the only Robin Hood film to have made a loss at the box office.

To an extent, this has always been the case. Whilst at least one noted authority on the legend has opined that the death narrative is "one of the most celebrated episodes in the entire Robin Hood saga," it was never the most popular story amongst the historical readership. Few original sources for the story survive and those that do are fragmentary or truncated, suggesting that they never circulated very widely. After all, the public appetite for tragedy has never been as pronounced as its taste for the picaresque.

Despite this public indifference, the death narrative remains a distinctive and powerful instalment in the Robin Hood myth cycle that deserves further attention. Not only is the tale unique in the outlaw's history, it is unique in the annals of medieval literature. It is a compelling story in its own right, featuring betrayal, brutality, tragedy and in the best-known variant, one of the most iconic and Romantic images in the canon. It has also left its mark on the landscape as few other aspects of the legend have done.

The story of Robin Hood's death, as it has been most commonly told since the legend was standardised in the 19th Century, opens with the outlaw life taking its toll on our hero. After decades living a harsh existence in the greenwood, with countless skirmishes both won and lost, he succumbs to a debilitating fever. In order to recover, he announces to his band of followers that he will repair to the nunnery at Kirklees to be healed, for in the medieval period medicine was concentrated in the hands of monastic communities.

His companions protest, arguing that it is too dangerous. But whilst Robin has always been an enemy of the corrupt Church, the Prioress at Kirklees was his kin – some say an aunt, some say a cousin – and he believed she could be trusted to take good care of him. Nonetheless, Will Scarlett sounds a further note of caution, reminding Robin that Sir Roger of Doncaster, also known as Red Roger, lives in the vicinity of Kirklees and has always been an enemy of the outlaw. Scarlett begs his leader to allow several men to accompany him on the journey, but Robin refuses, saying that he will only take his most faithful companion, Little John.

Upon their arrival at Kirklees Priory, Robin instructs John to take his leave and wait nearby, reassuring the loyal giant that he could be summoned with a horn should there be any danger. Robin proceeds to the gatehouse of the Priory alone and is greeted by his relation, the Prioress. He explains to her that he is in dire need of medical attention and offers a sum of money to the nunnery for their trouble. The Prioress consents and, as men may not enter the hallowed precincts of a nunnery, she takes him to a private room on the upper floor of the gatehouse, and seemingly proceeds to minister to his needs.

The treatment for maladies in the Middle Ages, when ignorance and superstition still reigned, was invariably a process of blood-letting, which was imagined to restore the balance of the bodily humors. To this end, the Prioress opens a vein in Robin's arm as he lies on the bed in that upper chamber, allowing his blood to drain into a cup beside him. As she does so, she tries to persuade Robin to repent his many sins and seek an official pardon, but he refuses. She then advises him that she must leave him for a while to attend to her other duties whilst the procedure takes effect and exits the room, surreptitiously locking the door behind her.

The Prioress leaves Robin to bleed for the length of the day. As the outlaw sees his blood growing ever thinner and feels his remaining strength ebbing away, he realises that treachery is afoot! Yet he lacks the strength to break down the door or make his escape through the narrow casement window, and eventually the Prioress returns, accompanied by Sir Roger of Doncaster. The Prioress is revealed as Sir Roger's lover and she has plotted to leave Robin at his mercy for the many wrongs the outlaw had done the Church over the years.

Sir Roger sets upon his intended victim but the conspirators have miscalculated, for even in his weakened state, Robin is the more skilful in combat and slays his adversary with a well-placed knife to the throat. Seeing the failure of her plan, the Prioress retreats (in some versions, she goes on to commit suicide), leaving Robin to expire from his blood loss. Summoning the last of his might, Robin blows a blast on his horn to call Little John, who upon hearing the sound races to the Priory, leaving broken doors in his wake.

Seeing the condition of his master, John is consumed by anger and grief. He begs Robin to permit him to burn the nunnery to the ground, but Robin refuses, saying that he has never harmed a woman in his life and nor will he allow such a thing to happen in death. He merely asks that his friend take his hand and hear his last confession, as he will not go to his grave unshriven. Finally, Robin takes up his bow and with Little John's assistance, fires an arrow through the gatehouse window with instructions that he should be buried where it falls.

The first arrow lands in the Priory precinct; the second in a nearby stream. The third, however, settles on a hillside around half a mile away and with this accomplished, Robin draws his final breath. Following his master's command, Little John carries Robin's body to the place where that last arrow came to ground and buries him there, with his bow by his side and his sword at his head. The spot is marked with a great stone and lying as it does overlooking the highway, it becomes a familiar site for travellers passing the fateful Priory of Kirklees.

This narrative has been stitched together from several different sources and even varies between more recent re-tellings. However, one element remains consistent in each version and that is the setting of Kirklees Priory. It is all too commonly assumed that as Robin Hood is a legendary hero in the vein of King Arthur or Finn MacCooill*, there must be numerous sites that claim to be his final resting place. Yet this is not the case. Although there are a few forgotten toponyms scattered here and there which suggest alternative locations, Kirklees is the only place that has been repeatedly associated with the outlaw's grave, in terms of both documentary sources and material remains, over several hundred years.

Not only that, but Kirklees Priory actually existed and is one of the very few specifically identifiable places in the earliest surviving ballads of Robin Hood. The only other example is Wentbridge, a small town near Pontefract, barely twenty miles from Kirklees. Both identifications support the hypothesis that the legend of Robin Hood originated in an obscure tract of the West Riding of Yorkshire known as Barnsdale, only spreading to encompass Nottingham and Sherwood in later centuries.

Kirklees itself refers to a shallow valley on the eastern fringe of the South Pennines, today surrounded by old mill towns such as Brighouse, Huddersfield and Dewsbury. Although in 1974 Kirklees Metropolitan Borough Council adopted the name, the valley itself does not lie within their boundaries and falls instead under the jurisdiction of Calderdale. For the purposes of this book 'Kirklees' will be used to refer solely to the valley in which Kirklees Priory once stood, and not the metropolitan borough of the same name, unless otherwise stated.

Like all other monastic houses, Kirklees Priory was abandoned in the 16th Century at the Dissolution of the Monasteries and very little evidence of its presence survives. Nonetheless, the legend of Robin Hood's death has embedded itself in the topography of Kirklees. Anybody who studies a map of the area will notice a site labelled 'Robin Hood's Grave', written in the Gothic script used to denote antiquities. Meanwhile, those fortunate enough to be permitted to visit Kirklees may be shown a room on the upper floor of a late medieval building referred to as the gatehouse of the old Priory, and told that it is the chamber from which the legendary outlaw shot his final arrow and then died. They may even be shown Robin Hood's grave itself and perhaps they will be disappointed to find the crumbling 18th Century folly overgrown and neglected in the woods nearby.

For whilst the existence of Robin Hood's grave is scarcely a secret, appearing on the definitive map of the area and referred to in countless non-fiction sources concerned with the legend of

---

* Fionn mac Cumhaill known in English as Finn McCool, was a mythical hunter-warrior of Irish mythology, occurring also in the mythologies of Scotland and the Isle of Man. The stories of Fionn and his followers the Fianna, form the Fenian Cycle (or Fiannaidheacht), much of it purported to be narrated by Fionn's son, the poet Oisin.

Robin Hood, for the last fifty years it has been regarded as nothing but an annoyance by its custodians. It lies on private land without any right of access and visitors are categorically discouraged. Whilst this situation has improved over the last decade, opportunities for anybody wishing to glimpse the burial site of this legendary hero remain few and far between. For Robin's modern followers, it has become an immensely contentious issue.

A relatively short time after the dissolution of Kirklees Priory, the land on which it stood was purchased by a local merchant family called the Armytages and it has remained in their possession ever since. As the family climbed the social ladder, eventually securing a baronetcy for themselves, they proceeded to turn Kirklees into a gentrified country estate befitting their new status. They built a grand hall and landscaped the surrounding valley, creating an Arcadian parkland with Robin Hood's grave as its centrepiece.

Whilst they were never exactly friends of the people, for many centuries the Armytages were content to exploit their connection with Robin Hood, maintaining the grave and permitting visitors freely. But during the mid-20th Century things changed. As the fortunes of the gentry class waned and the family were forced to turn their rolling parklands into a modern agricultural business, they were increasingly unconcerned with the fate of Robin Hood's monument. It was left to moulder amongst dense vegetation and Kirklees grew ever more isolated, prompting some writers to refer to its "insularity" and "mystery". Thousands of people passing by on the M62 motorway daily would never suspect its existence and even locals began to forget about the place.

One local woman, however, was determined that this should not be the case, and in 1985 Barbara Green founded the Yorkshire Robin Hood Society to promote the grave and protect it from decay. Initially, the Society was just a group of local enthusiasts intent on reminding the world of Robin's Yorkshire connections. But after several years of being stonewalled by Lady Margarete Armytage[*] and encountering nothing but indifference on the part of institutions from Calderdale Council to English Heritage, their aims became more militant.

With the advent of mass trespasses and a sustained campaign through the local press, the situation degenerated into a vitriolic war of words between the opposing parties that has endured to this day. Confronted by the refusal of local authorities to acknowledge the potential of the tourist site in their midst and the failure of a number of promotional projects, the Yorkshire Robin Hood Society began to talk of a conspiracy to suppress knowledge of the grave's location at Kirklees, either to appease the Nottingham tourist industry or protect Lady Armytage's interests. There was even talk of MI5 involvement.

During the same period, even stranger ideas began to circulate. As if the tragic death of Robin

---

[*] In April 2008 Séan Manchester wrote: "Maria Margarete, Lady Armytage, who died 4 April, 2008, aged 81, was the second wife and widow of Captain Sir John Lionel Armytage, 8th Baronet, of Kirklees Park, Brighouse, West Yorkshire. She was born *circa* 1926, the former Maria Margarete Tenhaeff, daughter of Paul Hugo Tenhaeff, of Bruenen, Niederhein, and married Sir John (whose GB Baronetcy was created in 1738) in 1949. He died in 1983. She leaves a daughter and a step-son, Sir (John) Martin Armytage, 9th Baronet".

Hood was not legend enough, there was now a rumour of a malevolent supernatural presence lurking in the woods near the gravesite. This manifestation was variously described as "a wraith with red eyes, staring and horrible", "a woman... her eyes... dark, mad, set in her pale face" and "like a bat... her black nun's robes flapping eerily while her eyes flashed red and venomous... her teeth bared sharp and white between snarling blood red lips". Soon it was an integral part of a contemporary legend, involving ley lines and occult groups seeking to exploit Robin Hood's grave for their own nefarious purposes.

The supernatural phenomenon was dubbed the 'Kirklees Vampire' and through this apparition Robin Hood's grave found itself embroiled in a bizarre and interminable dispute, which had started with a similar supernatural flap in north London in 1970, widely remembered as the 'Highgate Vampire' affair. Swiftly, Kirklees became a new symbolic battleground for Bishop Séan Manchester and David Farrant, who - in the opinion of many researchers including this author - have been arguing over who is best qualified to investigate the paranormal and occult ever since the twenty-four year old Farrant claimed to have witnessed a ghostly figure in Highgate Cemetery, all those years ago.

It is fair to say that today Robin Hood's grave is known for the acrimonious disputes in which it has become involved almost as much as it is known for the legend of the outlaw's death. However, very few attempts have been made to assess the many controversies connected to Kirklees objectively. Too much information is only available from partisan sources who have tailored facts to fit their own narratives. These have then been repeated uncritically by other writers, leading to a situation in which fallacies are continually stated as truths, thus perpetuating the confusion.

Of course, some might wonder why these issues need to be examined at all. One of the most common responses to mention of Robin Hood's grave is "But he didn't really exist, of course". There are many who take this attitude, including some academics and even the custodians of the grave itself, who have used it to deny public admittance over the years. To these people, the monument at Kirklees can be nothing more than an artificial folly, unworthy of further study. Equally, however, the grave has been cited by many commentators as material proof of the outlaw's historical existence, who firmly believe it should be accessible to those wishing to pay their respects.

Yet this debate misses the point. To obsess over the existence of Robin Hood is not only a failure to comprehend the wider importance of the legend, it represents a profoundly narrow understanding of the study of history, focusing on biographical detail to the exclusion of the way ideas have developed and endured over the ages. Consequently, this book will examine the evolution of the legend of Robin's death and the gravesite itself, without feeling the need to reach a conclusion regarding its origins. In the absence of further evidence, any such conclusion would be little more than an act of faith. But, even if the grave's genesis remains shrouded in mists of time, it has a history as venerable as many of the original Robin Hood ballads.

The subject of this book is a location rather than an individual. Countless volumes have been written on the topic of Robin Hood by some of the finest scholars of medieval history and literature in Britain and this tome does not seek to rival them. Arguments pertaining to the historical reality or otherwise of the outlaw will be discussed here only where they directly concern his grave. With regard to Robin Hood, the question for this book is not whether he is really buried at Kirklees but, for want of definitive proof either way, how that tradition became so firmly attached to the site. Hopefully, it will illustrate that Robin Hood's grave is a site of historical interest quite irrespective of its 'authenticity'.

For Kirklees certainly seems to attract strong beliefs, and in many cases changing perceptions of the site itself have coloured the content of those beliefs. Studying Kirklees and the various legends to have grown up around it allows us an insight into the reciprocal relationship between people and place. Of particular interest is the extent to which the state of Robin Hood's grave in the modern era and all the associated disputes have determined the interpretation of the paranormal phenomena witnessed in the vicinity of the site today. In this regard, it is a study in modern myth-making.

Moreover, this book comes at an opportune moment. Following the death of Lady Margarete Armytage in 2008, the future of Kirklees is uncertain and there is much local rumour that it is to be sold off. As the land has been in the hands of the Armytage family for over four hundred years this would undoubtedly represent the start of a new chapter in its history. Perhaps it will fall into the possession of an owner more amenable to making Robin Hood's grave accessible to the public, or perhaps it will precipitate a whole new campaign for the monument's preservation. Either way, this is an ideal juncture to remind ourselves just why the site is important, because whatever the future of Kirklees may be, it will always be haunted by the ghosts of its past.

CHAPTER ONE
Murder ballads

The earliest association between Robin Hood's death and Kirklees Priory is found in the original literary sources, although whether it had always been part of the legend remains uncertain. By the late 15ᵗʰ Century, the legendary outlaw was a familiar figure in ballads, plays and poetry, and whilst the earliest surviving manuscript (a copy of the ballad *Robin Hood and the Monk*) dates from circa 1450 [1], there is good reason to believe that by this point the myth had already been established for almost two centuries.

The earliest textual reference to Robin Hood is found in William Langland's famous allegorical poem, *William's Vision of Piers Plowman*, written sometime around 1377 [2], in which a figure representing Sloth is made to remark "I do not know my paternoster perfectly as the priest sings it / But I know the rhymes of Robin Hood".

For many years, this was considered to be the first concrete mention of the character and his legend. However, more recently David Crook and J.C. Holt have suggested that the name was well-known as early as the 1260s, in support of which he points to strong evidence that the appellation 'Robinhood' was used as a generic term for outlaws at this time [3]. As the example he cites comes from Berkshire [4], this suggests that the narrative had already seen plenty of opportunity to spread across the country from its birthplace in Barnsdale or Sherwood.

Bearing this in mind, it is possible that many of the literary sources could be substantially older than their first recorded instances. Certainly the ballads were probably sung by minstrels for many generations before they were ever written down [5]. With over two hundred years between the inception of the myth and the oldest surviving documents, the legend would have had considerable time to develop. As such, if there ever was a historical figure upon whose exploits the Robin Hood stories were based, it is now impossible to say which facets of the tales are authentic, and which are the product of subsequent romantic embellishment in the late Middle Ages.

With regard to the narrative of Robin's death, its very earliest mention as part of the legend occurs in the 1440s, in Walter Bower's renowned Scottish history, *Scotichronicon*, which briefly refers to "Robert Hood… whom the foolish populace are so inordinately fond of celebrating both in tragedy and comedy". This, of course, is only a passing allusion, but it is thought that the 'tragedy' can only refer to the tale of the outlaw's death, for no other story in the original canon displays such a character [6].

However, there is certainly no mention of Kirklees Priory in these early accounts, for which it is necessary to turn to the ballads. The ballads were probably not the earliest or most popular Robin Hood traditions – oral tales, village plays and proverbs all may have preceded them [7] – but they represent the fullest narratives to have survived from the medieval period. The corpus of literary sources was settled by Joseph Ritson in his seminal but flawed attempt at a historical study, *Robin Hood: A Collection of All the Ancient Poems, Songs and Ballads Now Extant,* first published in 1795 and subsequently consolidated in 1888 by Francis Child, first Professor of English at Harvard University, in the third volume of *The English and Scottish Popular Ballads.*

Few people familiar with the legend, as it is told today, would recognise the milieu of the earliest ballads. Although they exhibit a distinctly anti-authoritarian bent, the targets of the outlaw's mischief are primarily the Sheriff and a corrupt Church. Beyond a few brief remarks to the effect that Robin was kind to the dispossessed, the classic theme of robbing from the rich to give to the poor is barely developed. Customary characters such as Maid Marian and Friar Tuck are conspicuous by their absence, whilst Robin himself is always portrayed as a yeoman, rather than a peasant or disenfranchised noble and there is certainly no suggestion that he was a Saxon freedom fighter waging some guerrilla campaign against Norman oppressors [8]. Nor is he presented as infallible or the *de facto* leader of the group [9].

Child collected thirty-seven ballads dealing with Robin Hood and the ordering reflects a rough chronology, suggesting that he considers *Robin Hood and the Monk, Robin Hood and Guy of Gisborne, Robin Hood's Death* and *Robin Hood and the Potter* to exhibit the greatest antiquity [10], compared to later examples that merely provide variations on earlier themes.

However, their placement was determined by textual analysis rather than the actual provenance of the manuscripts, meaning the early dating for *Robin Hood's Death* is purely conjectural. The earliest known manuscript of this ballad is no older than the mid-18th Century, so whilst it might provide the fullest elucidation of this aspect of the legend, and may indeed have been the inspiration for all subsequent retellings, it cannot be definitively regarded as a primary source.

For the earliest reliable treatment of the death narrative, it is necessary to turn to the work that Child placed at the head of his collection - a poem most commonly known as *A Gest of Robin Hood* (Appendix 1). This 15th Century composition provides the most comprehensive account of the outlaw's career – the title comes from the Latin *res gestae* meaning 'things done' – although from its format it is clear that many of the individual ballads pre-date it [11], even if their surviving manuscripts do not.

Dating the *Gest* itself remains less controversial but still uncertain. Five surviving prints of the poem exist from between the late-15th and mid-16th Centuries, and typically the earliest two are combined to generate a full text, with the later examples used to provide occasional corrections and embellishments [12]. Of the two primary versions, an edition published by the Antwerp press of Jan van Doesbroch between 1510 and 1515, titled simply *A Gest of Robyn Hode*, is considered the more reliable transcription, but sadly it is only fragmentary [13]. The second, titled *A Lyttel Geste of Robyn Hode* is complete but harder to date positively, although Wynken de Worde, who published it, is known to have operated between 1492 and 1534 [14].

It is believed, however, that a copy must have been circulating prior to any of these. All five versions repeat exactly the same misprints and so it is believed that each was derived from an earlier manuscript, which has since been lost [15]. By how much this antecedent predates the surviving prints is a matter of speculation. The persistence in the text of a number of Middle English linguistic conventions which had died out by the end of the 15th Century has led some scholars to suggest a date as early as 1400 [16]. But more conservative recent estimates prefer to settle on 1450, believing it improbable that the poem could've been in popular circulation for a full century before a copy survived [17].

With four-hundred-and-fifty-six four-line stanzas divided into eight cantos or 'fyttes', the *Gest* is clearly a project with a much broader scope than the ballads, most of which deal only with individual incidents and lack any sort of commentary on the action. It also differs from the ballads in its form. Although exhortations to an audience at various points in the text make it clear that it was meant to be performed, it was probably designed to be spoken rather than sung [18].

Nonetheless, it is obvious that the *Gest* was compiled from a melange of antecedent sources [19]. From narrative parallels, these must have included those aforementioned ballads that Child regarded as the most authentic, hence why he prioritised them in the ordering. Comparisons are often drawn to Sir Thomas Mallory's similar attempt in the 15th Century to unite the various strands of the Arthurian mythos in a single chronicle with *Le Morte d'Arthur,* although arguably the anonymous author of the *Gest* lacks Mallory's deft touch [20].

The *Gest* frequently betrays its patchwork origins with a highly episodic structure and persistent topographical anomalies, which suggest that it was compiled from two separate geographical traditions [21]. On occasion, the action shifts between Barnsdale and Sherwood without reason, and characters appear to cover the fifty miles between the two in a matter of hours.

Opinions differ on the literary merits of the *Gest*. Knight and Ohlgren praise the work for its diversity of style and mood, and its healthy use of irony, concluding that it:

> "combines and develops materials of high potency and complexity into a genetically new whole of great future impact, which manages to convey and even enhance the source material's innate values and power" [22].

However, some regard the author's attempts to link the various episodes as too clumsy and some of the narrative is undeniably truncated compared to other sources [23].

This is certainly true of its handling of Robin's death, which appears naturally enough at the end of the poem, in the eighth fytte, between stanzas 451 and 456. Such is the synoptic nature of this passage, some commentators have suggested it could only be meant for an audience already familiar with the tale from other sources, either the ballad *Robin Hood's Death,* or a common antecedent [24].

The *Gest* tells how following a reconciliation with the king, Robin remained for some time in his service before growing restless and returning to the greenwood. There he survived for a further twenty-two years until requiring medical attention, when he travelled to 'Kirkesly' (Kirklees) to receive the common medieval treatment of bloodletting from the Prioress, who was obscurely related to him. However, under the influence of her lover Sir Roger of Donkesly ('Doncaster'), she betrayed her kinsman, and together they engineered the outlaw's death.

This is all the *Gest* has to say on the matter and it is clear that several integral details of the narrative are missing from this account. No motive is provided for the actions of the Prioress and Sir Roger, nor is it clear exactly how they despatched Robin. Moreover, whilst the *Gest* provides the earliest conclusively datable association between Robin's death and Kirklees, it does not explicitly mention his burial there. Doubtless, this is tacitly assumed, but there is certainly no reference to the circumstances of the grave itself.

However, over the course of the 16th Century, several antiquarian and topographical reports mention a grave at Kirklees, suggesting that not long after those early surviving copies of the *Gest* were printed, and perhaps even before, the monument was widely understood to be located there [25]. These early descriptions of the grave will be discussed more fully in Chapter 3, but one particular example is relevant here on account of its wide availability in its day and apparent use by subsequent writers trying to construct a biographical narrative of the legendary outlaw.

It is found in *A Chronicle at Large,* a 1568 work by Richard Grafton, who held the position of King's Printer under Edward VI. He wrote:

> "Robert Hood, beying afterwardes troubled with sicknesse, came to a certain Nunry in Yorkshire called Bircklies, where desirying to be let blood he was betrayed & bled to death. After whose death the Prioress of the same place caused him to be buried by the high way side, where he had used to rob and spoyle those that passed that way" [26].

Today Grafton is not generally regarded as a reliable source [27]. However, his report possibly influenced some of the detail in the next appearance of the story of Robin's death in the literature. This handwritten 'life of Robin Hood' is otherwise known as the Sloane Manuscript due to its discovery amongst the papers of physician and collector Hans Sloane, donated for the foundation of the British Museum upon his death in 1753 [28].

The text is believed to have been written sometime during the late 16th Century, as its most significant innovation is placing the outlaw's birth at Loxley, thus clearly predating the 1598 plays of Anthony Munday [29]. These plays established Robin as the Earl of Huntington, a spurious background that remained in currency throughout the 17th and 18th Centuries. The Sloane Manuscript represents the earliest known prose version of the legend and whilst much of its material is clearly taken from the *Gest* [30], it adds several further elements to the description of his demise.

It relates:

> "Being distempered with could and he had great payne in his lymmes, his bloud being corrupted, therefore to be eased of his payne, he repayred to the Prioress of Kyrkesly, who some say was his aunt, a woman very skilful in physique and surgery; who, perceiving him to be Robin Hood, and waying how fel an enimy he was to religious persons, tok revenge on him for her owne house and all others by letting him bleed to death; and she buried him under a greate stone, by the hy wayes side. It is also sayd that, that one Sir Roger of Doncaster, bearing grudge to Robin for some injury, incited the prioress, with whom he was very familiar, in such manner to dispatch him, and then al his companie was soon dispersed." [31]

Whilst this again cites Kirklees as the scene of the action and is at pains to include Sir Roger of Doncaster, it expands on the *Gest* in several respects. The manuscript clearly states that the Prioress murders Robin through exsanguination during the bloodletting procedure and that she was motivated by the injury he had done to the Church. This is consistent with a theme in many of the early ballads, in which Robin's principal animosity is directed towards the greed of religious houses [32]. Additionally, his burial and grave at Kirklees are specifically mentioned.

It is worth noting that, in this first mention of a grave as part of a complete literary narrative, it is the Prioress who chooses the site. Such an account is at odds with subsequent versions, in which Robin chooses his own resting place, a more romantic notion which has quite understandably endured in the popular consciousness, whilst the version in the Sloane Manuscript has not.

The description of the great stone next to the highway is apparently derived from Grafton's *Chronicle at Large*, although it is possible that they both obtained their information from a common earlier source, since lost. Certainly, Grafton claims that his own account is taken from "an olde and auncient Pamphlet" and as he includes detail missing from the *Gest*, he must be referring to something else. He also cites this pamphlet as the origin of an assertion that Robin was originally of noble blood, a divergent tradition from his status as a yeoman in the early ballads [33].

This pedigree was taken up enthusiastically by Anthony Munday in his two plays of 1598, *The Downfall of Robin Hood* and *The Death of Robin Hood*, which portray Robin as the disinherited Earl of Huntington, driven to banditry by political intrigue. Munday was not the first to associate Robin with aristocracy – this suggestion is found as early as 1521 in John Major's *History of Greater Britain* [34] – but he was certainly the most influential, and this perspective on the tradition has endured into the present day.

A leading playwright of his age and occasional collaborator with William Shakespeare, Munday's work would certainly have been popular and it is not surprising that these two plays are the only stage adaptations of the legend to survive from this period. The writer was keen to depict the legend as a tragedy and because the conventions of Elizabethan drama held that only the gentry were acceptable as tragic heroes, it became necessary to present the outlaw as a nobleman [35].

The two works tell a single story, Munday having produced too much material for just one play. As its title suggests, the second piece deals with Robin's death, although the event itself is over by the end of Act 1, and Munday's treatment of the episode differs from any account that had gone before. Here, in a narrative that fits better with the political concerns of the play, Robin is poisoned by his uncle - the Abbot of York - conspiring with the familiar figure of Sir Doncaster. The bloodletting, the Prioress and Kirklees Priory itself are all omitted.

The Earl of Huntington title was retained by Martin Parker some years later in his new ballad-epic, *A True Tale of Robin Hood*. This is arguably one of the most important literary sources in the development of the Robin Hood legend, as it was the first to stress, and so establish in the popular consciousness, the theme of Robin stealing from the rich to give to the poor [36].

Parker's work was originally published as a broadside; a ballad, often accompanied by a woodcut and the name of a common tune to which it could be sung, printed on a single-sided sheet of cheap paper and sold for as little as a penny [37]. With hundreds of thousands of broadsides sold annually, their popularity was such that after 1556 the Stationers' Company demanded their registration, and so Parker's publication can be conclusively dated to 1632.

Whilst many of the original ballads were also circulating as broadsides at the time, like the *Gest*, *A True Tale of Robin Hood* had much loftier ambitions. Parker was already a successful versifier, acclaimed by Poet Laureate John Dryden as the finest ballad writer of his day and renowned for his stirring compositions dealing with issues in the national interest, a tendency which reached its apotheosis with his Royalist ballads during the Civil Wars [38].

Hence, Parker was keen to establish Robin Hood as a figure worthy of biographical attention and so *A True Tale* reflects the concerns of the early 17th Century as much as it does the original legend. It is also likely that Parker was influenced by the emerging antiquarian movement, as he seems equally concerned to emphasise the historical veracity of his account [39], supplementing the already instructive title with an assertion that it is:

> "...carefully collected out of the truest Writers of our English Chronicles: And, published for the satisfaction of those who desire truth from false-hood".

However, whilst it is clear from the action in *A True Tale* that Parker must have been familiar with the *Gest* and at least some of the earlier ballads [40], he takes numerous liberties with the narrative provided by this source material. This is certainly the case when he comes to relate the circumstances of Robin's death. In Parker's narrative, the fever which precipitates Robin's trip to have his blood let is brought about by the desertion of his followers who have forsaken him to travel north, and fight for the king of Scotland. Robin travels to an anonymous nunnery, where the bloodletting procedure and subsequent treachery is the work not of the Prioress, but of a "faithless friar", although the motive is again revenge for the wrong the outlaw has done the Church.

Nonetheless, the Prioress turns up in subsequent stanzas to bury Robin "close by the highway-side". There is no mention of her being his relation, but it does curiously add that although she opposed Robin's deeds, she loved his memory and did not wish to see his fame die. To this effect, Parker claims that she erected a gravestone inscribed with the date of his death and an epitaph, which could be read "within this hundred years" but has since been weathered away.

After many further stanzas of rather didactic, valedictory fare, Parker even provides the wording of this epitaph.

> "Robert Earle of Huntington / Lies under this little stone / No archer was like him so good / His wildnesse named him Robbin Hood / Full thirteene yeares and something more / These northerne parts he vexed sore / Such out-lawes as he and his men / May England never know again."

Yet despite his insistence on the materiality of the gravestone, nowhere in *A True Tale of Robin Hood* does Parker specifically mention Kirklees. This is especially ironic when considering that the epitaph he cites – almost certainly a poetic invention on his part [41] – actually went on to provide the inspiration for the inscription which exists on the 18th or 19th Century folly at Kirklees today [42]. The wording of this epitaph is repeated in a late ballad, *Robin Hood and the Valiant Knight,* but here its location is conclusively stated as being at "Birkslay Monastery in Yorkshire". From the spelling, it seems the writer must have been familiar with Grafton's *Chronicle,* which he fused with Parker's account.

Broadside ballads continued to be a primary mode of transmission for the Robin Hood legend throughout the 17th and 18th Centuries, but despite the large number that must have been circulating, no full and discrete handling of the death narrative has been found before the mid-1700s [43]. The only ballad to have endured in this regard, commonly called *Robin Hood's Death,* provides the version of the story that most people will be familiar with today, although there are considerable problems involved in establishing its authenticity.

The difficulty is primarily that the ballad exists in two different forms that were both published around the same time, but whilst they describe broadly the story, there are some notable variations between them. However, as the first and more obviously archaic version only survives in a fragmentary fashion, it is usually combined with the second to create a complete sequence of events.

The first example is typically referred to as the Percy Folio, as it is taken from a sheaf of manuscripts saved from use as kindling in a Shropshire farmhouse by Thomas Percy, Bishop of Dramore in Ireland and described by him in the introduction to his 1765 collection, *Reliques of*

Ancient English Poetry[44]. The ballad covered several sheets of the original manuscript, but it was only discovered with the bottom portion of the pages torn away, leaving a fragment of twenty-seven stanzas which breaks after the eighth and eighteenth.

The Percy Folio version of *Robin Hood's Death* (Appendix 2) opens with Robin declaring to his men that he must travel to "Churchlees" to have his blood let. Will Scarlett sounds a note of caution and recommends that Robin travel with a retinue of at least fifty of his best archers, because a "good yeoman" resides in the vicinity who is bound to pick a quarrel. However, Robin dismisses these concerns and permits only Little John to accompany him.

Further portents of misfortune plague the outlaws on their journey and at the crossing of "black water", they encounter an old woman "banning" Robin. Banning is an archaic term, the exact meaning of which is disputed. Some re-tellings have translated it as 'cursing', but more often it is rendered as 'lamenting'[45]. A full account of their discourse is missing due to the damage to the original manuscript, but the text resumes with Robin assuring her that the Prioress is his cousin (his aunt's daughter, to be precise) and as such would not harm him.

Upon arrival at the Priory, the two outlaws are welcomed in by the Prioress, who Robin gives twenty pounds and promises more should she need it. They proceed to the bloodletting but as the Prioress lets his vital fluids ebb away, Robin apprehends treachery is afoot and appears just about to relate his suspicions to Little John, when the manuscript breaks again.

It recommences in the middle of a skirmish with "Red Roger", presumably the yeoman Will Scarlett warned Robin about in the opening stanzas, and an analogue of Sir Roger of Doncaster in the *Gest*. Roger skewers Robin in his side, but the outlaw is still sufficiently swift to mortally wound his adversary and leave his corpse lying on the ground for the dogs to devour.

Weakened by blood loss, Robin sees his end drawing near and asks Little John to perform the last rites. John begs his master to allow him to exact vengeance after his death and burn the nunnery to the ground, but Robin refuses, declaring that he would not harm a woman. He then asks John to carry him on his back to the highway and bury him there in a "fayre grave" with his sword at his head, his arrows at his side and his bow at his feet. This is the last we hear of the outlaw, for damage to the manuscript obscures the ballad's conclusion.

The second variation of *Robin Hood's Death* (Appendix 3) appeared in a compilation of broadsides from about 1779, titled *The English Archer, or Robert Earl of Huntington, Vulgarly Called Robin Hood.* As such anthologies were known as "garlands", this is typically referred to as the garland version. Possibly due to its overt references to the local site of Kirklees, this version was far more popular in the north of England than the south [46].

Here, Robin is depicted travelling to "Kirkly-hall" alone. Curiously, this ballad never makes it clear that this place is a nunnery until much later in the text, whilst the outlaw's treacherous cousin is referred to as female but not specifically as the Prioress. She proceeds to offer Robin food and drink, but he refuses until he has undergone the bloodletting. To this effect, he is taken to a private room and his cousin begins the operation, only to lock him in and leave him to bleed "all the live-long day".

The following noon, Robin attempts to escape by climbing through the window but finds himself too weak to move and instead, he blows three feeble blasts on his horn to summon Little John. John guesses from the weakness of those notes that his master must be approaching death and hurries to his side. Once again, John asks Robin to permit him to burn the nunnery to the ground and Robin refuses for the same reasons. Then, in what has become the most iconic scene of the narrative, he takes his bow and fires a final shot, requesting that John bury him where the arrow falls.

Dating *Robin Hood's Death* is a controversial matter. With regard to the Percy Folio, although it was not unearthed until the mid-18th Century, there is good reason to believe that the manuscripts were transcriptions of a much older work, largely due to the frequency of obvious copy-errors throughout [47]. The earliest surviving copy of the ballad *Robin Hood and Guy of Gisborne* was also found alongside it and from the evidence of a fragment of a play dating from circa 1475, which appears to tell the same story, it is thought this ballad must have been well-established by the late-15th Century [48].

Furthermore, the language of the Percy Folio ballads is much older than the date of their discovery [49], whilst the character of the narrative bears a much closer resemblance to the earliest ballads, rather than those written later than the 17th Century, which invariably show the influence of Munday and Parker [50]. It emphasises themes such as the corruption of the Church, Robin's strong Christian convictions and the fraternity of Little John, all of which are artefacts of the late-medieval sources [51].

The brutality of the ballad is also a typically medieval feature. Robin is mercilessly bled to death by his kinswoman, Red Roger's body is left for the dogs and Little John would happily slay all the nuns in the priory. Such cruelties are rarely found in later, sanitised narratives [52], but bear comparison with other definitively medieval ballads such as the aforementioned *Robin Hood & Guy of Gisborne,* in which the outlaw beheads and mutilates the eponymous antagonist.

Child certainly believed that *Robin's Hood's Death* was of a relatively venerable provenance, as reflected by the position he accords it in *The English and Scottish Popular Ballads.* Many Robin Hood authorities, including J.C. Holt [53], Dobson [54], Stephen Knight and Thomas Ohlgren [55], have argued that it predates the *Gest,* due to similarities in the action and because the *Gest* deals with the death in such a perfunctory fashion that it must have been intended for an audience already acquainted with the story. Indeed, all the sources from the *Gest* onwards, including Grafton, the Sloane Manuscript and Parker display a familiarity with the events described in *Robin Hood's Death,* which could not have been gleaned from the *Gest* alone.

At odds with this interpretation is the fact that it seems incredible that an extensive treatment of such an important aspect of the legend could have been in circulation for at least three hundred years before a manuscript survived. However, Knight and Ohlgren suggest that the ballad's apparent lack of endurance may be a consequence of public taste, which has always favoured conciliatory tales of adventure and derring-do over morbid tragedy [56].

All things considered – the thematic correspondences especially – it seems reasonably safe to suggest that the Percy Folio version of *Robin Hood's Death*, or at least an earlier ballad on which it is largely based, existed by the late medieval period. Conversely, the garland version appears to be a much more recent invention, albeit directly inspired by the earlier example [57]. There are numerous grounds for this conclusion, the most obvious of which is that the style of the work lacks the archaic features of the earlier version.

Meanwhile, the fact that the garland version neglects to make clear that Kirkly is a nunnery or that Robin's cousin is the Prioress there, suggests that the author assumed most people would be aware of these details. It is precisely the sort of mistake made by writers so familiar with the source material that they unconsciously neglect to elucidate it fully for their audience. The repeated reference to "Kirkly-hall" is also suspicious, as no hall existed at Kirklees until the 16th Century, following the dissolution of the Priory.

Most interestingly, it is the only version of the legend prior to Ritson's influential attempt to standardise the canon of literary sources, to feature that final arrow shot which determines the location of Robin's grave. Grafton, the Sloane Manuscript and Parker all emphasise that the Prioress selected the burial spot, by the side of the highway. Whilst the Percy Folio version of *Robin Hood's Death* implies that it was Little John who laid his master to rest, it still omits the story of the final arrow and indicates that the burial was in the vicinity of "yonder streete". Presumably, such a highway would not have run through the grounds of the Priory itself, yet the garland version clearly states, "they buried bold Robin Hood *within* the fair Kirkleys".

It therefore seems unlikely that the garland version predated its 1779 publication in *The English Archer* by any significant amount of time. The image of the final arrow is one of Romantic nobility, an ambience that is entirely absent from the late-medieval sources and only begins to colour the legend following the work of Munday and Parker. Nonetheless, it undoubtedly has far more dramatic impact than the alternatives. As such, it is scarcely surprising that it was favoured in many Victorian re-tellings and persists as a defining motif in the myth today.

There are other discrepancies between various interpretations of Robin's death worthy of comment. The involvement of Little John is only mentioned in both versions of *Robin Hood's Death*, although in the Percy Folio version he is present throughout, whereas the garland version has him answering his master's summons at the last minute. John's presence has been cited as a mark of the antiquity of the Percy Folio ballad [58], as many of the earliest ballads stress the brotherhood between the two outlaws and, indeed, were as much about Little John as Robin.

Similarly, the role of the figure known either as Sir Roger of Doncaster or Red Roger varies in all cases. The *Gest* mentions him but indicates that he is a knight, whilst insinuating that the Prioress is his lover, whilst the Sloane Manuscript proposes that her actions were largely a result of his influence. He also appears in the Percy Folio version of *Robin Hood's Death* but here is portrayed as a "good yeoman". There is no hint of his relationship with the Prioress, although this, along with the specific nature of his disagreement with Robin, may have been dealt with in the missing stanzas, for when the manuscript resumes at Verse 19, he is in the middle of a quarrel with the outlaw.

Their fight only occurs in the Percy Folio account and the wound Roger inflicts upon Robin may be as much responsible for his expiration as the bloodletting. However, despite its many parallels with the Percy Folio, Roger is omitted from the garland version of *Robin Hood's Death.* He is also absent in Parker's *True Tale,* although he may have been the confused inspiration for the anonymous friar who is actually responsible for Robin's death in the latter. Otherwise, there seems to be no reason for Parker to essentially duplicate the role of the Prioress, unless his high-minded attitude made it impossible for him to suggest that a woman could be responsible for such a heinous deed as murder.

Of course, it is worth noting that the actions of the Prioress would not have been regarded as murder under medieval law. Outlaws at this time were regarded as non-persons; they had no legal existence. To kill an outlaw was regarded as no different to killing a wolf and hence they were often given the title 'wolfshead'. This state of affairs persisted until the late 13th Century, but even after the law was revised they could still be legitimately killed for resisting arrest.

The method of dispatch is also interesting. Bloodletting was a common procedure in medieval medicine, based on the theory developed by the Ancient Greek physicians Hippocrates and Galen that all maladies were caused by an imbalance of the four 'humors' in the body. These were defined as blood, phlegm, black bile and yellow bile, of which blood was considered to be principal. As such it could easily build to excess, and so by draining a limited amount of blood, medieval healers sought to restore equilibrium between the humors.

In the narrative of Robin Hood's death, however, it becomes a distinctive and vicious mode of killing. Former district nurse Barbara Green comments in her book *Robin Hood: His Yorkshire Legend* that the description of the incident given in the Percy Folio version of *Robin Hood's Death* – "At first it bled, the thicke, thicke bloode / And afterwards the thinne" – is a remarkably accurate description of a fatal haemorrhage lending the episode even greater potency [59].

Bloodletting features in a majority of the literary sources, but perhaps the most notable constant in the various texts dealing with Robin's death is the association with Kirklees. It is variously given as Kyrkesly, Kirkly, Churchlees, Bircklies and Birkslay, but despite aspersions cast by those attempting to claim the outlaw for Nottinghamshire, there really is no doubt that Kirklees is meant. Spelling was far from standardised prior to the 16th Century so it is not unusual to find a wide divergence in the construction of words.

In the definitive work on the subject, *Place Names of the West Riding of Yorkshire,* A.H. Smith cites a range of variations for Kirklees, including Kyrkesley on several occasions as early as the 13th Century, and shows the name to be derived from a contraction of the Old English *kirkja* meaning 'church' and *lēah* meaning 'clearing(s)' [60]. It is thus clear how the Percy Folio ballad arrived at "Churchlees" whilst Grafton's "Bircklies" is probably a misreading of an earlier source.

Apart from a demonstrably prehistoric cairn near Oddendale in Cumbria, no other site claims to be the place of Robin's burial, either in the literature or in topographical references. This is rare for such a legendary figure; the number of alleged graves of King Arthur, for instance, is legion. It is also surprising when you consider the sheer quantity of other locales associated with Robin Hood scattered across the country. There are numerous features dubbed Robin Hood's Stone, Robin Hood's Well, Robin Hood's Chair, Robin Hood's Cave and so forth, places where he purportedly stopped to rest or spots where he supposedly hid treasure.

That Kirklees is the only site consistently connected with the death and burial of Robin Hood is testament to the strength of a tradition, which has probably persisted since the late Middle Ages. Indeed, the materiality of the site and its corroboration by the literary sources contributes to the veneer of authenticity surrounding the stories of Robin Hood, and Kirklees has often been invoked by those seeking a historical figure at the nucleus of the legend.

The question of which came first, the grave or its description in the ballads, is a vexed one and it is unlikely that a definitive conclusion will ever be settled upon. But whatever the answer, the narrative provided by the literary sources remains a potent and unique episode in the canon. Whilst J.C. Holt remarks that "it would be surprising if much of *Robin Hood's Death* were anything other than fiction", he is also moved to note that it is one of the most distinctive and durable tales, without any analogue in medieval literature [61].

Stephen Knight represents a dissenting voice, however, arguing that:

> "Unlike the deaths of King Arthur and most other major heroes, the tragic death of Robin Hood is not the necessary climax of the story, and indeed it seems to contradict the sense of vitality and free action that is inherent to the outlaw's myth" [62].

Knight is correct to the extent that regarded as part of that frequently picaresque epic, *A Gest of Robin Hood,* the episode seems tacked on and unceremoniously handled. However, this is a criticism of the author's ability to draw together the various themes of the legend into a unified whole as much as the episode itself.

If we turn to *Robin Hood's Death,* it is the very incongruous melancholy of the piece that lends it such force. Fran and Geoff Doel praise the "haunting, fatalistic, even ritualistic aura" which suffuses the Percy Folio ballad throughout and note its mythological resonances [63]. Divorced from the wider tradition, it is a compelling tragedy in its own right but regarded as a properly integrated facet of the legend, it the inescapable arrival of autumn after the summer revels, the chill note of nemesis whose inevitability prevents the other stories from seeming too glib. More importantly, it ensures that Kirklees is as integral to the mythology of Robin Hood as Sherwood or Barnsdale, the Sheriff or Little John.

CHAPTER TWO

The Foggy Ruins Of Time

Before discussing the monument that purports to mark the site of Robin Hood's grave, it is necessary to discuss the historical context of its location. An understanding of the chronology and topography of Kirklees Park will clarify certain issues concerning the history of the grave itself, and provide perspective on the access controversy that has developed over the last twenty-five years. It will also hopefully emphasise the site's compelling *genius loci* (spirit of place) and demonstrate that the locale is not merely a footnote in the legend of Robin Hood, but a unique cognitive landscape, which has been the focus of human activity and belief for thousands of years.

Despite being located on the periphery of West Yorkshire's heavy woollen district, near old mill towns such as Huddersfield and Brighouse, and barely a stone's throw from the busy M62 motorway, Kirklees Park seems completely isolated from the modern age. Entering the estate is like stepping back in time to a forgotten pastoral land and even the modern agricultural operations cannot dispel the impression created by the timbered barns and mill-ponds. A sense of serenity reigns there and you can understand why its owners have been so keen to protect it from the insidious bustle of the outside world. In a way, the cloistered atmosphere of the medieval Priory has never been broken.

The Park today occupies an area of a couple of square miles in a shallow valley formed by Nun Brook as it descends from Hartshead Moor to join the River Calder at Cooper Bridge. Atop the hillside to the north is the village of Hartshead, whilst the M62 now severs its connection with Clifton to the west. Historically, Kirklees has always been intimately associated with the ancient parish of Hartshead-cum-Clifton and the 17th Century antiquarian Roger Dodsworth recorded some once well-known lines of local doggerel:

> "Clifton standes on Calder banke and Hartshead on a hill, Kirkeleyes stands within the dale and many come there still." [1]

The south side of the park rises to a ridge of around three hundred feet overlooking the River

Calder. In the rangy landscape of the South Pennines it is scarcely worth dignifying such an elevation with the title of a hill, but nonetheless, it goes by the name of Castle Hill. And whilst it may be densely wooded today, in previous centuries it must have represented a fine vantage point, with sightlines along the Calder Valley to the east and west, and down the Colne Valley to the south.

Robin Hood's grave stands amongst the trees towards the crest of Castle Hill, but this is not the only point of interest here. At the summit, now almost entirely obscured by the dense vegetation, there is a five-sided earthwork consisting of little more than a ditch and a bank crudely constructed of loose stone, forming an enclosure between 0.8 and 1.2 hectares in size. [2] Never a substantial structure, there is even less to see today. The remains were disrupted by quarrying in the 19th Century and the construction of a summer-house at its centre in 1905[3], the eerie, ivy-clad ruins of which still draw the eye. However, this insignificant earthwork possibly represents the earliest phase of human activity in the area.

Opinions differ as to the exact provenance of the enclosure and in the absence of any datable evidence, it could have been built anytime between the Iron Age and the foundation of Kirklees Priory in the Middle Ages. An excavation by Sir George Armytage in 1906 failed to uncover any occupational evidence such as pottery, which has moved some people to suggest that it may have something as prosaic as a cattle enclosure for the Priory [4].

Yet something about the name of the site, 'Castle Hill', has always stirred the antiquarian imagination. It has been known by this title since at least the 16th Century. The Survey for the Possession of Kirklees Priory, carried out in 1539 during the Dissolution of the Monasteries, refers to the pasture on the flanks of the hill as 'Castle Field,' suggesting that the feature was already well-known and had been recognised by the name for some considerable time before that [5].

The first scholar to survey the site properly was Rev. John Watson, a curate at Halifax and Ripponden, in his seminal 1775 tome *The History and Antiquities of the Parish of Halifax.* Earlier commentators such as John Whitaker in *The History of Manchester* had regarded it as a Roman feature, possibly a station on the road between Manchester and Tadcaster that passed by the Second Century fort at Slack, some six miles to the south-west of Kirklees [6]. However, having attempted to trace the route of this road, Watson finds no evidence of it in the Kirklees area [7].

This did not prevent I.A. Richmond from including it in his 1925 survey *Huddersfield In Roman Times* suggesting that the enclosure was a marching camp on a trans-Pennine Roman road towards the next station at Meltham. He later dropped this theory when it became clear that the camp at Meltham was much larger at eight hectares with a more regular perimeter [8].

The latest thinking regarding the site is that it is some sort of defensive feature constructed during the Iron Age. This date would account for the lack of occupational evidence such as pottery, as Iron Age materials rarely survive in such soil. Meanwhile, the site's defensive nature is suggested by its strategic location at the summit of a hill, a position rarely used for purely agricultural enclosures [9]. It would also be in a direct line of sight from a major Iron Age hill-fort atop that more famous Castle Hill at Almondbury, above Huddersfield.

Although the earthwork may not provide evidence of Roman activity at Kirklees, there is some indication of settlement there in the Romano-British period. In 1796, two sherds of Samian ware, a characteristically Roman style of pottery, were discovered in a bed of clay some four or five feet down by estate workers digging a drain. They were identified as belonging to two bowls made in Lezoux, Gaul between 160 and 190 AD. One expert who examined the finds, proclaimed that their state of preservation suggested they had not been merely abandoned in the open, but were evidence of occupation of some kind, possibly a villa [10].

In 1965, D. Haigh of the Halifax Antiquarian Society successfully re-identified the place where the sherds had originally been found. Picturesquely documented as "the south part of Gringley Carrs called the Hirst, near Lawns Close," this proved to relate to a field at the extreme east of the estate above Nun Brook. Excavation failed to uncover any further evidence of activity in the Romano-British period, however, and due to the poor drainage of the clay soil, it is debatable whether it would be the most propitious site for settlement of any kind [11].

For the next thousand years or so, like so many places around the country during that period, the history of Kirklees remains obscure. The West Yorkshire Metropolitan County Council Archaeology Unit discovered some evidence of a deserted medieval village just north-west of the Priory site, indicated solely by some scattered and shallow earthworks. There is no documentary evidence of this settlement, suggesting that it had been abandoned prior to the foundation of the Priory [12].

Nor is it possible to say exactly when Kirklees Priory was founded. A copy of the foundation charter survived in the 17th Century, as William Dugdale quotes from it in his opus *Monasticon Anglicanum,* but he does not give a precise date, and the document has since been lost [13]. The 19th Century Huddersfield historian Charles P. Hobkirk, confidently states that the priory was founded in 1155 [14], the second year of the reign of Henry II, but he does not give a source for his information, and as some of his other assertions regarding Kirklees are demonstrably incorrect, this must be taken with a pinch of salt.

Nonetheless, the best guess for the date of foundation is certainly some time in the latter half of the 12th Century and the reign of Henry II, on land granted by Reyner Fleming, Lord of the Manor at Wath-upon-Dearne in South Yorkshire [15]. It was definitely well-established by the mid-13th Century as it is mentioned in the 1236 charter roll of Henry III, and in an undated charter of William de Warrene, 6th Earl of Surrey and Lord of the Manor of Wakefield, who lived between 1166 and 1240 [16].

The foundation charter printed by Dugdale states:

> "Be it known to you all that I Reyner Ffleming have given, granted and by this present Charter confirmed in free and pure and perpetual alms to God and to Saint Mary and to the nuns of Kirkales the place in which they

remain, to wit, Karkley and Hednesley, as the water of Kelder goes to the old mill as far as to the river and from Blakelana as far as the Wagestan and from the Wagestan so by the bounds of Liverseg, Herteshevet and Mirfield. All within the mentioned bounds and beside this 12 acres of land."

The place-names are relatively easy to distinguish. Karkales and Karkley are clearly Kirklees, the "church fields" themselves, whilst the water of Kelder is the River Calder, Liverseg is Liversedge, and Herteshevet is Hartshead. The Wagestan is the Walton Cross, a fifteen-foot high Anglo-Saxon preaching cross, dated to the 10th Century, the base of which still survives near St. Peter's Church, Hartshead. Blakelana, meanwhile, is thought to refer to the hamlet of Blakelaw, which was destroyed by the construction of the M62 in the 1970s.

A sheltered and fertile tributary valley with a good water supply, the Priory site is typical of many such locations in the north of England [17]. You have to wonder if the sequestered atmosphere Kirklees Park retains today is an enduring product of the isolation the Priory must have brought, a segregation the aristocratic Armytage family were only too happy to uphold in later centuries. Or did this sense of place perhaps already exist in the valley and draw the nuns to it?

The Priory was dedicated to the Blessed Virgin Mary and Saint James and belonged to the Cistercian Order [18], a strict monastic philosophy that had been founded in 1098 at Cîteaux in France by a Benedictine monk named St. Robert of Molesme. By the 12th Century, the Cistercians were the dominant religious influence in western Europe and one of the wealthiest, as their agricultural skill brought them great commercial success in the wool-trade. Many of the major medieval abbeys in Yorkshire such as Fountains, Rievaulx, Byland and Kirkstall were Cistercian institutions.

Cistercians adhered to the Rule of St. Benedict, a canon of precepts for cenobitic living set down in the 6th Century and noted for its austerity. Followers of this tradition were commanded to live communally under the absolute authority of an abbot and once admitted, postulants had to take vows of chastity and poverty, which they were expected to hold for the rest of their lives. Although, contrary to popular belief, there was no explicit vow of silence, Benedictine rule instructs its disciples to speak only when necessary, or when spoken to.

The lives of Benedictines were strictly regulated, in obedience to a command always to keep occupied with acts of worship or labour. Fieldwork and domestic chores were a significant component of their day, as were the regular communal prayers known as Canonical Hours; Lauds before daybreak, Prime in the early morning, Terce around mid-morning, Sext at midday, None in the mid-afternoon, Vespers at twilight and Compline towards midnight. Benedictines were also entreated to tend to the sick and elderly, which explains why the Prioress of a Cistercian house would be practiced in an art such as bloodletting.

The Cistercians were often known as the White Monks or Ladies due to the colour of their unlined woollen habits, over which they would wear a black scapula (apron). They were only permitted two sets of clothing, to allow for washing, and typically these would have been woven by the monks or nuns themselves. Doubtless, such austere vestments proved quite inadequate during winters at Kirklees, as we know that the majority of windows in the Priory were unglazed [19].

Although the Priory structure has been completely destroyed, thanks to a survey of Priory holdings carried out in 1539 during the Dissolution of the Monasteries, and archaeological excavations carried out in 1863 and 1902 by Sir George Armytage, it is possible to say - with a reasonable degree of confidence - what the building must have been like. In addition to the absence of glazed windows, it seems that many of the small and poorly-constructed buildings also lacked a chimney, even in the kitchen [20].

At the centre of the Priory complex was the cloister, a courtyard some forty-foot square with a slate-roofed arcade running around it. On three sides there was a variety of two-storied buildings. The chapter-house and parlour were located on the eastern wing, over which was the dormitory. To the south of the cloister, there were a number of domestic buildings such as the larder and gyle-house (where vinegar was made) with the refectory above, and an infirmary at its nether end. Meanwhile, the bulting-house (where the grain was sifted) and several miscellaneous cells, probably for work or study, were located on the western flank.

The church stood north of the cloister and was inevitably the largest of the Priory buildings, eighty feet long and twenty-one feet wide. It was also one of the few buildings with glazed windows, although they would not have been stained-glass, as Cistercian rule forbade any such decoration. Its centrepiece would have been the High Altar, possibly adorned with a simple crucifix, whilst there were two subsidiary altars in the choir and twenty-two stalls for the nuns [21]. We also know that the church possessed a bell-tower, thanks to a Will of 1480 leaving money for its upkeep [22].

Such bequests were one of the primary sources of income for the Priory, and various gifts were donated to the institution over the course of its existence. For instance, in 1350, Sir John Savile of Elland, whose daughter Margaret would one day become Prioress, granted them 40s plus an annual quarter of corn and stone of wool for each nun [23]. Many of these endowments came from local gentry like Savile, doubtless keen to secure their passage to Heaven. It was certainly the motive of Sir John Hall, who in 1526 requested burial at Kirklees and granted the nuns all income from his lands around Huddersfield, on the condition that every year they conducted a requiem mass for his immortal soul [24].

Unusually, the Priory does not seem to have had any actual land granted to it, beyond eight acres in Saddleworth from Robert de Stapleton in the 1270s [25]. But whilst the Priory was evidently not considered fit for donations of land, it was deemed adequate for the offloading of people, which gives some insight into the priorities of a feudal society. Hence, in 1349, Sir John de Flemying presented the nuns with a serf named Alice Dounger of Clifton, along with the right to all her "heirs and chattels". She would probably have been used as a domestic servant, although unlike her mistresses, she would have retained the right to marry [26].

The Priory's most lucrative asset arrived in 1403 when the Archbishop of York gifted them the church and rectory at Mirfield, entitling the nuns to all tithes collected in that parish, namely sheaves of corn, hay and fallen wood, along with possession of the dwelling-house. In return, the Priory had to allow the local vicar use of the rectory and "bear all burdens… incumbent on the church" [27].

Nonetheless, unlike many other Cistercian houses in Yorkshire which grew rich on the back of the wool-trade, Kirklees Priory was never very wealthy, and despite their various grants, the nuns probably enjoyed little more than a subsistence living. According to the survey made at the time of the Dissolution, the nunnery's assets were worth a meagre £19.8s per annum [28], their last significant acquisition having been the Mirfield rectory over a century earlier.

The very obscurity of Kirklees has led some commentators to regard it as corroborating evidence for the authenticity of the Robin Hood legend. They argue that if the story was fabricated, its author would have chosen a more celebrated location for such a pivotal episode. If the death narrative was intended to continue the *Gest's* indictment of the corruption of the Church, then it certainly makes little thematic sense to use such a humble institution when there were plenty of richer examples nearby [29].

Meanwhile, the portrayal of the faithless Prioress may not have been entirely far-fetched. By the 14th Century, decadence was creeping in to the Cistercian Order. Whilst in its early years, the Order was composed solely of those individuals who would willingly choose such an ascetic lifestyle in the interests of religious devotion, monastic communities increasingly became a clearing-house for the dispossessed of medieval society. Rather than bastions of piety, nunneries were now a refuge for widows, spinsters and orphaned girls, who had little incentive to live by the unforgiving Rule of St. Benedict.

In the early part of the 14th Century, the Registers of the Archbishop of York are littered with edicts hinting at widespread insubordination throughout the monastic communities of Yorkshire. Nineteen out of twenty-seven religious houses in the county are mentioned in connection with some indiscretion on the part of their inmates, Kirklees foremost amongst them [30]. Indeed, the Archbishop of York seems to have needed to exert an unusual degree of authority over Kirklees, despite the degree of autonomy granted to the Cistercian Order [31].

To this effect, the Register for 27th August 1306 reads:

> "The archbishop to the prioress and convent of Kirklees. Turning our attention to the miserable state of Alice Raggid, your fellow nun, the bearer of these presents, who, often deceived by the allurements of frail flesh, in levity of mind hath gone from her house into the world, and hath wandered in great peril, having long ago put off her religious habit. In virtue of obedience, and under canonical penalty which those contravening our mandate may, not without cause, dread, we firmly enjoin and command you that you freely admit to the bosom of mercy and mercifully treat in the bowels of love the aforesaid Alice, who returns to you in the spirit of humility…"

Several years later on 11th September 1313, we find another entry:

> "The archbishop hath absolved Elizabeth de Hopton, nun of Kirklees, from the sentence of greater excommunication which she had incurred for apostasy and rash change of her habit, and she is to be admitted according to the discipline of the order, and she is to be at Kirklees on or before the feast of St. Michael then next under pain of a return of her sentence."

However, the state of affairs at Kirklees was evidently not mollified by such indulgence on the part of the Archbishop and by 10th October 1315, the situation had clearly deteriorated further. The Register records:

> "The archbishop having heard that there are scandalous reports in circulation about the nuns of Kirklees, and especially about Elizabeth de Hopton, Alice le Raggede and Joan de Heton, that they admit both clergy and laymen too often into secret places of the monastery and have private talks with them, from which there is suspicion of sin, and great scandal arises.
>
> He commands the prioress to admonish the nuns and especially those above named that they are to admit no one, whether religious or secular, clerk or layman, unless in a public place and in the presence of the prioress or sub-prioress, or two of the other ladies. The archbishop also forbids the religious and secular persons, concerning whom the aforesaid scandal and suspicion have arisen, from presuming to approach the said ladies or any of them under penalty of excommunication.
>
> Johanna de Wakefield, your fellow nun, is also admonished to quit the chamber which she inhabits contrary to the proper credit of religion, and to follow the convent assiduously as well in choir, cloister, refectory and dormitory as in other fit places and times. Any rebellious or misbehaving nuns are to be punished according to the discipline of the Order. The names of those who shall refuse to admit the discipline and castigation of the prioress are to be sent by her to the archbishop by letter under your common seal."

The same Register also yields the nature of Joan de Heton's transgression, noting that she was:

> "...judicially convicted before the archbishop of the crime of incest with Richard de Lathe and Sir Michael called Scot a priest, and by us absolved therefrom..."

Meanwhile, the Register for 5th November 1315, indicates that nine years after her earlier disobedience, Alice le Raggede was still not reconciled to the monastic lifestyle. It states:

> "The prioress and convent are to receive Alice le Tragged, their fellow nun, who on her own confession before the archbishop has been convicted of incontinence with William de Heton of Mirfield."

The Prioress at this time was Alice de Scriven, who appears in the Wakefield Manor Court Rolls for 1314, accusing the Chaplain of Hartshead of stealing the Priory's cattle. Her name is mentioned again in 1327, when she was summoned for non-payment of a debt to Thomas de Toothill of Brighouse [32]. Considering these facts in tandem with the disorder that apparently wracked Kirklees Priory during her tenure, we must conclude that she was either a very ineffectual, or unusually worldly, Prioress. Indeed, in light of such data, a Prioress who takes a lover and murders her own cousin does not seem entirely improbable.

A fine example of the procedure by which women typically came to the nunnery at this time is the case of Elizabeth de Staynton, who would eventually become Prioress sometime in the mid-14th Century, although her exact dates are uncertain. Elizabeth has assumed great importance in the history of Kirklees as her grave is one of the very few to have endured, moving Hobkirk to suggest that she was the founder of the Priory [33], along with her sisters, Mary and Agnes, but this has since been conclusively disproven.

In fact, according to the antiquarian J.W. Walker, she entered the Priory in 1344 at the age of twelve, unusual in itself as the Cistercian Order did not typically admit children, on the grounds that they were not yet capable of freely choosing such a life [34]. She was one of four daughters of John de Staynton, a landowner at Wooley-moor-house. Following John's death, his wife Joan remarried Hugh de Toothill of Toothill Hall near Brighouse. Two of the Staynton girls, Isabel and Joan, married Toothill's sons, but the remaining pair, Elizabeth and Alice, were despatched to Kirklees Priory so that Toothill could enjoy their late father's full estate, which had been left equally to all four daughters [35].

However, the Will had appointed Joan's brother, William de Notton, as the girls' guardian and he began proceedings to extricate Elizabeth and Alice from the Priory. He argued that they were too young to take holy orders and complained that Hugh de Toothill had not entered them out of piety or charit, but for material gain. William de Staynton, the girls' paternal uncle and Prior at Monk Bretton, accepted Notton's case but unusually, Elizabeth pleaded with them to permit her to remain at Kirklees. This was agreed, on condition that Hugh de Toothill pro-vide the girls with an allowance from their family estate [36].

So, whilst Elizabeth de Staynton herself clearly demonstrated unusual religious devotion from an early age, she provides an instructive example of how, by the late Middle Ages, many women were forced into nunneries through patriarchal politics and necessity, rather than pursuing it as a vocation. It is scarcely surprising that the likes of Alice le Ragged, Elizabeth de Hopton and Joan de Heton rebelled against the strictures of a lifestyle they may never have voluntarily chosen.

The grave of Elizabeth de Staynton was rediscovered in 1706, alongside two others [37]. The table-tombs still stand behind decaying railings to the north of the feature known as the Orchard Wall, itself one of the few surviving relics of the Priory. The area would formerly have been to the east of the Priory church. The inscription on her gravestone reads, "Sweet Jesu of Nazareth, grant mercy to Elizabeth de Staynton, formerly Prioress of this house", in Norman French and a Lombardic script characteristic of the 14th Century [38].

This entreaty for mercy has led some commentators to suggest that Elizabeth de Staynton was the Prioress who murdered Robin Hood, and many have sought connections between the Staynton family and their favoured historical candidates for the outlaw [39]. However, if Elizabeth did not enter the Priory until 1344 at the age of twelve, she would not have been eligible for the role of Prioress until at least 1362 under Cistercian law [40], which is only fifteen years prior to the first textual reference to Robin Hood and therefore, probably far too late.

The unruliness, which infected the Cistercian Order during the 14th Century, led to extensive reform, and whilst these measures certainly seemed to quell such rebellions at Kirklees, the Order had slipped into irreversible decline. Monastic communities were increasingly alienated from the general populace and failing to fulfil their spiritual needs. As a result, revenues and the number of new postulants steadily dwindled through the 15th Century and by the time the end finally came, only eight inmates remained at Kirklees Priory [41].

In 1531, Henry VIII renounced the authority of the Roman Catholic Church and declared himself Supreme Head of the Church in England, triggering a sequence of events that resulted in the Dissolution of the Monasteries. The initial act of defiance was prompted by Pope Clement VII's refusal to annul Henry's marriage to Catherine of Aragon. However, the ensuing programme of transformation was driven as much by a wider urge to root out moribund religious institutions in the wake of the Protestant Reformation sweeping Western Europe, and the rather less virtuous desire to seize monastic land and income for the Crown.

The process began in earnest in 1535, when parliament passed the Act for the Dissolution of the Lesser Monasteries, ostensibly on the damning evidence of first minister, Thomas Cromwell, who had been commissioned to inspect standards of propriety in religious houses across the country. The legislation allowed for the disbanding of any monastic establishment worth less than £200 per annum and the expropriation of its holdings by the monarch. Commissioners were then despatched through England and Wales, with the authority to execute the closures.

With a yearly income of only £19.8s, Kirklees Priory was certainly amongst those eligible for suppression in this first round. However, the Act also allowed monasteries to petition the King, who could grant an extension at his discretion, and the Patent Roll of 1538 records a Grant for the Continuation of Kirklees Nunnery [42]. Signed by the Prioress, Cecilia Topcliffe, and Richard Layton, a clerk of Chancery, it permits the nuns to remain at Kirklees, but they must surrender title to the property and submit to the authority of Henry VIII over that of the Pope [43].

However, following a mass uprising against the Dissolution known as the Pilgrimage of Grace, Henry increasingly began to regard the monasteries as troublesome and punitive measures were imposed to coerce more institutions into voluntary surrender. In 1539, parliament passed the Second Act of Dissolution, which made provision for the suppression of all remaining religious houses. Kirklees Priory was finally handed over to the Commissioners on 4th November 1540 by the last Prioress, Joan Kyppes [44].

All surviving nuns were subsequently pensioned off. Kyppes and one Joan Leventhorpe were provided with an annuity of £2, whilst the others received £1.13s.4d each [45]. Following their eviction, Leventhorpe, Cecilia Topcliffe and Katherine Grice are believed to have founded a hostelry named the *Three Nuns* which still stands on the perimeter of Kirklees Park beside the A62 [46]. Meanwhile, Isabella de Hopton, Agnes Brook, Isabella Rhodes and Isabella Saltynstall went with their former Prioress to live at the now-demolished Paper Hall in Mirfield [47]. The grave of Joan Kyppes can still be seen at Mirfield Church.

The Priory and its lands were originally sold to William Ramsden in 1547 [48], passing through the hands of a succession of owners over the course of the following two decades, until 26th October 1565 when it was purchased by John Armytage of Farnley Tyas near Huddersfield [49]. Armytage was a wealthy clothier and export merchant, no doubt keen to establish himself amongst the local gentry, and indeed with the purchase of Kirklees Priory, he achieved exactly that. The estate remained in the hands of his family for over five hundred years.

It is difficult to establish exactly when the Priory was demolished and Kirklees Hall constructed. A plan from the 16th Century indicates that the former nunnery stood for several decades following the Dissolution and was employed as a domestic residence [50]. In his excavations of 1863 and 1902, Sir George Armytage discovered plasterwork bearing the family crest amongst the remains of the Priory, suggesting that the buildings were still used as a dwelling by the first Armytage at Kirklees [51].

The destruction of the Priory and the foundation of Kirklees Hall were probably symbiotic acts, as there is evidence to show that the Hall was built with materials plundered from the Priory site [52]. Many stones in the fabric of the Hall bear masons' marks identical to those found on the few known surviving Priory features, in a sense making the Hall itself the principal material relic of the Priory's existence still extant. However, the Hall lies on higher ground some distance west of the original Priory site. All that remains *in situ* are the nuns' graves, the Orchard Wall, a dry-stone wall to the east and a number of outbuildings. These include a timber-framed barn and more controversially, the structure known as the Gatehouse [53]. Local lore holds that this building originally formed part of the entrance to the Priory and contains the room in which Robin Hood expired. Yet any mention of a gatehouse is conspicuous by its absence from the remarkably thorough 1539 survey, which even went to the lengths of recording dry-stone walls [54].

The architectural evidence is more confusing still. A timbered section on the first floor, now encased in stone, probably dates from some point during the 16th Century, but the rest of the building is constructed from a different type of stone, in the style of a later date. The external staircase providing access to the first floor was certainly not added until the 19th Century as it does not appear on an engraving of the building from that period [55].

One suggestion, which reconciles the 16th Century fabric with its absence from the 1539 survey, is that it was constructed as a gatehouse after the Dissolution when the Priory was still being used as a residence [56]. An alternative hypothesis is that it did in fact exist prior to the Dissolution and corresponds to an almshouse next to Nunbrook mentioned in the survey [57]. There is, however, no evidence at all of it ever having been used as a gatehouse and this tradition may have been taken from the Robin Hood legend rather than the other way round.

Construction of Kirklees Hall probably began in the late Elizabethan period [58]. The west-wing is believed to date from that time and one chamber called the Oak Room has been described as "the perfect example of an Elizabethan drawing room". Then around 1610, a Jacobean front was added by another John Armytage, grandson of the first Armytage at Kirklees (the names John and George were immensely popular in the family). Unusually, this façade is north facing, allegedly because John "could not bear to turn his back on the Church" and so it is designed to look towards St. Peter's at Hartshead [59].

Charles I first conferred title upon the Armytage family on 15th December 1641 when Francis Armytage became the first Baronet of Kirklees, in the parish of Hartshead, County of York, England [61]. A baronetcy is a curious and archaic honour. It is not a peerage and those bearing the title are not eligible to sit in the House of Lords. Hence, baronets are not considered members of the nobility. Like knights of the realm, they are permitted to style themselves 'Sir' but in contrast, the honour is hereditary and the baronetcy outranks most knighthoods. It has few material advantages.

The Armytage family wasted no time in throwing themselves into the role of local gentry. In addition to acting as a Justice of the Peace, Sheriff of Yorkshire and Captain of a Troop of Horse in the Civil Wars, the Second Baronet, Sir John Armytage (1629-1676/7), was instrumental in the campaign against religious dissent in the region [61]. He was the scourge of Rev. Oliver Heywood, one of the most notorious Non-Conformists in northern England at the time, who ministered at Coley and Northowram nearby. Thanks to Heywood, we know that Sir John died following a drunken fall from his horse in the vicinity of Robin Hood's grave, an event the good reverend records in his diary with barely concealed satisfaction [62].

All three of John's sons, Thomas, John and George, succeeded to the title and all three died childless, allowing it to pass to their cousin, Thomas, who only enjoyed the position for a year between 1736 and 1737. As he similarly passed away without issue, the first Baronetcy of Kirklees came to an end. The estates passed to Samuel Armytage of Keresforth Hill, the great-grandson of the younger brother of the first Armytage at Kirklees, and in 1738 a new Baronetcy was created for Samuel, with the title slightly modified to the Baronetcy of Kirklees, in Hartshead, County of York, Great Britain [63].

His son, Sir John inherited the title in 1747 but enjoyed it for only eleven years, dying in the Battle of Saint Cast, France, as a volunteer in the Seven Years' War [64]. As he was yet another Armytage to die childless, he was succeeded by his brother, Sir George, and it was during this man's tenure that Kirklees Hall and Park assumed their present form. An extensive programme of renovation throughout the 18th Century converted the Hall into the E-plan Georgian dwelling seen today [65].

In 1759, the illustrious Yorkshire architect John Carr, whose résumé included work on buildings as grand as Harewood House, Chatsworth House and Castle Howard, was brought in to set the tone of the project [66]. He was responsible for the remodelling of the doorway, passage and arcade, but perhaps most famously, he added the remarkable hanging staircase, designed to have no visible means of support [67]. Many of the improvements to the Hall carried out over the next thirty years were influenced by this initial work by Carr.

Extensive additions were also made to the grounds during this period. Between 1766 and 1770, a walled garden was created to the north of Nun Brook [68] - and is still there today - whilst in 1769 the Leeds ironmonger, Maurice Tobin, constructed a seventy-two foot iron bridge over the ornamental pond. Although this edifice does not survive, it is noteworthy in representing the first iron bridge in England, predating the more famous (and admittedly still standing) example over the River Severn at Coalbrookdale in Shropshire [69].

The Armytages continued to revel in their position as quasi-feudal lords of the manor. Both Sir Samuel and Sir George acted as MP for York, whilst nearly all holders of the title through the 18th and 19th Century served terms as either Deputy Lieutenant or High Sheriff of Yorkshire. The fourth new baronet, also called Sir George, even commanded the Huddersfield Fusilier Volunteers, who put down local food riots in 1794, whilst he later led the offensive against Luddite activity in the region [70].

Perhaps the most energetic, however, was the sixth baronet, Sir George John Armytage, who held the title from 1899 to 1918. A trained civil engineer, he was director of the Lancashire and Yorkshire Railway, responsible for the operation of countless tracks in the area, including the Leeds-Manchester Railway, which runs on the far side of the River Calder from the estate. He was also noted for his scholarship. A Fellow of the Society of Antiquaries, he was a founder member of the Yorkshire Archaeological Society and served as its president for a time. It is to his two excavations in 1863 and 1902 that we owe much of our present knowledge concerning Kirklees Priory.

The last Baronet to live permanently at Kirklees was Sir John Lionel Armytage (1901-1983), who became the Eighth Baronet in 1953. Initially a military man, serving as a Captain with the King's Royal Rifle Corps, he later became a keen agriculturalist, active in both the Royal Agricultural Society and the Country Landowners' Association. It was largely during his tenure that the estate developed into the modern farming operation it remains today, trading under the name of Armytage and Webster.

Commercial interests prevailed and, ostensibly to prevent disruption to the smooth running of the agricultural business, access to Robin Hood's grave became harder than it ever was. The grave was largely forgotten, even by local people. One doubts that the Armytages were particularly displeased with this situation. Despite the relative insignificance of their title, they always relished their position as landed gentry, lording over the common man. Their opposition to popular movements such as Non-Conformism and the Luddites nicely demonstrates their historical antagonism towards the masses. It was also during Sir John's time that the name Kirklees was adopted by the new Metropolitan Borough created in 1974 by the merger of numerous councils in West Yorkshire's heavy woollen district including Huddersfield, Dewsbury, Spenborough and Batley. The name was chosen from over fifty suggestions despite Kirklees Park itself falling within the Metropolitan Borough of Calderdale. Despite some controversy, Calderdale

Council successfully persuaded the Boundary Commission that the historical ties between Kirklees and Brighouse meant it should remain in their jurisdiction [71]. This much was true, as a great deal of the modern town of Brighouse was constructed on land sold by the Armytages in 1816 [72].

The Armytage dynasty at Kirklees came to an end in 1983 with the death of Sir John. Although he had one son by his first marriage, Sir Martin Armytage, he resides in Gloucestershire, whilst the estate passed to Sir John's German second wife, Maria Margarete Tenhoeff, who continued to be known as Lady Armytage. Sir Martin inherited the title to become the Ninth Baronet, but as he is childless, the baronetcy may finally come to an end when he dies.

Lady Armytage continued to run the estate as a thriving agricultural business. However, in March 1987 she made the decision to sell Kirklees Hall along with twenty acres of surrounding land. By this time, she was living alone at the Hall in a private apartment in the south-east section [73]. The majority of the building was shut up and falling into disrepair so the sale was probably inevitable, but eyebrows were raised at the relatively paltry £450,000 at which it was placed on the market [74]. Meanwhile, Lady Armytage moved into a carbuncular modern residence newly built on the estate, adjacent to the Priory site itself with the nuns' graves in the back garden.

Kirklees Hall was initially purchased by a successful hotelier name Michael Craig Dent, who in the early 1980s had been described by the *Observer* as one of the most promising chefs in England. He originally had big plans to turn the Hall into a thirty-room hotel and gourmet French restaurant [75]. However, perhaps spying an easy profit, Dent sold the hotel barely a couple of years later in March 1989 for £1.2 million [76], almost three times the price at which he had purchased it.

A hotel scheme was also proposed by the new buyers, albeit on a much grander scale. In 1990, they submitted an application for planning permission to turn the Hall into a forty-room hotel, complete with a bridal suite, training rooms and bar, with a two-hundred-and-seventy seat auditorium in the coach house. However, by 1994, Calderdale Council were forced to withdraw the planning permission after correspondence regarding some necessary alterations to the access routes broke down, and it became clear that work was unlikely to go ahead on the Hall at any time in the near future [77].

In 1998, English Heritage was forced to add Kirklees Hall, a Grade One listed building, to their Buildings at Risk Register, along with the Priory barns and gatehouse, which were still owned by Lady Armytage and located within the boundaries of the Kirklees Park Estate. Despite proposals in the last decade to turn the gatehouse into a holiday cottage, this historically significant building remains in a lamentable state of repair [78].

Kirklees Hall, at least, was finally saved from dereliction by a consortium named Kirklees Hall Ltd who purchased it in 1997 and converted the Hall and adjacent stable block into fifteen luxury residences. The scheme was completed in 2000 at a cost of over £3 million, including a £430,000 grant from English Heritage [79]. Unique features such as the hanging staircase, the oak panelling in the Elizabethan drawing room and a famous ceiling in the music room were retained, largely preserving the heritage value of the building.

Meanwhile, the future of the Kirklees Park looks uncertain. Lady Armytage passed away in 2008 and whilst her daughter will presumably inherit the estate, it is currently in the care of a board of trustees until substantial death duties are settled. In order to pay for these, property is currently [2011] being sold off, including buildings such as Mock Hall Farm, a 16th Century farm-house owned by the Armytage family since they originally purchased the Priory lands [81]. Whatever ultimately becomes of the larger estate, we can only hope that the new owner has a more enlightened attitude towards Robin Hood's grave and the visiting public.

Kirklees Hall, the seat of the Armytage baronetcy, in the Nineteenth Century (Unknown)

CHAPTER THREE

Confusion Will Be My Epitaph

Located in dense woodland towards the brow of Castle Hill, the monument known as Robin Hood's grave is at present a sorry sight. The brickwork is crumbling, whilst iron railings added over two hundred years ago to deter souvenir hunters, rust and twist inwards to litter the enclosure itself. Scant light penetrates the canopy of evergreen yew trees above, and so the grave festers in the dank and gloom, reeking of neglect. It is certainly an atmospheric place, but such dilapidation cannot be perceived as anything less than an unfortunate fate for a site of such historical significance.

Of course, there are many who would deny that claim to historical significance, including the grave's most recent custodians. However, the basis on which they reject its importance is rooted in a reductive and ultimately deficient understanding of how the history of antiquities is shaped. Their concern is purely with empirical origins and authenticity. They take the moment of inception and exalt it to the extent that it eclipses all subsequent development, ignoring historical process in favour of the myth of historical stasis, as if the meaning of a site remains fixed over centuries. It is a fundamentally stagnant view of history, which focuses on the materiality of an artefact rather than how countless generations have perceived and interacted with it, and it is an approach which will always fail to do justice to a site such as Robin Hood's grave.

Bearing this in mind, it is necessary to examine the full and complicated chronology of the monument to demonstrate that whilst its origin might be eternally shrouded in mystery, that genesis is but one instant in a much longer and perpetually dynamic biography. Moreover, when the authenticity of a relic is destined to remain ambiguous, its history can only be understood through historiography, the study of how successive writers have interpreted their subject. This meta-narrative is often more fruitful than the empirical facts in creating an understanding of how a site evolved to become what it is today,

Even the Yorkshire Robin Hood Society, who actively promote the belief that a medieval outlaw who was known as Robin Hood lies buried somewhere in Kirklees Park, accept that the monument currently standing is largely an 18th Century folly [1]. The issue, therefore, becomes not about authenticity, but about the antecedents and established attitudes that motivated the construction of such a memorial. The folly did not emerge *ex nihilo*. It is a testament to an already existing belief complex and the strength of that tradition is itself a matter of historical importance, regardless of the precise origins of the alleged grave.

As Chapter 1 demonstrated, Kirklees has been associated with the death of Robin Hood since the late 15th Century at least. However, it is clear enough that the inscribed epitaph set into the low stone wall of the enclosure of the grave today dates from much later than the late medieval period. The script is clearly that of a later century, whilst the language, although obviously intended to imitate Middle English, does not correspond to any known medieval spelling or dialect [2]. The lines are given below, with a translation alongside:

Hear underneath dis laitl stean,	Here underneath this little stone,
Laz Robert earl of Huntingdon,	Lies Robert earl of Huntingdon,
Neer arcir ver az hie sa geud	Never was there an archer so good
An pipl kauld im Robin heud,	And people called him Robin Hood,
Sick utlauz az hi an iz men	Such outlaws as he and his men
Vil England niver si agen.	Will England never see again.
Obiit 24 Kal Dekembris 1247	Died 24 Kalends of December 1247

The style in which the date is written is that of the Roman calendar, never used in Britain even in the medieval period. Furthermore, no such date as 24 *Kalends* December existed in the Roman calendar. The *Kalends* represents the first day of a new month and the Romans counted the days up to rather than away from this marker. Therefore, the date indicated would actually have been in early November. But more importantly, the Roman calendar was based on a lunar cycle. The *Kalends* denoted a New Moon, but the calendar also marked the Full Moon (*Ides*) and Half Moon (*Nones*) and counted dates in relation to these too. Hence, the Romans themselves would not have counted as far back as twenty-four days from the *Kalends*. Such a date would be given in terms of the *Nones* [3].

It seems odd that whoever composed the inscription had enough Classical learning to be familiar with the style of the Roman calendar, but would then make such an elementary mistake. I suggests the date was designed as an obvious pseudo-archaism to lampoon those scholars who were easily impressed by the mere artifice of antiquity [4]. If this is the case, we can assume that the rest of the epitaph was intended in the same spirit, which explains why it is so unconvincing. It was never really meant to fool anybody.

Yet whilst the inscription is demonstrably a fake, this does not mean that the whole monumen can be so easily dismissed. Textual references from as early as the 16th Century indicate tha there was some sort of memorial on the site and that the current edifice was designed as replacement for a decaying original. Attentive visitors will notice that on the floor of the enclosur lies an inconspicuous and eroded lump of sandstone. It doesn't look like much, but it is likely that this is all that remains of the original grave slab, reduced to this state by the depredation of weathering and vandalism over several hundred years [5].

The first allusion to a grave comes from John Leland's *De Rebus Britannicis Collecteana,* a series of notes compiled in the 1530s, but not published until 1770. The original Latin reads *"Ebor. Kirkley monasterium Monialium, ubi Ro: Hood nobilis ille exlex sepultus"* which translates as "Yorkshire: Monastery of Kirkley, where the noble outlaw Robin Hood is buried." [6] Whilst this does not refer directly to a tomb and he could arguably have obtained the information purely from ballad sources, it is likely that at some point in his career, Leland visited Kirklees, or at least communicated with those who had personal knowledge of it [7].

Leland is widely regarded as the father of antiquarianism. He was certainly the first person to officially identify himself as such and prior to his work, no large scale survey of the material antiquities of England had been attempted [8]. Indeed, not only is the mention in *Collecteana* the earliest reference to a grave of Robin Hood at Kirklees in a self-consciously factual context, Leland's writings are arguably the first place such a reference could have occurred.

Much of the *Collecteana* derives from Leland's tour of religious houses in England between 1533 and 1538, undertaking a commission from Henry VIII to catalogue the libraries of these institutions prior to their Dissolution. David Hepworth argues that the entry for Kirklees probably dates from 1534 when Leland travelled to York.

Although he would again visit Yorkshire in November 1539 whilst composing his more famous *Itineraries* (which unlike the *Collecteana* was published in his lifetime), the absence of any mention of Kirklees in this detailed topographical volume suggests that he did not reacquaint himself with the area [9].

It is equally possible, from the lack of further detail in the *Collecteana,* that Leland never visited Kirklees at all. It was, after all, an insignificant house and probably lacked a library of any consequence. If so, then he must have received the information second-hand.

For the *Itineraries,* he certainly relied on oral sources for some entries, although he tended to qualify such accounts with the phrase *"in hominum memoria"* meaning "it is widely believed" *[10]. Leland is not thought to have been overly credulous in his use of oral testimony and modern scholars regard him as an unusually reliable primary source, suggesting he would not have included the reference to Robin Hood's grave had he lacked faith in its veracity [11].

At the very least, Leland's mention of Kirklees implies that there may have been a material grave at Kirklees even before the final surrender of the Priory in 1539. It is merely necessary to remember that the trustworthiness of such a conclusion depends on two assumptions. Firstly, that the *Collecteana* reference dates from his tour of monasteries in the 1530s rather than his subsequent travels for the *Itineraries* between 1539 and 1542. And secondly, that Leland obtained his information personally or at least from a reliable source.

But whilst Leland's note is the earliest mention of the grave at Kirklees, as it was never published until the late 18th Century [12], it does not represent the first reference to have been available to

---

* The literal translation is "upon of men memory", but one gets the gist.

a general audience. This distinction goes to the controversial Richard Grafton, in the second edition of his *Chronicle At Large*, published in 1569.

He writes:

> "Robert Hood, beying afterwardes troubled with sicknesse, came to a certain Nunry in Yorkshire called Bircklies, where desirying to be let blood he was betrayed & bled to death. After whose death the Prioress of the same place caused him to be buried by the high way side, where he had used to rob and spoyle those that passed that way. And upon his grave the sayde Prioresse did lay a very fayre stone, wherein the names of Robert Hood, William of Goldesborough and others were graven... at eyther ende of the sayde Tombe was erected a crosse of stone, which is still to be seen there at this present." [13]

This is the first recorded physical description of the grave, although from where Grafton got his information is unclear. From the reference to "Bircklies" it seems clear that he never personally visited Kirklees and misread the name from another source [14]. He cites "an olde and auncient Pamphlet" but this has not survived. The biographical details provided by Grafton are corroborated by the Sloane Manuscript, which also appears to date from the late 16th Century. However, it is impossible to tell whether the writer of this manuscript took his material from Grafton or if both independently obtained it from this earlier pamphlet.

Knight and Ohlgren surmise that such a pamphlet never existed and Grafton has certainly never been regarded as a reliable source [15]. He has been described as "a compiler of useless books, an unskilled pretender in history, an inaccurate and credulous plagiarist whose facts and dates even for the reigns he lived through, were often as not wrong," whilst his "carelessness with texts... shows a remarkable incompetence... an incompetence indeed that seems to have increased with age" [16]. Even in his own age, Grafton was regarded with suspicion and found himself embroiled in a protracted feud with rival antiquarian John Stow, who accused him of plagiarism.

On the other hand, whilst Grafton may have been little more than a compiler and a plagiarist, he has not been specifically accused of fabricating material. Indeed, the comprehensive and often incongruous detail in his description of the grave suggests that it was not an invention. For instance, there seems to be no compelling reason to mention that the stone was also inscribed with the name of William of Goldesborough, a name that does not appear in connection with Robin Hood in any other context, unless it was a true report.

A word must be said regarding the highway beside which both Grafton and the Sloane Manuscript claim Robin was buried. The main thoroughfare running in the vicinity of Kirklees during the Middle Ages, referred to in later years as Nun Brook Lane, ran from a landmark known as the Dumb Steeple at Cooper Bridge, through the woods on the southern flank of Castle Hill, until it met Blake Law Lane descending from Clifton and thence continued to Brighouse [17]. Until 1815, when the Elland and Obelisk Turnpike was constructed further down the hillside (now the modern A644), this was the only route along the north bank of the River Calder between Cooper Bridge and Brighouse for many centuries.

Following the opening of the turnpike, the road fell into disuse and the land passed into the hands of the Armytage family, but its route can still be traced - both on old maps and on the ground. At its closest point, it ran sixty-six yards, or three chains, from the current site of Robin Hood's grave. Whether this can be considered "by the highway side" is debatable. In an article on the subject for the Yorkshire Archaeology Journal, W. P. Crump certainly thought it deserved to be regarded as such [18], but other commentators have argued that the monument may have been moved to its present location from a spot more obviously adjacent to the old road.

After Grafton, the next mention of the outlaw's grave at Kirklees, can be found in the final edition of William Camden's classic work of topography, *Britannia*, published in Latin in 1607 and translated into English by Philemon Holland in 1610. In the section on the West Riding of Yorkshire, Camden notes simply:

> "The Calder runs to Kirkley, heretofore a nunnery, thence to Robin Hood's tomb, a generous robber and very famous on that account." [19]

Sadly, Camden's reference has been the source of much confusion regarding the precise location of the grave. Following its original publication, *Britannia* was successively republished with additions and 'improvements' by later antiquarians, and a number of authors writing on the subject of the grave have failed to distinguish Camden's own words from later embellishments. This has caused them to make some erroneous claims regarding what Camden tells us about the grave, which are not supported by the primary text.

It starts innocently enough, with the 1695 edition published by Bishop Edmund Gibson, which also includes the statement:

> "The famous robber, Robin Hood, lies buried in the park near Kirklees Nunnery, in the West Riding, under a monument which remains to this day" [20].

This is not substantially different to Camden's original phrasing and although it has been mistakenly attributed to Camden himself, it has not therefore caused any difficulty. However, a far more damaging revision occurs in the 1789 edition published by Richard Gough. It reads:

> "At Kirklees nunnery Robin Hood's tomb with a plain cross on a flat stone is shewn in the cemetery. In the ground at a little distance by two grave stones, one which has the inscription for Elizabeth de Staynton, prioress there." [21]

Despite the 1789 edition being specifically marked as "Enlarged by the latest discoveries by Richard Gough", several writers have fallen into the trap of crediting this passage to Camden writing in 1607 rather than Gough in 1789. This trend apparently began with J.W. Walker, a President of the Yorkshire Archaeological Society, who really ought to have known better [22].

From that mistake, a couple have concluded that in the early 17th Century, the grave was not located on Castle Hill as it is today, but in the Priory cemetery in proximity to the nuns' graves [23].

A number of features should have alerted them to the fact that it was not the work of Camden. It is certainly not composed in Camden's style, which mostly "sets out to evoke what exists only in fragments, if at all – in half-lines inscriptions and shards" [24]. Nor is there any other evidence to suggest that Elizabeth de Staynton's grave was known in the early 17th Century. Indeed, the fanfare that heralded its rediscovery by Sir Samuel Armytage in 1706, suggests that it had been lost for at least as long as the Armytage family had owned Kirklees.

Yet the most damning evidence against the misattribution of Gough's account to Camden is that we know exactly where Camden obtained his information concerning Kirklees and that source is cited in Joseph Ritson's *Robin Hood*, one of the most famous historical works on the outlaw. In a letter dated 25th December 1589, local antiquary Sir John Savile writes to Camden:

> "Kirkleys Nunnery, in the woods whereof Robin Hood's grave is, is be-
> tween Halifax and Wakefield" [25].

This reference clearly locates the grave in the woods rather than in the Priory cemetery, and Camden's grasp of this fact is reflected in his wording in 1607. "The Calder runs to Kirkley… *thence* to Robin Hood's tomb" indicates that he understood the grave to be beyond the Priory complex rather than within in.

Nor is it likely that Sir John Savile was mistaken in his original assertion, for not only was he an antiquarian of some repute living only a couple of miles away in Elland, the Savile family also had old ancestral ties to Kirklees. Sir John was descended from the John Savile who, in 1350, granted an endowment to the Priory and whose daughter Margaret acted as Prioress between 1350 and 1361 [26]. Meanwhile, the Patent Roll of Edward VI indicates that between 1544 and 1547 a cousin, Nicholas Savile, owned the land at Kirklees, several years before it came into the possession of the Armytage family [27].

It seems probable that a man with such strong connections to Kirklees as Sir John would be intimately familiar with the topography of the site, and - given that he was born in 1545 - may have been aware of the site for many years before his letter to Camden. From this, we can conclude that in 1589 Robin Hood's grave was definitely in the woods on Castle Hill, probably in exactly the position it is seen in today.

The next reference to Kirklees as the location of Robin Hood's grave in an antiquarian context, occurs in Song 28 of Michael Drayton's epic topographical poem *Poly-Olbion*, published in 1622. Lines 67-70 run:

> "…But thence as Calder comes along / It chanced she in her course on
> Kirkley cast her eye / Where merry Robin Hood, that honest thief doth
> lie."

This does not impart any new information regarding what was known of the grave in the 17th Century, but it does demonstrate that the association between Kirklees and the outlaw's burial was becoming established in the collective consciousness beyond the ballads and broadsides.

For more detailed evidence, we must wait until 1669 when the Pontefract physician, pamphleteer and antiquarian Nathaniel Johnston visited Kirklees to attend to the wife of Sir John Armytage IV. Whilst there, he and his brother Henry sketched a number of antiquities for a mooted history of Yorkshire, including the slab supposed to mark Robin Hood's grave. The reputation of the Johnston brothers as accurate draughtsmen is well-attested and so this drawing is believed to be the first reliable representation of the stone itself [28].

The sketch shows the slab was engraved with a three-stepped Calvary, typical of many medieval gravestones, with a thin stem and knop on the cross shaft, rising to a floriated cross. Around the edge of the cross is an inscription similar to that given by Grafton, "Here lies Robart Hude, William Goldbugh, Thoms…" Meanwhile, there appears to be another smaller stone adjacent to the grave slab, which could represent the remains of one of the crosses Grafton claimed stood at either end of the tomb.

If this sketch is accurate, it is almost too good to be true. It corroborates Grafton's description a century earlier and suggests that the grave slab was a demonstrably medieval artefact; the Calvary cross carved upon it corresponds to a design that was common throughout Yorkshire during the 13th Century, but which had largely died out by the 14th [29]. However, whilst Johnston himself might be an unimpeachable source, David Hepworth has shown that the image attributed to Johnston ever since its first publication in the Yorkshire Archaeology Journal of 1902, is not actually the original 1669 sketch [30].

The published version is certainly a hand-drawn copy. It had been sent to Sir George John Armytage by Rev. Harris Fleming St. John of Dinmore Manor, Herefordshire, who discovered it accompanying a manuscript of 1720 by the antiquarian William Stukeley. As St. John did not feel comfortable lending the originals, he had his wife copy the sketch, assuring Sir George that her work was accurate [31]. However, there is further evidence to suggest that the drawing amongst the Stukeley papers was itself a copy.

Not only would this make the published version of Johnston's sketch a copy of a copy, with all the potential for error that this entails, it throws the whole accuracy of the representation into doubt. Nathaniel Johnston is a reliable source, but William Stukeley is widely regarded as a romanticist and mythologiser. He has form for the fabrication of material concerning Robin Hood, with his invention of a pedigree identifying the outlaw as the fictitious Robert Fitz Ooth [32], whilst his contemporary, Thomas Hearne, observed that:

> "…what he does hath no manner of likeness to the originals. He goes all by fancy" [33].

Stukeley similarly has form for potentially embellishing the work of Nathaniel Johnston. In the second edition of *Itinerarium Curosium*, published in 1764, he includes a landscape engraving, which he attributes to Johnston. Entitled 'A Prospect of Kirkleys Abbey', which includes features such as the Priory itself, the Hall and a mysteriously turreted gatehouse. As these buildings never stood contemporaneously, it is clearly a fanciful reconstruction, uncharacteristic of Johnston, but very typical for Stukeley.

Nonetheless, the depiction of Kirklees Hall is accurate enough to suggest the work of somebody acquainted with the building, whilst the style of the hand is thought to satisfactorily correspond to Johnston's. As a result, David Hepworth believes that the landscape as it appeared in the 17th Century was indeed drawn by Johnston, but the Priory buildings were inserted later by Stukeley, and suggests that an inspection of the original will confirm that the penmanship is different [34].

Such evidence indicates that Stukeley's copy of Johnston's 1669 sketch of the gravestone cannot be wholly trusted. It seems likely that it was definitely a copy of Johnston's original, rather than being wholly conjectural, but how closely it followed it remains uncertain. Knight and Ohlgren have described the sketch as resembling an artist's impression of Grafton's account, [35] and whilst Hepworth has shown that Johnston almost certainly drew the grave first-hand, he does not think it improbable that Stukeley added certain details, such as the inscription, to ensure that it better conformed to Grafton's account [36].

By the late 17th Century, knowledge of the grave's exact location was clearly widespread. In March 1677, local Nonconformist preacher Oliver Heywood mentions it in his diary whilst describing the death of his old adversary Sir John Armytage IV:

> "A second time he fell, just by Robin Hood's grave; his man lifted in vain,
> cast his cloak over him, went back to Nunbrook for help, but found him
> dead, his neck being broken" [37].

Heywood is an esteemed source of social history and despite his puritanical tendencies, he often commented on the vulgar customs of his flock. It seems likely that, if he was aware of the grave's existence, then its fame would have been considerable amongst the local populace and it was probably during this period that many of the superstitions associated with the tomb arose, ultimately leading to its enclosure. There was certainly an explosion of irrational 'magical' thinking during the 1600s of which such practices are typical.

From the beginning of the 18th Century, the material history of the grave becomes much easier to trace, possibly because the Armytage family themselves begin to take an active interest in the monument and use it to promote their family name. It certainly aroused the curiosity of a young Samuel Armytage, even before the estate and baronetcy passed to him in 1737. Several later sources record a tradition that in 1706 he excavated the grave but failed to discover any evidence of a burial. [38]

The wording of these reports, however, is ambiguous. Richard Gough in 1786 wrote that Armytage:

> "...caused the ground under to be dug a yard deep and found it had never
> been disturbed" [39].

This does not make it clear whether they simply failed to find any human remains, or if they recognised that nobody had ever disturbed the soil there. It is unlikely that the stratigraphy techniques of the early 18th Century were sufficiently sophisticated to draw such conclusions, so it probably just means that they failed to find any bones.

However, a later commentator, writing in *Bradford Antiquary* in 1897 writes:

> "...a careful examination of the ground has revealed that the cross (which undoubtedly did stand here) rests on solid natural rock, precluding all possibility of interment" [40].

Sadly, no source is provided for this information, so it is not clear on what authority such a claim is made. It seems odd that such damning evidence is not discussed more fully in any other publication, and the possibility exists that it is merely an extrapolation of the reports of the excavation by Samuel Armytage in 1706.

If this excavation did indeed reach the natural rock without discovering any human remains, then that would be strong confirmation that the ground had "never been disturbed". However, it seems unlikely that they could have reached such a layer at a depth of only one yard. Given the densely vegetated character of the site, there must have been substantial soil accumulation over the years, and an excavation of merely one yard would barely have penetrated this. Indeed, it seems unlikely that the 1706 investigation dug nearly deep enough to uncover human remains. Medieval burials were often placed at least a yard deeper and when soil accumulation is accounted for, any bones could have been several yards beneath the surface even by the 1700s. It is also important to consider that depending on the acidity of the soil, any bones may already have entirely decayed. Taking all these factors into account, Samuel Armytage's excavation seems to prove very little.

Barbara Green also uncovered evidence that sheds further light on the failure of this excavation, although - as it derives from an oral source - it cannot be treated as wholly reliable. She refers to a Hartshead resident, Richard Hobson, who preserved a family tradition that one of his ancestors, Robert Barr, was with Samuel Armytage when the excavation took place. He told her:

> "My grandfather told me the story... They dug on the site of the grave but they found nothing. They were both well in their cups!" [41]

If this last sentence is true, it suggests that the 1706 excavation was far from a serious endeavour and was hardly likely to have proceeded with the sort of rigour necessary to uncover anything.

In 1715, in the appendix of *Ducatus Leodiensis,* the antiquarian Ralph Thoresby first records the epitaph found at the grave today. He describes the inscription in his time as "scarce legible" but claims he found the lines amongst the papers of Thomas Gale, who served as Dean of York between 1697 and 1702 [42]. The stone currently set in the monument was undoubtedly carved later in the 18th Century, based on this epitaph given by Gale via Thoresby, whose word was probably trusted.

However, as a noted scholar it seems unlikely that Gale would have taken the pseudo-medieval dialect and manufactured date seriously, and it seems possible that it was the good Dean himself who invented it, perhaps as some bookish prank, based on the equally contrived epitaph given by Martin Parker in his *True Tale of Robin Hood* [43]. Robin Hood enthusiasts have observed similarities between the two since Joseph Ritson, and whilst he believed this correspondence to prove its authenticity [44], it seems now that Parker's was almost certainly an original invention.

A letter to Thoreby written in 1715 by his fellow scholar Richard Richardson offers further information on the state of the grave in the early 18th Century, and seems to confirm that the epitaph quoted by Gale was a fabrication:

> "The inscription upon Robin Hood's grave was never legible in my time; and is now totally defaced; insomuch that neither the language nor the character is to be distinguished; only you may perceived it was written about the stone. I have heard Dr. Armytage say... that he could read upon it '*Hic jacet Robertus Hood, filius Comitis de Huntingdon*' but I must own, tho' he was a person of merit, I gave little credit to this report" [45].

An even more curious reference to the grave is found in Thomas Gent's *Ancient and Modern History of the Famous City of York*, published in 1730. He relates:

> "That his (Robin Hood's) tombstone, having his effigy thereon, was order'd, not many years ago, by a certain knight to be placed as a hearth-stone in his great hall When it was laid over-night, the next morning it was "surprisingly" removed one side; and so three times it was laid, and as successively turned aside. The knight, thinking he had done wrong to have brought it thither, order'd it should be drawn back again; which was performed by a pair of oxen and four horses, when twice the number could scarce do it before" [46].

This is the first mention of supernatural phenomena associated with Robin Hood's grave, the significance of which will be discussed in later chapters, but as a historical record it is very dubious. Gent himself adds the caveat "This is a story only, it is left to the reader to judge at pleasure", which seems to indicate that he had it purely at hearsay, possibly several times removed. There is no suggestion in the text that Gent had visited Kirklees himself and, therefore, the description of the tombstone as bearing Robin's effigy cannot be regarded as a reliable description as some scholars have attempted to do. It may be that the process of oral transmission had confused the gravestone with a statue of the outlaw, which was known to have stood at the entrance to Kirklees Hall in the 18th Century [47].

Given the fanciful and folkloric nature of the story, it is also unwise to treat it as an accurate account of the removal of the original grave slab. It is possible that it represents a folk memory of Samuel Armytage's excavation of the grave in 1706, when presumably the stone could have been moved to another place for safe-keeping [48], but it certainly cannot be used to give much credence to the idea that the exact site of the grave has been successively moved over the centuries.

Even if the story contained a grain of truth, it reports that the knight replaced the stone where it had originally lain.

Nonetheless, this narrative nicely embodies the theme of interference with the grave, which recurs throughout many of the written sources. That molestation did occur to some extent, however, is a historical fact and had led to the enclosure of the grave during the 18th Century. The first widely published reference to this contingency is found in *The History of Brighouse. Rastrick and Hipperholme* by local historian J. Horsfall Turner, published in 1893 who says simply that it was "strongly railed to a great height... to keep vandals away, who for various reasons, one being as a charm against toothache, desired fragments of the stone" [49].

However, in 1944, J.W. Walker extrapolated on this, writing:

> "When the Lancashire and Yorkshire railway was being constructed in the second quarter of the nineteenth century pieces of the gravestone were carried away by the navvies engaged on the work" [50].

This was repeated by J.C. Holt [51], and as a result it became orthodoxy that the current monument was only erected during the 1800s. However, more reliable sources suggest that it was actually built around seventy-five years earlier. and if it was indeed navvies responsible for any of the damage, then they would not have been building the Lancashire-Yorkshire railway in the late 1830s, but the Calder and Hebble Navigation canal in the early 1760s.

There is unpublished evidence that the construction of the enclosure began even earlier than this. This information comes from the diary of Joseph Ismay, who had served as tutor to the children of Sir Samuel Armytage and was subsequently appointed as Vicar of Mirfield, a position he held from 1739 to 1778 [52]. His entry for 14th April 1752 refers to:

> "...ye sepulchral Monument of Robin Hood near Kirklees which has lately been impaled in ye form of a Standing Hearse in order to preserve the stone from the rude hands of the curious traveller who frequently carried off a small Fragment of ye stone, and thereby diminished its pristine beauty" [53].

Ever curious regarding local antiquarian matters, Ismay sketched the grave twice, in 1754 and 1759. Given his close connection with the Armytage family, it is certain that he worked directly from the monument itself and so his sketch is the only absolutely reliable representation of the original gravestone, given that Johnston's may have been embellished by Stukeley. Sadly, Ismay was not an especially skilled draughtsman, but whilst his drawing is crude, its principal features largely tally with the earlier sketch by Johnston [54].

Ismay shows a Calvary cross with a knop on the shaft, although the arms do not appear to be floriated, and it is impossible to tell how many steps the Calvary has. However, David Hepworth believes these discrepancies may simply be due to the weathering the stone suffered in the century since Johnston's drawing [55]. Ismay also provides the dimensions of the slab, which he records as six foot by four foot by three foot, making it a sizeable object that could not have been easily moved [56].

Several years later in 1758, the Halifax curate and historian John Watson was shown around Kirklees Park whilst gathering material for his *History and Antiquities of the Parish of Halifax*, although his notes on Robin Hood's grave remained unpublished. He describes it as:

> "...at some distance from Castle Field, in an inclos'd Plantation... nothing but a rude stone not quite two yards long and narrow in proportion; it has a figure of a cross, cut in a manner not common upon it; but no inscription, nor does there appear ever to have been any letters upon it, notwithstanding Mr. Thoresby has published a pretended one found amongst the papers of Dr. Gale, Dean of York" [57].

Watson's estimation of the size of the slab seems to concur with Ismay's description, whilst the fact that he saw no evidence of an inscription is instructive. Previous testimonies, especially the letter from Richard Richardson to Ralph Thoresby, indicate that there had once been an inscription of some sort, albeit too worn to read in 1715. This suggests that by 1758 it had wholly eroded away or had been obliterated by vandals, whilst the replacement epitaph seen at the site today had yet to be erected.

Exactly when this new epitaph was placed at the grave remains uncertain, but it seems to have been at some point during the second half of the 18th Century. Watson's description indicates that it was not an original part of the enclosure, which Ismay's diary entry indicates had begun prior to 1752, nor was it placed there in February 1755 when account books indicate that Sir John Armytage VI spent money on the maintenance of the grave prior to his death in the Seven Years' War [58].

The most likely date is April 1773, when as part of his grand estate improvements, Sir George II paid two labourers £3.11s.8d for work building 'Robin Hood's Monument' [59]. Further work was carried out in August 1785, but this largely appears to have been for the iron railings [60]. It is uncertain whether the inscription was added as a replacement, in the mistaken belief that the Gale/Thoresby epitaph had indeed once adorned the gravesite. It may simply have been a knowingly artificial device to embellish the picturesque qualities of the monument.

The grave would have already been in its current enclosed state when the antiquarian Richard Gough included the misleading reference to it being near the grave of Elizabeth de Staynton in his revision of Camden's *Britannia* in 1789. Quite how Gough made such an elementary error is not clear. He was generally known as a rigorous researcher, and the first to criticise antiquarians who failed to check their sources, writing:

> "Injudicious and sedentary compilers find it much easier to arrange matters put into their hands than to ramble about and examine every remnant of antiquity. Whoever sits down to compile the history and antiquities of a county or town should confirm the evidence he collects from books and manuscripts by inspection of the places described" [61].

Gough's mistake in *Britannia* also throws further into doubt the accuracy of the engraving of the grave slab he published in 1786 in *Sepulchral Monuments of Great Britain*. Although it reproduces the Calvary steps and knop shown by Johnston and Ismay, the cross arms end in fleurs-de-lys, a detail included by no other source [62]. Some commentators such as Maurice Keen in *The Outlaws of Medieval Legend* have regarded this as evidence that Gough had seen an entirely different gravestone, and used this supposition to throw the whole chronology of the monument into doubt [63].

But, whilst Gough fancied himself as a meticulous chronicler, he was not an accomplished artist and all the engravings in *Sepulchral Monuments* were drawn by others (including some by the young William Blake) which impacted on their accuracy. As his successor, Charles Stothard, observed in 1817:

> "The delineating part is so extremely incorrect and full of errors that at a future period, when the originals no longer exist, it will be impossible to form any correct idea of what they were... Had Mr. Gough been draughtsman sufficient to have executed his own drawings, he might have avoided the innumerable mistakes... He could not transfer that enthusiasm which he himself felt to the persons he employed" [64].

By the late 18th Century, the controversy over the authenticity of the grave was already in full swing. In his *Reliques of Ancient Poetry* of 1765, Bishop Percy had expressed doubts regarding the genuineness of the Gale/Thoresby epitaph, opining that it "appears to me suspicious. The most ancient poems of Robin Hood make no mention of his earldom". The bishop also questioned whether the epitaph had ever been on the grave, although from his phrasing it seems that he did at least believe the monument itself to be *bona fide* [65].

Twenty-one years later, in *Sepulchral Monuments*, Gough reaffirmed Percy's misgivings regarding the epitaph, stating:

> "The inscription (is) illegible. That printed in Thoresby... from Dr. Gale's papers was never on it" [66].

However, Gough is dubious about the authenticity of the supposed burial site at Kirklees altogether. Referring to Samuel Armytage's excavation in 1706, he concludes that the stone:

> "...was probably brought from some other place and by vulgar tradition ascribed to Robin Hood" [67].

In his 1816 work *Loidis & Elmete*, the local historian Thomas Whitaker finds a middle way. He avows the legitimacy of the location, writing:

> "It is no small confirmation of this opinion that the spot pointed out as the place of interment is beyond the precincts of the nunnery and therefore not on consecrated ground. He was buried as a robber and an outlaw – out of the peace of the Church".

However, he then goes on to cast doubt on the stone itself:

> "At the dissolution of the nunnery, many ancient gravestones would remain and that the place of the outlaw's interment still being notorious and popular, one of these might be removed thither to mark a place which perhaps an older memorial had ceased to record."

As confirmation of this supposition Whitaker offers the evidence that:

> "A cross without a sword can originally have covered none other than the grave of an ecclesiastic,"

suggesting that the stone had originally belonged to one of the nuns at the Priory [68].

Such debates have raged ever since and inevitably, the attitude a writer adopts towards the gravesite very much depends on their own personal bias. Those seeking to claim the outlaw for Yorkshire such as Joseph Hunter, J.W. Walker and Barbara Green display few qualms about its authenticity, whilst Nottinghamshire writers invariably assume an opposing stance. Academic writers seeking to demonstrate that Robin Hood is nothing more than a medieval legend take a similarly sceptical position.

Yet even such supposedly objective commentators in our own time have traded on the confused history of the site to allow them to draw erroneous inferences in support of their own pet theory. For instance, Maurice Keen in *The Outlaws of Medieval Legend,* suggests there have actually been four different stones exhibited at Kirklees as Robin Hood's grave. That mentioned by Richard Grafton and drawn by Nathaniel Johnston; the one with the epitaph reported by Thomas Gale via Ralph Thoresby; the slab bearing the effigy described by Thomas Gent; and finally the example featured as an engraving in Richard Gough's *Sepulchral Monuments* [69].

Such a conclusion, however, can only be reached as the result of a failure to properly interrogate the reliability of the sources. No other modern writer is willing to accept the Gale epitaph as anything other than his own invention, whilst the context of Gent's description of the gravestone means that it cannot be taken seriously as historical evidence. Equally, the engraving printed by Gough is sufficiently similar to Johnston's sketch to conclude that they represent exactly the same stone, with only some minor artistic discrepancies.

Indeed, when examined properly, the history of the site at Kirklees reveals a remarkable continuity of tradition. John Leland's reference to it suggests that the grave has existed since at least the 16th Century, possibly prior to the Dissolution of the Monasteries. It definitely stood in the woods on Castle Hill in 1589 when Sir John Savile described it in his letter to William Camden. The stone featured a Calvary cross of a type common in the 13th Century when Nathaniel Johnston sketched it in 1669, possibly with the inscription described by Richard Grafton hundred years earlier.

Johnston's sketch is confirmed by those of Joseph Ismay and Richard Gough during the 18

Century, although by this time the inscription had weathered away. Vandalism caused the gravestone to be enclosed during the mid-18th Century, and 19th Century accounts from the likes of J. Horsfall Turner indicate the original gravestone is the lump of sandstone that still lies on the floor of the enclosure today, now so badly defaced as to be unrecognisable. All this suggests that there has only ever been one gravestone, probably carved in the 13th Century, which has been in its present location at Kirklees for nearly five hundred years at least.

This similarly discounts a theory propagated in recent years by the Yorkshire Robin Hood Society that the original grave slab now lies forgotten in the cemetery at nearby St. Peter's Church in Hartshead. The stone to which they refer can be found set into the ground beside the verger's entrance to the church. It is partly grassed over but although a certain amount of the stone is obscured, it clearly bears a three-stepped Calvary cross in much the same style as that sketched by Nathaniel Johnston in 1669 [70].

The initial identification of the stone as belonging to the grave of Robin Hood came from a colourful character called John Pope de Locksley, whose story was published by the *Brighouse Echo* on 27th December 2002. Locksley claims descent from a medieval outlaw who has been posited as one of the many candidates for the 'historical' Robin Hood, and refers to an oral tradition passed down in his family for generations recognising St. Peter's Church as the place of his burial. This information came from his cousin Beryl who, in the mid-1950s, had stayed with some relatives at Hartshead named Bottomley, and had been taken with them every Sunday to lay flowers at what they said was Robin Hood's grave. However, the stone to which they paid their respects was the one in St. Peter's churchyard, not Kirklees Park [71].

However, it is unlikely that the stone at Hartshead is the original slab from Robin Hood's grave, the Bottomley family tradition notwithstanding. Despite superficial similarities to Nathaniel Johnston's sketch, David Hepworth has shown that the Calvary cross motif was far from uncommon in Yorkshire during the 13th and 14th Centuries, and it would be quite consistent to find similar examples in the surrounding area. Moreover, all the textual evidence seems to support the rather prosaic truth that the stone still lies in the grave enclosure at Kirklees, albeit wholly disfigured.

Perhaps the only aspect of the Kirklees legend that remains dubious is the involvement of the Gatehouse, an upper room of which is pointed out as the chamber from which Robin fired his final arrow and then died [72]. Countless writers have observed that the gravesite is approximately six hundred and fifty metres uphill from the Gatehouse, almost three times the distance that a medieval archer in full health could have been expected to shoot [73]. With the restrictions of the narrow casement windows and Robin's supposed blood loss, it would have been entirely impossible [74].

Nottinghamshire Robin Hood enthusiast Richard Rutherford-Moore even went to the length of recreating the shot and demonstrating that the arrow could not have fallen more than eighty metres away. However, quite why Rutherford-Moore went to such lengths is a mystery, as even by his own acknowledgment [75] the motif of the final arrow shot was not appended to the narrative until the 18th Century garland version of *Robin Hood's Death*. None of the earlier ballads include this detail and indeed, they claim he was buried by the highway side, which more or less corresponds to the site where the grave has always been shown.

Nor is there any textual support for the legend that the outlaw died in the Gatehouse. This assumption - no doubt - arose from the fact that as a man, Robin could not have entered the Priory complex itself, and - therefore - the Gatehouse represented the most likely place to which he would have been taken. However, this is not explicitly mentioned in any of the ballads. Furthermore, as discussed in Chapter 2, the Gatehouse shown at Kirklees today may not have been part of the Priory at all. It is unclear when this building was first exhibited as the scene of Robin Hood's death, but it does not appear in any published sources until the 19th Century.

Yet the flimsy evidence for the involvement of the Gatehouse cannot be used to discredit the provenance of the gravesite itself. The association between Robin Hood's death and Kirklees stretches back as far as the late 15th Century at least, and records of a physical grave begin to appear in the 16th. For those commentators who claim that this is too late, you have to wonder exactly what it would take to demonstrate the venerability of the site, given that prior to the birth of antiquarianism with John Leland, such monuments were rarely recorded by chroniclers.

Of course, the question of whether the grave belongs to a historical figure that corresponds to the legendary outlaw Robin Hood remains shrouded in mystery, and it is improbable that this conundrum will ever be resolved. Even if a modern archaeological excavation uncovered human remains of the appropriate vintage, it would be impossible to confirm their identity without the emergence of corroborating textual evidence from some hitherto overlooked source. It is not even possible to say whether there was such a historical figure as Robin Hood.

Meanwhile, if we adopt the deflationary perspective and argue that the outlaw was a purely literary creation, brought forth from the imagination of medieval balladeers, then a new enigma presents itself. Namely, were the ballads tailored to fit the existence of a grave at Kirklees or was the grave artificially created to trade on the existing association with Kirklees in the ballads? If the ballads came first, why associate Robin's death with an obscure religious house some distance from the scene of the main action? Yet if the grave came first, to whom did it really belong?

Whichever attitude you adopt towards the grave, it continues to present an impenetrable mystery and as the poet Sacheverell Sitwell so rightly observed, "In the end it is the mystery that lasts and not the explanation" [76]. This is why reductive empirical questions regarding the grave's 'authenticity' are largely moot. The origin of the monument is but one chapter in a much longer narrative. It has become a locus of belief for scholars and the masses alike, invested with significance by countless generations and for this reason alone, it is a site worthy of our attention and respect.

CHAPTER FOUR

They Seek Him Here, They Seek Him There

This is a book about a place, not a person. The question of whether there ever truly was a historical figure upon whom the Robin Hood legends are based is not only irrelevant to the thesis presented here, but to dwell on such a conundrum would be to miss the entire point. The object is not to demonstrate that any such personage as Robin Hood lies buried in Kirklees Park, but to map how layers of related belief have accreted around the site and account for the persistence of those traditions in terms of what might be described as the 'cognitive landscape'.

To regard the question of the grave's authenticity as paramount would be to stand guilty of what Stephen Knight dismisses as "reductive biographic empiricism" [1], amounting to a denial of that flexibility and symbolic resonance which is the very essence of legend. In its crushing literal-mindedness, the historical debate invariably neglects the rich mythic significance invested in the site by popular folk-belief, and fails to grasp that material facts are not necessarily the only source of that nebulous concept dubbed 'truth'.

Nonetheless, as the aim is to study the various shades of belief that have been projected on to Kirklees Park over the ages, it is impossible to avoid the fact that the debates of Robin Hood scholars represent a fertile source of discussion about the site. Their attitudes towards the grave and the myriad ways in which they have fitted the site into their personal schemata are no less important than local feeling, and just because such debates tend to occur in an academic context, that does not necessarily exclude them from the realms of folk-belief.

The annals of Robin Hood scholarship have yielded three principal ways of interpreting the legend [2]. For the purposes of this book, the least noteworthy is the literary school, which began with Francis Child and has so far found its apotheosis in the work of Stephen Knight today. These writers argue that the outlaw was a fictional character created solely by the balladeers of medieval England and as such, the existence of the grave at Kirklees rarely features in their arguments.

However, advocates of both the other traditions of interpretation – the historical and the mythological – have deployed either the materiality of the grave or other aspects of the death narrative to justify their positions. During the 19th and early 20th Centuries, supporters of these two positions were often in direct conflict, but whilst the mythologists have largely died out today, the historical standpoint endures and now finds itself fending off attacks from the literary faction.

In scholarly terms at least, the idea that that Robin Hood was a genuine historical figure is generally regarded as the more venerable tradition. All the early mentions of the outlaw by chroniclers such as Bower in 1440 or John Major's reference in his *History of Greater Britain* of 1521 assume his historicity, a notion which persisted through influential contributions to the legend such as Parker's *True Tale of Robin Hood,* William Stukeley's manufactured pedigree of 1746, and Joseph Ritson's *Robin Hood*[3].

Yet it is wise to note that despite this scholarly conviction, the idea that Robin Hood was a purely fictional or mythological character may have circulated amongst the general populace from an early date. A source dating from the first decades of the 15th Century, *The Reply of Friar Daw Topias to Jack Upland,* features the proverb "many men speak of Robyn Hode / That shotte never in his bowe" [4]. The meaning can be variously interpreted, but some commentators have used it to support the hypothesis that Robin was always regarded as an artefact of legend, with the implication that historical interpretations are a betrayal of the folk tradition.

It is also necessary to remark that until the mid-19th Century, the historical case for Robin Hood was actually based on very shoddy scholarship, drawn from little more evidence than what is contained in the ballads, and often a great deal of conjecture, hearsay and outright invention. Even Ritson in his grand attempt to collect all the available sources of the legend is distinctly uncritical in his analysis of their provenance, and his attempt to derive a coherent biography from these texts is scarcely convincing.

As research standards matured in the Victorian period, antiquarians realised that if they were going to provide a compelling case for the historical reality of the legendary outlaw, it was necessary first to evaluate the validity of the ballads as reliable sources and then seek corroborating evidence in independently verifiable documents such as medieval court rolls, or amongst the putative material remnants of his life. As such, the grave lends itself to any historical account of the Robin Hood legend. The existence of a monument of this nature, and the fact that from an early stage Kirklees is the only location consistently associated with the hero's death, is for many a convincing argument for the authenticity of both the grave and the man. To a mind already inclined to believe in the historicity of Robin Hood, it can appear to be the only surviving material artefact of his existence, and it is accordingly difficult for attempts at a historical account to resist engaging with the grave, even if it is to deny its importance.

However, many cases for a historical Robin Hood which depend on the grave for support, have invariably succumbed to the lure of circular argument. They use the existence of the site at Kirklees to support their favoured historical candidate and then substantiate the authenticity of the grave with reference to that very same figure. Fortunately, the grave is usually only one component in their reasoning, which weakens the circularity somewhat, but the dangers of this tendency should always be recognised.

Arguably, the first example of a persuasive and credibly researched hypothesis for the existence of a historical figure behind the Robin Hood legend is found in Joseph Hunter's clumsily titled publication of 1852, *The Great Hero of the Ancient English Minstrelsy of England: Robin Hood*. Although Hunter's theory has since been disproved by the emergence of evidence to which he could not possibly have had access at the time [5], it remains an impressive attempt to provide a certifiable historical account.

Hunter was born in 1783, the son of a Sheffield cutler, and following theological training in York, served as a Presbyterian minister in Bath from 1809 to 1833, during which time he wrote several highly regarded works on South Yorkshire topography. In 1833, he secured a position as a commissioner of public records at the newly established Public Records Office and rose to become assistant keeper from 1838 until his death in 1861. In this capacity, he was responsible for compiling and publishing the records of medieval government, a role that provided him with an unparalleled opportunity to pursue his interest in Robin Hood [6].

Hunter's fascination undoubtedly owed something to his Yorkshire heritage, as rather than search for his historical Robin in Nottinghamshire, where most 18th and 19th Century literary sources placed him, Hunter followed the earliest ballads and assumed that Robin's principal haunt had not been Sherwood Forest, but an obscure tract of the West Riding of Yorkshire known as Barnsdale.

In the late medieval ballad *Robin Hood and Guy of Gisborne,* the hero introduces himself as "Robin Hood of Barnsdale" in Verse 35, whilst Verse 11 mentions that Little John is "gone to Barnsdale / The gates he knows eche one." Meanwhile, *A Gest of Robyn Hode,* quite clearly one of the earliest surviving sources of the outlaw's exploits, is set predominantly in Barnsdale, stating in the very first fytte "Robyn stode in Bernesdale". Although Nottingham and Sherwood do feature here, it is clear from the compilatory nature of this text that these have been incorporated from a separate body of tales [7].

There are several good reasons for thinking that Barnsdale represents a more authentic tradition than Sherwood, not least the accuracy of the topography described in the *Gest*. Verse 18 of the first fytte contains the lines:

> "And walke up to the Saylis / And so to Watlingr Strete / And wayte after
> some vnkuth gest / Vp chance ye may them mete."

"Saylis" has been identified, by Dobson and Taylor, as Sayles Plantation, the name of which can be traced back to at least the 17th Century [8]. It is an area of woodland on the hilltop overlooking a steep valley where the Great North Road (here referred to as Watling Street) once crossed the River Went (now the settlement of Wentbridge). Clearly, this is an ideal location for bandits to watch for travellers to waylay [9].

There is also clear historical justification for thinking that the legend of Robin Hood originated in Barnsdale. It is the site of the first recorded place-name associated with the outlaw, namely Robin Hood's Stone, which was referred to by the monks at nearby Monkbretton Priory as a boundary marker in a document of 1422 [10]. The exact location of this stone is now lost, but it is thought to have been in proximity to Robin Hood's Well, John Vanbrugh's 1720 domed shelter, which still stands beside the A1 at Barnsdale Bar today [11].

Perhaps more tellingly, during the Middle Ages Barnsdale was notorious for its outlaws. In 1306, when the Bishops of St. Andrews and Glasgow were travelling from Scotland to Winchester by the Great North Road, their guard was increased from eight to twenty men between Pontefract and Tickhill, a contingency which the account books of the period state was "on account of Barnsdale" [12].

The exact extent of the district known as Barnsdale during the medieval period is contentious. However, it seems to have been a relatively small area of approximately ten miles across, bordered by the River Aire at Ferrybridge to the north and the Doncaster-Wakefield Road to the south, bisected by the River Went and the Great North Road [13]. But perhaps most significantly from the perspective of this book, the area lies less than twenty miles from Kirklees Park, as opposed to the fifty-five miles to Nottingham. There can be no doubt that in the context of the death narrative, Barnsdale makes far more sense as Robin's base of operations than Sherwood.

Of course, it is not difficult to understand why Nottinghamshire succeeded in claiming the legend as its own. Barnsdale always was an obscure, ill-defined area, and that is even more true today. Unlike Sherwood, it was never a royal forest, and possesses no substantial settlement to act as a centre for the associated tourist industry. Not only is Nottingham a county town, the edifice of Nottingham Castle provides a potent reminder of its feudal history (notwithstanding the fact that the current structure is no older than the 17th Century) [14]. Nor is it impossible to believe that a band of medieval outlaws ranged quite widely, operating in both Barnsdale and Sherwood at various points.

However, whilst the popular consciousness continues to associate Robin Hood with Nottingham and Sherwood, most academic historians dealing with the legend today emphasise its possible origins in Yorkshire. Less edifyingly, the debate has also become the focus of entrenched regionalism, dismissed by J.C. Holt as "pseudo-history expressing local patriotism" [15]. And, for many determined to establish, beyond doubt, the outlaw's Yorkshire heritage, the evidence first presented by Joseph Hunter in 1852 for "Robert Hood of Wakefield" has become the foundation of an entire belief complex.

Hunter himself was relatively tentative in his conclusions, accepting that the information he had uncovered represented little more than a series of intriguing circumstantial correlations. But in the mid-20th Century, the case was revived and embellished by the antiquary J.W. Walker, a president of the Yorkshire Archaeological Society. His arguments were first presented in a 1944 article for the journal of that organisation, and subsequently in 1952 for a full-length book, *The True History of Robin Hood*. As may be surmised from that title, Walker was rather more forceful in his speculation than Hunter. Today, their arguments are often conflated in a single hypothesis, and indeed, the majority of Walker's work simply attempts to offer corroborating evidence for suggestions Hunter had already made.

The case begins with Hunter's presumption that, due to its apparent topographic and chronological precision, the *Gest* was - to some extent - a reliable historical account of the outlaw's deeds [16]. This is not as absurd as it sounds. The narrative of a 14th Century dispute local to Kirklees, known as the Elland Feud, or the Elland Tragedies, was long preserved in ballad form (coincidentally, the Armytage family owned one of the earliest surviving manuscripts) [17]. At least one 18th Century antiquarian refused to include the story in his book on the grounds that it couldn't possibly be true. However, corroborating documentary evidence was discovered in the Public Records Office in 1890 [18].

In particular, Hunter concentrates on an episode described in the seventh and eighth fyttes of the *Gest*, in which Robin is reconciled with the king. Touring his parks in the north of England, the King – named as Edward – demands to know why the game is so poor. Informed that it is due to the activities of Robin Hood, the monarch determines to bring this menace to justice and so, donning an ecclesiastic disguise, enters the forest and allows himself to be captured by the outlaws. However, the King is ultimately so impressed by Robin's conduct that when he reveals himself, the King pardons the band and takes Robin back to court with him. Robin remains there for several months before he pines for the freedom of the greenwood, and returns to live out a further twenty years as an outlaw, culminating in his terminal visit to Kirklees.

Hunter observed that if this account is regarded as a report of a genuine historical event, then it corresponds with only one royal tour. Edward I never visited the north during his reign, whilst Edward III was not there until the late 14th Century, by which time the allusion in *Piers Plowman* indicates that the legend was already well established. Therefore, it could only refer to Edward II's tour of the northern counties in 1323 [19].

Leaving Westminster on April 18th, Edward arrived in York on May 1st and stayed at the Archbishop's palace until July, during which period he surveyed the royal park of Plumpton, two miles south of Knaresborough. Significantly, v357 of the *Gest* names "Plomton Parke" as the site where the king laments the depredation of his venison and determines to travel to Nottingham to seek out Robin Hood [20]. Meanwhile, Nottingham is where the historical Edward II ended his tour, staying in the area from November 9th to 24th [21]. Nor do the coincidences end there.

In the royal household accounts, Hunter discovered a record of payments of 3d per week to a porter named Robyn Hode between April 16th and 22th November 1324 [22]. The entries, from the Norman-French *Journal de la Chambre*, are sadly fragmentary prior to the former date, which made it impossible for Hunter to prove exactly when this Robyn Hode entered the King's service [23]. However, he is certainly not recorded after November 1324 [24]. Hunter took this synchronicity as proof of the *Gest's* historical veracity, arguing that the named porter was *the* Robin Hood, who must have joined the King's household during Edward's November 1323 sojourn in Nottingham, and departed a year later when his longing for his former life grew too great, hence why the wage payments ceased [25].

The *Gest* states that Robin lived in the greenwood for twenty-two years following his departure from court. If Hunter's identification is correct, and Robin left the King in November 1324, and if the *Gest* is regarded as a reliable historical source, then this could easily make the year of Robin's death 1347 [26]. Some commentators have suggested that as the date given on his grave at Kirklees Park is 1247, this could represent a simple copy-error, especially if details displayed in the current epitaph were transcribed from an earlier stone [27].

Feeling confident that he had successfully identified a historical figure on which the legend of Robin Hood was based, and so conclusively dating the legend to the first half of the 14th Century, Hunter turned his attention to trying to find evidence of the man prior to his reconciliation with the King [28]. This is where the Yorkshire connection comes in, for with the *Gest* now cemented in his mind as a reliable historical source, Hunter was sure that the geographical evidence of the text indicated that he should concentrate on the vicinity of Barnsdale.

Sure enough, Hunter found in the Court Rolls of the Manor of Wakefield (a town adjacent to Barnsdale), several references to a man named Robert Hood in the early 14th Century [29]. He went somewhat further than the evidence, however, in suggesting that such a man may have fought for Thomas, Earl of Lancaster, also Lord of the Manor of Wakefield for a brief period, in the 1321-2 Contrariant rebellion against Edward II [30]. Following their defeat at the Battle of Boroughbridge on March 16th 1322, all those Contrariant followers who were not killed in combat were outlawed, and their property confiscated.

Robert Hood was also married to a woman called Matilda, who Hunter had speculated may have subsequently become Maid Marian [31]. This corresponds with the naming of the character in Anthony Munday's two plays of 1598, *The Downfall* and *Death of Robin Hood.* He rather casually sidesteps the issue that Munday represents a late source for the legend, and none of the earlier ballads mention the character of Marian, who is thought to have only found her way into the narrative through the May Games in the 16th Century [32].

A further correspondence mooted by Hunter is the tenure of Elizabeth de Staynton at Kirklees Priory and her possible identity as the murderous Prioress. Chapter 2 has shown how Elizabeth came to be installed at Kirklees, but prior to this misfortune, the Staynton family were well-established in the early 14th Century as tenants-in-chief of both the Manor of Tickhill and Pontefract [33]. Hunter points to evidence in the Court Rolls and family deeds that the Stayntons were very loosely connected to the Hoods through business transactions. He also finds Godfrey de Staynton listed amongst those fined for Contrariant sympathies in the wake of Boroughbridge [34]. Hunter hopes that this evidence suggests a possible familial relationship between the Hoods and Stayntons, given that the *Gest* records the Prioress as Robin's kin.

However, there are substantial problems with this supposition quite beyond the paucity of the connection. Not least that Elizabeth could only have been fifteen in 1347 when Robin would have died, according to Hunter's case, and despite her apparent piety, the Cistercian Order did not allow nuns to ascend to that position of authority until they were older than thirty [35].

It is also a fine example of the circular logic, which prevails in so many of these hypotheses.

There is no particular reason to think Elizabeth de Staynton was connected with the death of Robin Hood other than the fact that her grave is the only other sepulchre found at Kirklees today. The argument then runs that she must have been the relevant Prioress because her family can be associated with Robert Hood, but the Stayntons can only be so associated if a connection is already presumed. Each side of the argument is used to support the other, and consequently both are without foundation.

Despite these tendentious leaps of reasoning, Hunter only makes the Wakefield connection tentatively and it is Walker, almost a century later, who follows up Robert Hood of Wakefield. Walker suggests that the man was born sometime between 1285 and 1295, probably the son of Adam Hood who appears in the Court Rolls from 1274 to 1314 [36]. There is no direct evidence for this link and it is merely the first in a series of weak correlations, which Walker presents as indisputable fact.

All references suggest that the family were relatively prosperous, which tallies with the ballads' assertion that Robin Hood was of the yeoman class. In 1316, Walker finds reference to Robert's handmaid, and also the purchase of land at Bichill, near the marketplace in Wakefield, to build a five-roomed house, both of which suggest a certain degree of wealth [37].

Walker is also very concerned to show that despite his status, Robert Hood of Wakefield had always enjoyed an uneasy relationship with the authorities. He notes that in both 1308 and 1315 Hood was summoned to appear before the Court for taking firewood in contravention of forest law, for which offense he was reprimanded and fined. He was also fined in 1316 for failing to attend a muster of troops called by Lord of the Manor of Wakefield, Earl de Warrene, for Edward II's campaign against the Scots [38].

Due to a feud between the two families, Warrene was succeeded by Thomas, Earl of Lancaster as Lord of the Manor of Wakefield and Walker suggests that Hood may have been similarly conscripted when Lancaster raised troops for the Contrariant rebellion in 1321. He points out that, whilst no record of those who fought survives, there is evidence of those who were fined for failing to attend, and that because Robert Hood's name does not appear amongst them, he must have served [39]. Walker also draws attention to the fact that Hood's five roomed house at Bichill is apparently mentioned in an audit of Contrariant property to be seized following their defeat. He regards this as confirmation that Hood was outlawed following his part in the rebellion [40].

Walker finds no mention of Hood again until the Court Rolls of 1335, when he was summoned, along with a couple of others, for "resisting the lord of the manor" [41]. If Robert Hood of Wakefield and Robyn Hode of Edward II's household staff were one and the same person, as Walker infers, then this would fit in with his return to outlawry for twenty-two years following his departure from court, according to the *Gest*. Walker also notes that in the Court Rolls of 1357, the house at Bichill is still identified as having once belonged to Robert Hood, as if that name was once notorious [42].

Further support for the Robert Hood of Wakefield hypothesis came from Percy Valentine Harris, not long after Walker's publication, in a book with the equally confident title *The Truth About Robin Hood*. In addition to lending his tacit support to the claims already made by Hunter and Walker, Harris attempts to bolster their case by finding a figure to correspond to the Sir Roger of Doncaster mentioned in the *Gest* (also known as Red Roger in *Robin Hood's Death*).

Indeed, Harris discovered two mentions of a possible candidate living in Yorkshire in the early 14th Century. The first occurs in a deed of 1301, witnessed by "Roger de Doncastre, chaplain", from Hornygton, eight miles south-west of York. Harris is sure to point out that if Roger was indeed a man of the cloth, this would account for his ability to enter a nunnery and maintain a relationship with its Prioress. The second, from the Wakefield Manor Court Rolls of 1327, indicates that one Roger de Doncastre owned land within ten miles of Kirklees [43].

These references are certainly contemporary with Robert Hood of Wakefield, but there is no evidence that Roger de Doncastre is the same individual in both cases. Harris may think it unlikely that there were two men of the same name in Yorkshire in the same period, but that is a moot point and probability is not proof. Moreover, if Roger de Doncastre had already attained the priesthood in 1301, then he must have been of advanced age by 1347, the suggested date of Robin's death [44]. Whilst he could conceivably have still been capable of an affair with the Prioress, it makes it doubly unlikely that the Prioress in question would have been the fifteen-year-old Elizabeth de Staynton.

Taken as a whole, the Robert Hood of Wakefield hypothesis is undoubtedly seductive. Many of the correspondences appear significant and in the absence of contradictory evidence, much of which has not emerged until far more recently, there really is no case more compelling. Meanwhile, Joseph Hunter should, at least, be given credit for being the first person to mount a genuinely scholarly attempt to locate Robin Hood in the historical record.

Ultimately, however, the argument falls apart. Returning to Hunter's initial speculations, there are a couple of purely methodological problems just to begin with. Despite the evidence of the Elland Feud, it is improbable that many scholars would regard the *Gest* as a reliable historical source, for all its topographical accuracy [45]. For instance, it is not unlikely that artefacts of the period of its composition were projected onto the narrative it describes. Accordingly, if there was a historical Robin Hood, there is no guarantee that he would have been contemporary with a king named Edward. It may have been the original balladeer who lived under such a monarch, and had inserted him into the story for purposes of audience identification [46].

A further difficulty is that the connection between Robert Hood of Wakefield and Robyn Hode, porter to Edward II, relies entirely on conjecture. The slight difference between the names is not itself problematic, as Robyn was originally a Norman diminutive of Robert and Hode a common variant spelling of Hood in the medieval period [47]. However, neither Hunter nor Walker have been able to demonstrate conclusively that they were one and the same man. All they have is a pleasing coincidence. Admittedly, Hunter is careful to point out that he is merely drawing attention to an interesting synchronicity [48], but even that meagre correlation has now been undermined.

In recent years, J.C. Holt has discovered a further reference to Robyn Hode in the *Journal de la Chambre* which throws into question a central tenet of Hunter case. It shows that this individual was paid a wage as King's porter on 27th June 1323, several months before the visit to Nottingham during which the *Gest* claims the King encountered Robin Hood [49]. It is possible to argue that the *Gest* may have been wrong about the exact time and place of the encounter, but this then weakens the contention that the *Gest* can be used as a reliable historical source.

This reference was discovered through ultraviolet analysis of a damaged document, a technique obviously unavailable to Hunter, so he cannot be blamed for his failure to heed it. But it is easier to blame him for his failure to consider the full implications of the final mention of Robyn Hode in the *Journal de la Chambre* on 22nd November 1324, which explicitly states "To Robyn Hode, formerly one of the porters, because he can no longer work, five shillings as a gift, by command" [50]. These details suggest that by 1324, Robyn Hode was already aged and infirm, making it improbable that he could have lived for a further twenty-two years in the woods as an outlaw.

Holt also challenges J.W. Walker's attempts to show that Robert Hood of Wakefield was ever an outlaw. He begins by pointing out that there really is no evidence that Robert Hood fought for the Contrariants. The fact that Hood's name is not listed amongst those fined for failing to appear at the relevant troop muster is not proof that he did in fact attend. It is just as likely that he was never called in the first place [51]. Moreover, it is questionable whether the Wakefield Manor Court Rolls for 1322 ever survived for Walker to have consulted them, as they are currently missing [52].

There are similar problems with Walker's claim that Hood's property at Bichill was repossessed following the Contrariant defeat. Holt shows that the suggestion that this was necessarily a five-roomed house is speculative. The most that can be claimed are five "stalls" and it is not even clear that these are associated with Hood's land [53]. Even more damningly, the assertion that it appears on the 1322 list of confiscated properties appears to be false. Rather, it seems to be counted amongst the "ordinary revenues", which would actually contradict Walker's argument [54].

Holt has also successfully demonstrated that the first half of the 14th Century is too late a date to be looking for a historical figure on whom Robin Hood was based, as the legend was already in wide circulation by the mid-1200s. Between 1261 and 1296, at least eight instances of individuals with the compound surname "Robinhood" have been found in the records [55]. More significantly, five of these are explicitly associated with an outlaw, suggesting that it was an appellation commonly applied to denote their status [56]. This proves that any candidate for the historical Robin Hood after 1261 cannot have been the original. It's possible that the exploits of successive outlaws to whom this nickname was given, subsequently contributed to the narrative but the basis for the legend clearly existed before the 1260s [57].

Accordingly, Robert Hood of Wakefield could not have been *the* Robin Hood and it is unlikely that he was ever even outlawed. The suggested death date of 1347 is similarly untenable. The date of 1247 given by the epitaph on his grave today is still feasible, although it remains questionable whether the legend could have spread as far as south-east England, where the 1261 reference was discovered, in such a short period of time. Meanwhile, the case for Elizabeth de Staynton being the relevant Prioress, or for Roger de Doncastre's involvement, is also rendered unsound. It is still reasonable to suppose, however, that the legend may have originated in the West Riding of Yorkshire [58].

For those who dispute the historicity of the outlaw, Hunter's case has at least provided an interesting possibility for the origin of the grave. It is notable that whilst the modern folly is clearly not the original tomb, all the early references to the inscription at Kirklees indicate that it read: "Here lie Roberd Hude, William Goldburgh, Thomas..." [59]. As such, it sounds as if it could have been the grave of an ordinary person who just happened to have a name similar to Robin Hood.

Hunter's research in the Wakefield Manor Court Rolls showed that the Hood family was already well established in the Wakefield area by the time of the earliest surviving Roll in 1274. Hence, it would not be incongruous to find the grave of an individual with that surname in the cemetery of a religious house, barely ten miles away. Given that there was no date included in the earlier epitaph, it could even be the resting place of the Robert Hood cited by Hunter and Walker.

David Hepworth has recently proved compelling supporting evidence for this supposition. He notes that Robert Hood's property at Bichill in Wakefield purchased in 1316, bordered land owned by a man named Thomas Aleyn who, in later life, also held something called a "corrody" at Kirklees Priory [60]. Corrodies were a medieval form of insurance, according to which a religious institution promised to care for an individual if they ever succumbed to infirmity or disease, in return for a regular donation. A corrody often included accommodation within a monastic house and, therefore, it is quite possible that Thomas Aleyn ended his days at Kirklees Priory [61].

Hepworth also considers it possible that Robert Hood could have held a similar corrody, details of which have not survived, or else visited his former neighbour Thomas Aleyn at Kirklees and died whilst there [62]. It may also be significant that the Nathaniel Johnston/William Stukeley sketch of the grave shows the names "Roberd Hude... Willam Goldburgh... Thomas..." However, as the reliability of that drawing is in doubt [63], this evidence should be accepted only with caution. It also remains to be explained why the site of the grave should lie so far from the former Priory precincts.

Another suggestion recently mooted by John Paul Davis is that the grave marks the burial of a disenfranchised adherent of the Poor Fellow-Soldiers of Christ and the Temple of Solomon, more commonly known as the Knights Templar. Templar pseudo-history is very much in vogue at the moment, and this is a typically fanciful contribution to the canon, depending as it does on Hunter's now discredited faith in the *Gest* as a reliable historical remembrance of Edward II's 1323 tour of the north [64].

The Templars were a Christian military order originally formed in 1129 to protect pilgrims to

Jerusalem following the First Crusade. However, their wealth and influence grew to such an extent that they found themselves regarded as a threat to the authority of the Vatican, and were excommunicated by Pope Clement V in 1307, five months into the reign of Edward II. However, the order was not enforced in England until January 1308, giving many knights in the country an opportunity to escape. Only one hundred and fifty three, primarily elderly, members of the Order were arrested in England, suggesting that many fled into the forests to survive as outlaws, a life which would not have been difficult for such highly trained warriors [65].

Davis argues that the Robin Hood of the *Gest* shows many qualities typical of a Templar knight, including his religious devotion, knowledge of banking and his observance of chastity and poverty [66]. If his reconciliation with the King did indeed occur during Edward II's 1323 tour of the north, then the chronology also fits. He also draws attention to the 1665 drawing of the Kirklees grave slab attributed to Nathaniel Johnston, which shows a three-stepped Calvary, a design commonly found on the grave of Templar Knights across Europe [67].

Of course, there are two substantial problems with Davis' theory. The first is that whilst the three-stepped Calvary may indeed be a customary motif on Templar graves, it was a popular image on sepulchral monuments in the 13th and 14th Centuries generally [68]. A similar point has been made in order to dismiss speculation that the original grave slab from Kirklees could now be found in the cemetery at St. Peter's Church, Hartshead.

Secondly, the case for the *Gest* representing an accurate record of Edward II's northern tour has been wholly undermined by Holt's evidence that the legend predates this episode by at least seventy years. As the reconciliation with the King is an episode unique to the *Gest,* it is vaguely possible that it was grafted on to the story of Robin Hood at a later date, but still acts as a reliable historical source pertaining to the activities of some other outlaw. However, this would be very difficult to prove and without any other evidence to this effect, the principal of parsimony discounts such an *ad-hoc* justification.

So much for the historical cases for the legend of Robin Hood, but what of the mythological interpretations and the role of the grave therein? When Joseph Hunter first presented his attempt to cast the *Gest* as a legitimate historical source, his introduction suggests the project was primarily a reaction against the ascendancy of the mythologists. He fulminates against:

> "...those writers who, acting in the wild humour of the present age, which
> is to put everything that has passed into doubt, and turn the men of former
> days into myths, would represent this outlaw living in the woods as a
> mere creature of the imagination" [69].

The mythological analysis has subsided somewhat today but throughout the 19th and early 20th Centuries, this interpretation was very much in academic favour, as can be seen by Sir Sidney Lee's description of Robin as a "mythical forest elf" in Volume 27 of *The Dictionary of National Biography*, published in 1891 [70]. This followed the emergence of folklore and mythology as an academically respectable discipline in the early part of the 19th Century, thanks to the efforts of writers like Jacob Grimm.

Indeed, it was Grimm in his 1835 work, *Deutsche Mythologie,* who first suggested a mythological source for Robin Hood when he associated the outlaw with the German forest spirit Hodeken, which he argued was itself a corrupted remembrance of the Teutonic deity Woden [71]. Ten years later, the German philologist Adalbert Kuhn reinforced this notion by arguing that "Hood" was a direct corruption of "Woden", whilst "Robin" came from "Ruprecht," a German familiar name for the deity [72].

The first English antiquarian to endorse speculation of this nature was Thomas Wright in his 1846 work, *Essays Concerned with the Literature etc. of England During the Middle Ages,* in which he argues that Robin Hood is a corruption of "Robin with the Hood". He regards this derivation as proof that the outlaw is merely a vestige of the Anglo-Saxon belief in woodland *genii,* on the grounds that such elfish figures are often imagined as wearing hoods, whilst offering further examples of similar mythological corruptions from across Europe which prove to be equally dubious [73].

The precariousness of Wright's reasoning scarcely needs spelling out, but he does at least augment the etymological argument with a further contention that:

> "...one of the strongest proofs of the mythic character of Robin Hood is the connexion of his name with mounds and stones, such as our peasantry always attributed to the fairies of popular superstition" [74].

This is a theme taken up again in the mid-20th Century by the Scottish folklorist Lewis Spence, who explicitly includes the gravestone at Kirklees amongst those "mounds and stones" [75].

Today, the speculation of Wright, Lee and Spence is taken seriously by very few people. Partly this is because the notion that popular legends and customs represent a fossilised relic of the religion of our pagan ancestors has long since fallen out of vogue in academic circles [76]. However, there are also some obvious particular problems in the case of Robin Hood, which the suggestions of the Victorian folklorists failed to consider.

Firstly, there is the parsimonious objection that because Hood was a common surname in the medieval period there is no need to believe that it is a corruption of anything else [77]. Moreover, numerous characters in the *Gest* are described as wearing a hood, including antagonists such as the monk, so to regard "Hood" as a title taken from an attribute unique to Robin is to overrate the significance of this garment in the texts [78]. It is also questionable how Wright can claim that "Robin with the Hood" was once the name for an Anglo-Saxon forest spirit when the name Robin, a diminutive of Robert, is taken from Norman-French [79].

The "connexion of his name with mounds and stones... always attributed to the fairies of popular superstition" is similarly problematic, for the ballads of Robin Hood apparently predate his association with place-names [80]. As previously mentioned, the earliest known place-name connected with the outlaw is Robin Hood's Stone near Barnsdale, recorded in 1422, by which time the ballads were undoubtedly already in circulation. Indeed, none of the locations whose names now refer to Robin Hood appear to have been so titled prior to the 15th Century, suggesting that such sites were not already dedicated to some pagan spirit from which the legend emerged, but simply reflected the popularity of the ballads in the late medieval period [81].

Despite difficulties with the folkloric case being recognised early on, its most monolithic formulation emerged in 1936 in *The Hero: A Study In Tradition, Myth and Drama* by Lord Raglan, peer of the realm, independent scholar and president of the Folklore Society. Not only does Raglan support a variation on the etymological hypothesis, suggesting that the name is derived from Robin-in-the-Wood [82], he attempts to demonstrate that the outlaw is but one manifestation of a global vegetation deity, and the entire legend is a corrupted remembrance of the ritual worship of this figure.

Raglan's argument was greatly inspired by that seminal opus of comparative mythology, *The Golden Bough: A Study In Magic and Religion* by Sir James Frazer, published and successively revised between 1890 and 1922. This tome founded the influential myth-ritual school of scholarship and whilst Frazer's grand synthesis is largely discredited today due to its lack of credible supporting evidence [83], it dominated the fields of anthropology, folklore and even literature until well into the 1960s.

Frazer suggested that many of the principal deities of early Mediterranean and Near Eastern civilisations such as Osiris, Attis and Dionysus were expressions of an Indo-European fertility god archetype, whose story symbolised the pattern of the seasons. This figure is referred to as the 'dying-and-reborn god' for his myth involves his death as the land falls barren with the onset of winter, and subsequent resurrection in the spring. Notoriously, early editions of *The Golden Bough* also associated Jesus Christ with the dying-and-reborn god.

Frazer went even further by suggesting that many of these societies also hoped to ensure the continued turn of the seasons through sympathetic magic, and so selected a member of their community to act as an earthly embodiment of the dying-and-reborn god. This 'divine king' would then himself be sacrificed and the vegetative spirit he represented symbolically resurrected in the body of his successor. Frazer believed this ritual to have been widespread through the ancient world, and many early 20th Century folklorists began to see echoes of the rite in all manner of places, from seasonal customs such as the Morris Dance to architectural motifs like the foliate head.

Whilst Frazer largely confined his speculation to the pantheons of antiquity, in *The Hero*, Lord Raglan extended the hypothesis to cover a whole range of legendary figures from across the world including King Arthur, Moses, Watu Gunung, Siegfried and of course, Robin Hood [84]. He proposes that none of these were ever authentic historical characters, but dim echoes of the dying-and-reborn god whose symbolic legend fuelled the primitive fertility ritual of the divine king.

In support of this argument, Raglan provides a check-list of twenty-two criteria, a majority of which any genuine 'hero' archetype will adhere to [85]. Robin Hood is supposed to meet thirteen of these conditions, six of which pertain to the narrative of the outlaw's death [86]. However, a common criticism of Raglan's work is that he often bends the criteria substantially to allow aspects of various legends to fit, and this is particularly obvious in the case of his application of them to the death narrative.

For instance, the seventeenth characteristic on the list is that the hero is driven from his kingdom, which Raglan perceives as corresponding to Robin finding himself forced to leave Sherwood through illness. Clearly, this is a very loose fit. It is debatable that Sherwood could ever be considered Robin's 'kingdom' as such, and departing on account of illness is scarcely being driven from his position in the same way as Classical hero figures such as Romulus, Oedipus and Heracles.

The eighteenth facet of the 'hero' archetype is that the character must meet a mysterious death. Again, this is debatably applied, as, whilst the version of the story provided by the *Gest* may be somewhat opaque, other accounts leave very little doubt as to the precise circumstances of his demise. The only sense in which it is mysterious lies in the oft-remarked incongruity of the death narrative with the rest of the Robin Hood legend. However, this is not clutching at straws nearly as much as Raglan's suggestion that, because the outlaw meets his death in an upper room, it thereby meets his nineteenth criterion, that the hero typically meets his death at the top of a hill.

The story of Robin's death also demonstrably fails to fit the twenty-first feature of the archetype, namely that there is confusion over the exact place of his death and burial. Raglan claims that the location of Robin's end is "variously given", yet as we have seen, Kirklees is arguably the only spot consistently associated, not only with story of the outlaw's death, but with the legend of Robin Hood as a whole, and has been since at least the late Middle Ages. The only criterion Robin's death fulfils is the twenty-second, stating that miracles were performed at his tomb. His grave at Kirklees has been the site of numerous strange events, which will be fully explored in subsequent chapters.

An even more controversial mythological hypothesis was presented in 1933 by the anthropologist Margaret Murray in *The God of the Witches,* a follow-up to her 1921 tome, *The Witch Cult In Western Europe.* Although Murray's background was in Egyptology, she is principally remembered for these works, in which she posits that the witch-trials of medieval Europe, rather than being the product of superstition and mass hysteria, were actually an attempt by the Church to suppress a genuine surviving pagan religion. This cult, she argued, worshipped a Horned God who was subsequently associated with the Devil by Christian propagandists.

Furthermore, Murray suggests that Robin Hood was, in fact, a disguised aspect of this horned deity. Wright's derivation of the name from "Robin-with-the-Hood" is revived, but this time the hood motif is associated with representations of the Devil [87]. She goes on to cite examples of medieval grimoires that record Robin as one of the names of the Devil and even drags in the popular Tudor trickster spirit, Robin Goodfellow. Evidence from the ballads is also presented, such as Robin's animosity towards the Church, and the fact that his band totalled thirteen, the same number as a witches coven [88].

Murray's arguments were wholeheartedly endorsed by the author and poet, Robert Graves, in his monumental work of comparative religion, *The White Goddess* [89], but despite such high profile support, the assertions are demonstrable nonsense. Murray's methodology and conclusions have been criticised across the board and few today accept her claim that pagan religion survived into the medieval period as a witch-cult, or that the witch trials of the period were a conscious attempt by the Church to extinguish it [90]. Her credibility is even waning amongst the neo-pagan traditions she inadvertently helped to found.

Barbara Lowe in her 1955 essay *Robin Hood In the Light of History*, directs attention to some particular problems with the identification of Robin Hood with a horned god and shows how Murray distorted the literary evidence to her own ends. For instance, Murray's insistence that Robin's band numbered thirteen is supported nowhere by the texts, in which the hero has anything from six followers to seven score [91]. Equally, his animosity towards the Church in the ballads is purely towards its corrupt officialdom and, in fact, Robin is frequently shown to be a devoted Christian, a portrayal which presents a substantial stumbling block for anybody arguing that he is a disguised pagan icon [92].

Murray's powers of reasoning are also called into question. It is certainly bad logic to suggest that because *some* characters called Robin were associated with the Devil in the Middle Ages, then *all* characters called Robin must have been. Any connection with Robin Goodfellow is easily dismissed, as there is little evidence for this spirit before the 16th Century, and none of the stories associated with him bear any relation to the stories associated with Robin Hood, unless there is a lost canon of ballads in which the now inexplicably cloven-hoofed outlaw plays tricks on milkmaids [93].

There is, however, one aspect of Murray's argument which remains interesting, and that is her analysis of an episode in *Robin Hood's Death*. She writes:

> "In one of the earliest ballads of this popular hero, there is a description of how he went to be let blood by his cousin, the prioress of a convent of nuns; she treacherously left the wound unbound and he bled to death. Part of the account shows, however, that his death was expected for his route to the priory was lined with people, mourning and lamenting for his approaching death. The resemblance to the death processions of Joan of Arc and Gilles de Rais cannot be overlooked" [94].

Murray's implication is that Robin went willingly to his death as a sacrificial victim in the supposed fashion of the pagan god-kings of antiquity. This argument is still problematic, not least because damage to the Percy Folio manuscript at this point makes it difficult to determine the full significance of the episode. It may simply have been that the women were lamenting because Robin was clearly unwell. It certainly introduces a degree of foreshadowing into the narrative, which functions well purely as a literary flourish.

Nonetheless, it remains a curious and unique incident in the ballads, contributing to the "haunting, fatalistic, even ritualistic aura" which Fran and Geoff Doel see in *Robin Hood's*

Death. They go on to remark:

> "This is the one surviving scene in a Robin Hood ballad which clearly gives a strong atmosphere of ritual, mythology and fatalism and which hints at another possible dimension to the significance of the Robin Hood legend" [95].

The fact that the "banning" woman is encountered at the crossing of the "black water" (which, presuming a proximity to Kirklees, could well be intended as the River Calder) may be relevant. John Matthews does not fail to notice the similarities to a manifestation of the Celtic 'bean-sidhe' (often Anglicised as 'banshee') known as the Washer at the Ford, a premonitory spirit said to haunt river crossings rinsing the blood-stained garments of those who were about to die [96]. Even if this strict identification is not accepted, it is still notable that in many pre-modern cultures river crossings were regarded as liminal points where Otherworldly encounters often took place.

A common argument against a mythological interpretation of Robin Hood is that, unlike Arthurian legend, his story takes place in a firmly naturalistic milieu [97] and on the face of it, there are no clearly magical elements to any of the original narratives (the revisionism of the 1980s television series *Robin of Sherwood* notwithstanding). However, if we accept that the women lamenting on Robin's route to Kirklees do so in foreknowledge of his death, then the episode does indeed represent an instance of the supernatural entering the legend.

Whilst this scene alone is not sufficient evidence to support a mythological interpretation of the hero, it could be a case of a mythic tableau inserted into the narrative for dramatic effect. To deny the analysis of Robin Hood as a 'fossilised' pagan deity does not necessarily mean that the legend entirely lacks motifs and imagery, which had been imported from more obviously mythological traditions for the sake of a good story and audience recognition. Intertextuality may have been as much a facet of literature in the medieval period as it is today.

The Robin Hood legend as a whole undeniably possesses mythic attributes, even if Robin himself is not a mythological godhead. Whilst mythology is often colloquially used to refer to the religious traditions of ancient pagan societies across the world, a more technical understanding of the concept "myth" recognises it as a metaphorical narrative, the purpose of which is to express a certain worldview [98]. It need not refer to a religious tradition at all and, in fact, the majority of myths operating in our society today are entirely secular.

Moreover, an influential essay by Joseph Nagy, called *The Paradoxes of Robin Hood*, has observed numerous liminal correspondences in the Robin Hood legend. Liminality is a significant mythic motif that deals with thresholds, both literal and metaphorical. The folklorist Bob Trubshaw describes it "about being 'betwixt-and-between', a transitional phase to something or somewhere else" [99]. Narratively, it often represents ambiguity and reversals, an appreciation of which is an integral aspect of the existential human condition. It is hardly surprising that it is so widely represented in myth, and often embodied in social rites-of-passage.

Nagy cites many examples of liminality in the original Robin Hood narratives. The outlaw himself is a figure who occupies the space between society and the wild, order and chaos [100]. Meanwhile, the ballads often feature examples of reversals through disguises such as the King concealing himself as a peasant in the *Gest*, or Robin adopting the mantle of Guy of Gisborne in the eponymous ballad [101]. Such stories may have inspired Robin's role in the 16th Century May Games, which saw him replacing the Lord of Misrule to preside over a liminal period of tolerated social disorder.

The death narrative also exhibits several liminal symbols. The lamenting woman at the crossing of the water has already been mentioned, but the Prioress is also profoundly liminal in the tale. She represents both the spiritual realm of the Church, but also the material world of lust and corruption in her collusion with Roger of Doncaster [102]. Today, Kirklees remains a liminal location. It lies at the borders of the urban and rural, and since the Dissolution, the former Priory site exists between the sacred and profane. Arguably, this liminality has influenced many of the later traditions associated with it, and as a later chapter will argue, it is still used for the modern rite-of-passage known as 'legend-tripping'.

Nagy concludes:

> "Liminality, a state in which normal distinctions and order are transcended, is a context for the recreation and reformulation of order... In the context of liminality cultural concepts and values appear in unique, paradoxical, almost chaotic forms. The confusion of separate categories is a means of reinforcing separateness... The reaffirmation of social values in a liminal context through paradoxes is apparent in the Robin Hood tradition... The ballads present a liminal world where basic social values are juxtaposed and even mixed with their seeming opposites. Thereby, these values are highlighted and endowed with new richness and complexity" [103].

Ultimately, whilst it may not have originated as such, it is now reasonable to say that the Robin Hood legend has become mythic, that is to say, a narrative which communicates ideals and concepts which our culture recognises as valuable [110]. Themes such as redistributive justice and the freedom of the greenwood embody persistent human preoccupations, which continue to resonate in modern society, and the liminality of the legend, which the death narrative adeptly embodies, reinforces these through paradox. This may be one of the fundamental reasons why the story has endured for so many centuries, whilst so many other medieval tales are unknown to all but scholars.

CHAPTER FIVE

Tear Down The Walls

D espite its historical significance as a focus of popular belief for almost five centuries, today Robin Hood's grave remains on private land, unloved by its guardians and unvisited by the public. Or at least unvisited in any legitimate capacity, for in the last twenty-five years the site has been the battleground for a militant campaign which has become as much about overturning anachronistic feudal privileges, as securing public access to a culturally important monument.

The continued failure of these efforts, despite regular press interest and popular support, has led to persistent trespass by members of the local community in an emulation of the outlaw hero's own attitude towards authority, with Lady Armytage unflatteringly cast as a modern day Sheriff of Nottingham. As even one respectable public source has noted "Robin Hood would, of course, have blithely scaled the wall, Keep Out notice or no Keep Out notice" [1].

However, it was not always thus. Earlier generations of the Armytage family, from Sir Samuel onwards, seemed perfectly happy to exploit their association with the Robin Hood legend. As much can be observed from their efforts to protect and beautify the gravesite in the mid-1700s. Kirklees historian David Hepworth points out that the fashion amongst landed gentry in the 18th Century for extensive landscape gardens, complete with a showpiece folly would have made the grave a very desirable feature indeed [2], and one which the Armytages were, no doubt, keen to show off to their peers.

The provisions to deter souvenir hunters introduced in 1785 [3] suggest that the public were able to visit the grave with impunity at this time. Given the closer proximity of the old road to the monument, this is perhaps understandable. It may have only been with the construction of the Elland & Obelisk Turnpike in 1815 that it became easier for the Armytages to consolidate the borders of their estate, and discourage people from coming and going to the grave as they saw fit [4].

Yet at one time Kirklees seems to have been bristling with adverts for its connections with the outlaw. From the 17th to 19th Centuries, a life-sized wooden representation of Robin Hood with Little John, Will Scarlet and Much the Miller's Son, occupied a prominent position at Kirklees Hall, and was often remarked upon by visitors [5]. The display appears to have been removed some time in the early 20th Century, to be once more unearthed in 1987 upon the sale of the Hall, and included in the auction of its contents [6].

A number of Robin Hood "relics" were also on display in the library at the Hall. Such artefacts were a popular phenomenon in earlier centuries – a number were similarly exhibited at St. Anne's Well in Nottinghamshire [7] – but doubtless the provenance was entirely spurious, their reputation manufactured by the Armytages for the amusement of credulous visitors.

Originally, principal amongst these "relics" was a bow said to have belonged to Robin Hood, but this was lost in the confusion following the death of Sir John Armytage VI at the Battle of St. Cast in 1758 [8]. Later research has shown that it fell into the possession of a Mr. Bartlett of Barlborough Hall near Chesterfield in Derbyshire. When this house and its contents came to be sold in the 1930s, the bow was purchased by the writer Sir Osbert Sitwell and went on display once more, this time at *his* ancestral home, Renishaw Hall [9]. A new bow must have appeared at Kirklees, however, as a writer for the *Brighouse Echo* in 1952 recalls seeing such an artefact during his childhood, along with the purported boots and staff of the outlaw [10].

Perhaps the most curious Robin Hood relic kept at Kirklees Hall was his helmet. Somehow, a tradition had become attached to this item that whoever tried it on would shortly afterwards lose all the hair on their head. The story is told that Hugh Brontë braved this curse whilst visiting his brother Rev. Patrick Brontë, who from 1811 to 1815 served as curate at St. Peter's Church in Hartshead [11]. Upon returning to Ireland, Hugh would frequently boast about his feat, but - sure enough - his hair soon began to fall out with great rapidity, and he was left entirely bald [12].

Later, Patrick's daughter Charlotte Brontë would do her own bit for the promotion of the Robin Hood legend at Kirklees, with the publication of her novel *Shirley* in 1849. Although Charlotte was born after her father's tenure at Hartshead, she was intimately familiar with Kirklees herself. This acquaintance began in 1831 when she was a pupil at Roe Head School in Mirfield [13], which was within sight of the Armytage estate. She returned to the school as a teacher between 1835 and 1838, and even stayed at Kirklees Hall in 1848 whilst researching material for *Shirley* [14].

The novel is largely based on Patrick Brontë's recollections of his involvement with the 1811-12 Luddite uprising whilst he was curate at Hartshead, and the topography corresponds precisely to the area around Kirklees and the neighbouring Spen Valley. Kirklees Park itself is thinly disguised as "Nunwood" and described as "one of Robin Hood's haunts" [15].

In her 1857 *Life of Charlotte Brontë*, fellow novelist Elizabeth Gaskell exposed this subterfuge with a rhapsodic passage describing:
"The park of Kirklees, full of sunny glades, speckled with black shadows of

immemorial yew-trees; the grey pile of building, formerly a "House of professed Ladies'; the mouldering stone in the depths of the wood, under which Robin Hood is said to lie" [16].

Such a picturesque sketch contrasts starkly with some of the more recent descriptions of the locale, as if over the course of the 20th Century the spirit of place has curdled through neglect.

Gaskell's portrayal is certainly not unusual for writers visiting the site in the 19th Century. Around the same time, another (anonymous) author reported:

"I had the strangest emotions when I first stood over the grave of this old forest hero. I stood there and had no words, nor can I now find any to tell what my feelings were. Brave-hearted Robin! Thou hast a fit resting-place in this glorious park, amongst these solemn yews and silent trees" [17].

Again, this is a far cry from the lamentations which tend to accompany descriptions of the grave today.

Of course, Robin Hood was always a favourite icon for many second and third generation Romantic writers, the outlaw having evolved into a character who embodied many of their most enduring concerns. This fascination began with John Keats' *Robin Hood (To a Friend)* [18] and Leigh Hunt's *Robin Hood, An Outlaw* in 1820 [19] and arguably persisted through the next century, reaching its culmination in Alfred Noyes' oft-quoted 1911 verse, *Song of Sherwood* [20].

Many of these works dwelt on the Sherwood association, finding in the Nottinghamshire forest a home-grown counterpart to the Classical notions of Arcadia which the Romantics so admired. It is scarcely surprising, therefore, that many lesser-known writers, often with a local background, found similar inspiration in Kirklees Park whilst seeking to carve out their niche. At the height of its splendour, such a landscape could hardly fail to rouse those of a poetic persuasion, and whilst none of the odes it prompted show any great artistry, they remain a testament to its potent *genius loci*.

Kirklees had already been immortalised in verse in Richard Griffith's poem of 1760, *Kirk-Leas*, although this was primarily a eulogistic piece composed to celebrate the achievements of Sir John Armytage VI following his death in battle [21]. Later works, more firmly in the Romantic tradition, included *At the Grave of Robin Hood* by the minor Scottish vagabond poet John Ramsay, and *Robin Hood's Grave In Kirklees Park* (or *The Gala at Kirklees* in an earlier draft) by George Searle Phillips [22]. Phillips was editor of the *Leeds Times* and a well-known Victorian literary critic in both Britain and the United States.

The Armytage family continued to exploit the potential of the grave into the early 20th Century. Between 1904 and 1907, Sir George Armytage V spent £39.9s.1d on restoring "Robin Hood's Room" in the Gatehouse [23]. It was possibly at this time that many of the relics, which had once been exhibited in the library at the Hall, were moved into the upper room of the Gatehouse and placed in display cases, along with various materials outlining the legend of Robin Hood's death at Kirklees, effectively creating a small museum.

During the early decades of the century, the public were permitted to visit the grave on certain Sunday mornings [24] and it made a fine attraction at the countless garden parties, galas and summer fairs which took place on the estate, with attendees typically charged 3d to see the monument. Perhaps the most memorable of these events was a Conservative Party fundraiser held on Saturday 26th July 1930, one of the largest gatherings the area had ever seen. Party leader and three-time Prime Minister, Stanley Baldwin, gave a speech, whilst other lures included two performances by the Brighouse and Rastrick Brass Band, a Punch & Judy show, displays by the Yorkshire Aero Club and a gang of trick motorcyclists [25].

The local community did not fail to capitalise on their Robin Hood connections either and, unlike in recent years, it does not appear that the Armytage family objected to any of them. Robin Hood Mill and Little John Mill had operated in Clifton since 1786 [26], whilst a pub named *The Robin Hood* opened in Brighouse in the late 19th Century. Most spectacularly, in 1922 a mosaic of the outlaw was erected atop a twelve foot stone structure at a prominent junction in Clifton. Known as "Ye Olde Kirklees," it had been constructed following a competition in the *Daily Mail* inviting readers to send in designs for village signs. It was dismantled in World War Two, when all such markers were removed for fear of German invasion [27].

It was apparently with the increasing influence of John Armytage VII, who ultimately succeeded to the baronetcy in 1953, that the family began to distance themselves from the Robin Hood legend. In contrast to his romantically-minded ancestors such as Sir Samuel and Sir George V, he seems to have had no particular interest in the story himself, and his desire to transform the estate from parkland into a modern agricultural business probably rendered tourists an unwelcome distraction.

In the 1980s, elderly Mirfield resident Tommy Dransfield told Barbara Green:

> "I remember going into the gatehouse in 1951. There were several glass topped showcases in a terrible state. I approached Sir John with a proposition regarding the scattered bits of relics that he might let me clean them up and re-label them, and put them on display in Mirfield library for the Festival of Britain but he refused" [28].

This sort of behaviour was clearly the beginning of a trend, which saw the Armytage family not only discourage people from visiting the grave, but from any knowledge of its existence. There were a few articles discussing the site in the *Brighouse Echo* during the 1950s possibly inspired by the publication of J.W. Walker's *True History of Robin Hood*, which briefly reawakened interest in the Yorkshire aspects of the legend, but following these there was scarcely a mention of the monument in the newspaper for almost twenty-five years.

By 1983, Sir John Armytage VII was on his death bed. Barbara Green, a Clifton resident then in her late thirties, was the district nurse sent by Calderdale Health Authority to attend to him [29].

Whilst Green had been told of the existence of Robin Hood's grave by her parents during her childhood, this was to be her first personal exposure to the grandeur of the Kirklees estate. It was to prove the inception of both an enduring fascination, and an acrimonious controversy.

As somebody already interested in local history, Green inevitably grew increasingly curious about the site and eventually asked Sir John's wife to show her the grave. The former nurse recalls:

> "Having helped Lady Armytage in the care of her husband and struck up what seemed to be an amicable friendship, I felt quite comfortable about asking her if I could have a look at the famous grave. I had no idea at the time that there could have been the possibility of her refusing my request, but in the event, she very graciously complied and a date was arranged" [30].

However, at first, securing public access to the decaying monument was not the primary focus of Green's attention. Following her first, and only official visit to the grave, she devoted her energies to investigating the wider links between the Robin Hood legend and the West Riding of Yorkshire, spending a great deal of time in Wakefield City Archives further researching the Robert Hode of Wakefield hypothesis originally postulated by Joseph Hunter and J.W. Walker [31].

The outcome of these efforts was the twenty-six page *Marion's Christmas Rose,* a retelling of the Robin Hood legend for children with an emphasis on its Yorkshire aspects. Published towards the end of 1984, ironically by a Devon-based company, Merlin Press, it was printed in a limited run of 3,500 copies to be sold at various local bookshops across West Yorkshire and, of course, in Nottingham, the centre of the Robin Hood tourist trade [32]. Indeed, early press coverage of Green's interest upon the publication of the book tended to concentrate on the conflict between Nottinghamshire and Yorkshire.

Together with her neighbour, Ruth Harrington, Green embarked on a promotional campaign for *Marion's Christmas Rose* through the summer of 1985, out of which the Yorkshire Robin Hood Society would ultimately be born. Their strategy largely consisted of running a stall at various public events across the region such as the Brighouse Gala, selling copies of the book and providing further information on the outlaw's Yorkshire connections, often with Green and Harrington in costume [33]. Occurring at the height of silly season, this attracted widespread interest in the local press and even a national mention in the *Daily Star* [34], focusing on the fact that the photogenic Harrington was forced to dress up as Robin herself due to a dearth of men willing to suffer the indignity of wearing green tights.

The Yorkshire Robin Hood Society (herefoth abbreviated as YRHS) was officially formed following a particularly eventful attempt to sell *Marion's Christmas Rose* at the medieval fair held annually in Nottingham. Green explains:

> "It seemed that we had touched a sensitive issue with our Robin Hood of Yorkshire theme because suddenly the medieval market place was in

uproar – because of us! The Chief Town Councillor... rounded on us in no uncertain terms... Horde(s) of wrathful Nottinghamites descended upon our stall while we tried not to laugh" [35].

Green claims that they were informed of the dismay of the actual Sheriff of Nottingham at their activities, and were asked to cover up the Yorkshire references on their stall following complaints from attendees. However, the Sheriff, Councillor Tom Harby. subsequently denied any knowledge of the dispute in the Yorkshire press:

"I knew nothing about it. We don't really know at this stage which councillor it was that complained... If I had known about it (the YRHS stall) at the time I don't think I would've been that annoyed" [36]

The aims of the newly-formed Society were stated as:

a) To promote the Yorkshire connections with Robin Hood;
b) To save Robin Hood's grave and the priory gatehouse from destruction;
c) To promote tourism in Calderdale with the cooperation of local councils if this can be obtained" (37).

A regular hand-made magazine was produced for members detailing Robin Hood's association with Yorkshire and the history of Kirklees, along with frequent press releases distributed to the local newspapers [38]. However, in those pre-internet days, raising awareness of the Society was difficult and its membership would never number more than one hundred [39].

Barbara Green appointed herself as President of the Society, and whilst Lady Armytage was asked to become its patron, she refused [40]. It was the first in a long line of snubs. Green eventually settled on the patronage of Seán Manchester (who at that time had yet to take holy orders and was referring to himself only as Lord Manchester) following their meeting at the Barnet Carnival in May 1987 [41].

Press coverage of the YRHS was initially very favourable. Although some newspapers continued to dwell jokily on the perceived Yorkshire/Nottinghamshire conflict, many local commentators took it more seriously. An opinion piece in the *Halifax Evening Courier* in June 1986 notes:

"The growing feud between Yorkshire and Nottinghamshire claimants to Robin Hood may seem like a pleasant little diversion but in an age where tourism is increasingly important to local economies there may be more at stake" [42].

There was also a mild degree of television interest. In 1985, Green and Harrington had been filmed for a slot on BBC1's regional news programme, *Look North,* although the shooting took place in Shibden Park as the producers could not secure permission to film at the grave [43]. A later BBC documentary called *Facts* encountered the same problem, and resorted to filming the pair poring over books at Wakefield Library, although in the end, this was never actually broadcast [44].

Lady Armytage was certainly not pleased with the increased publicity, even though at this stage the campaign was still in its infancy. Following a request from the YRHS to operate a stall at the 1986 Kirklees garden party, Lady Armytage and her personal assistant paid Barbara Green a visit at her home in Clifton. According to Green's recollection of events, the PA did most of the talking, and was particularly upset about the way in which *Marion's Christmas Rose* promoted the site of the grave at Kirklees. She was concerned that this would encourage people to visit the monument, and for the first time it became very clear that wider public access was not on Lady Armytage's agenda. The YRHS were naturally refused permission to attend the garden party [45].

This marked the turning point in Barbara Green's attitude towards Lady Armytage. Whereas previously Green had been amicable, if not deferential, such a dismissive response to her labours and enthusiasm led to an increased resentment towards the class privilege which Lady Armytage represented. As Green herself perceived it, "War had been declared" [46]. From this moment on, both parties grew ever more entrenched in their respective positions. For Green this meant running an increasingly militant campaign for access to the grave through the YRHS and the local press, whilst Lady Armytage simply persisted in ignoring the situation altogether.

It was soon after this incident that the YRHS first began to express concern regarding the dilapidated condition of the grave and gatehouse. An article was published in the November 1986 issue of the National Trust's magazine, *Out of Town*, drawing attention to the existence of Robin Hood's grave and particularly its poor state of repair [47]. The Society also began to contact organisations such as English Heritage and the Yorkshire Archaeological Society, along with MPs and various local councils to express dismay at the continued neglect of the historical monuments at Kirklees [48].

Increasingly, the YRHS attempted to quash the media narrative regarding a supposed feud between Nottinghamshire and Yorkshire, in order to direct attention specifically towards the grave. They sent a letter to the *Nottingham Evening Post* saying "We would like to make it clear that we are not out to steal Robin Hood but simply to promote his Yorkshire connections" [49]. This was at odds with some of their earlier rhetoric, in which they had insisted that the historical evidence for a Yorkshire Robin Hood was far stronger than Nottinghamshire's. Nonetheless, they were now building bridges and in a conciliatory gesture made Jim Lees, President of the Nottingham Robin Hood Society, an honorary member of the YRHS [50].

When the sale of Kirklees Hall was announced in early 1987, many believed that a chance to secure access to the grave had finally arrived. Even though the land on which it stood would remain part of Lady Armytage's estate, the prospect of the Hall being converted into a hotel led to repeated suggestions in the local press that the time was ripe to fully exploit the tourist potential of the area's connection with the Robin Hood legend. In an editorial, the *Brighouse Echo* opined "It's a wonderful opportunity for this area and one which should be taken without delay" [51].

There were even promising signs coming from the administrators of the Kirklees estate itself. The *Huddersfield Daily Examiner* reported that:

> "Talks have been going on between estate officials, council officers and representatives of bodies like the English Tourist Board to find ways of raising money for a complete restoration – after which the monument would be open for the public to view [52]. 'There are some developments, but nothing definite as yet,' estate manager Martin Webster said."

Meanwhile, Lady Armytage remarked to the *Brighouse Echo*, "Eventually we hope that the site will be open to the public" [53].

A couple of months later the newspaper reported that Barbara Green and Ruth Harrington had been invited to Kirklees Hall (where Lady Armytage was still living until the sale was completed) to discuss plans for public access to the grave. Green told the *Echo*:

> "We were very pleased to be invited to the hall by Lady Armytage. It was indeed a step towards cooperation concerning future plans but I think we have a long way to go. There still seem to be a lot of problems that need sorting out such as finance and access to the site. We have left the meeting feeling unsure that anything had been achieved, but it was certainly a start" [54].

Yet in her 2001 self-published book, *Secrets of the Grave,* Green paints quite a different picture of the meeting. She claims that Lady Armytage started the conversation with the statement "This Robin Hood business is becoming rather a nuisance" and went on to insist that the prospect of vandalism and the logistical difficulties, combined with the demands of running an agricultural business, made it unlikely that unfettered public access to the grave would ever be a possibility. Vague promises were made to allow parties of YRHS members to visit to the grave accompanied by estate staff, but these were subsequently reneged upon, with Lady Armytage claiming she would now be "extremely busy with several projects" [55].

Nonetheless, speculation about the tourist potential of Kirklees's Robin Hood connections rumbled on in the local press. In early 1988, the Old Corn Mill on the banks of the River Calder, almost within sight of the grave, was purchased from the Kirklees estate by developer John Akins with plans to turn it into a restaurant and hotel complex. The *Brighouse Echo* reported "The development, based on the theme of Robin Hood, will be known as the Robin Hood Hamlet... 'The whole thing is going very well indeed' said Mr. Akins, 'There is a lot of interest in the Robin Hood theme and we all feel it has potential'" [56]. The YRHS were even invited to provide information on Robin's local links for the scheme [57].

Similar plans were mooted for the Trusthouse Forte hotel, which was constructed on green-belt land off Coal Pit Lane at Clifton, close to Junction 25 of the M62. However, whilst both of the developments themselves went ahead successfully, the proposed Robin Hood themes never materialised. The manager of the Trust House Forte allegedly later told Barbara Green that:

> "He didn't want to upset Lady Armytage. He went on with painful chivalry that there was no point in promoting the Robin Hood legend as no one could visit the grave and they must respect her ladyship's privacy" [58].

Still, guests at the hotel were provided with a leaflet entitled *Forte Hotel Brighouse: An historical note* written by local historian and Kirklees estate employee, David Nortcliffe, which mentioned the outlaw's grave [59]. It did not provide any detail regarding its location other than to say it was "just over one mile from this hotel" but given that the monument appears on Ordnance Survey maps of the area, such ambiguity is unlikely to have confused anybody with a genuine interest. Thus, whilst the hotel may not have adopted a Robin Hood theme, contrary to Green's claims, it certainly promoted the gravesite.

Despite their perception of institutional indifference towards the area's folkloric heritage, the YRHS were undeterred. Indeed, it spurred their campaign on, in the conviction that they were the only ones who seriously cared about the Kirklees legend and the monuments there. They continued to lobby heritage organisations and the local press, whilst Barbara Green had compiled her historical researches into a new non-fiction book, which she hoped to persuade Calderdale Council's Leisure Service to publish.

Inevitably, after having kept the manuscript for almost a year, Calderdale Council did not prove to be enthusiastic about the venture. Tourism Officer Jane Branton told Green, "It has been deliberate policy to keep the Robin Hood connection at a fairly low profile because of Lady Armytage's desire to keep the site of the grave private." However, she cited the fact that a book on Robin Hood of Yorkshire was beyond their publication remit as the primary reason for failing to take it on [60].

It was also during 1988 that the YRHS became increasingly involved with the interests of their patron, Seán Manchester and his cumbersomely titled organisation, the International Society for the Advancement of Irreproducible Vampire and Lycanthropy Research. A full account of the Kirklees Vampire 'flap' will be given in a later chapter but it is worth noting here that press coverage connecting the YRHS with these paranormal speculations – of which there was a great deal from 1988 onwards – made it far easier for their opponents to portray them as cranks, whose arguments and activities need not be taken seriously.

Meanwhile, in July 1988, Barbara Green, and increasingly active YRHS member Evelyn Friend, agreed to appear on the BBC1 show *People*. The programme, hosted by former tabloid journalist Derek Jameson, focused on eccentric individuals and it is scarcely surprising, therefore, that Green and Friend felt they were misrepresented [61]. Everything they said about the Kirklees legend was edited out and Friend was left with a single line "I am Robin Hood in drag!" It is significant that the producer was Peter Bazalgette, later to make a substantial fortune out of judicious editing in his role as Chairman and Creative Director of Endemol, the company responsible for *Big Brother*.

Nonetheless, the documentary did include footage of Robin Hood's grave, although there was nothing in the programme to suggest its whereabouts, or connect it with the activities of the YRHS. Bazalgette told the *Brighouse Echo*:

> "The grave is on private land and the owner made it a condition that we
> didn't say exactly where it was situated. Lady Margarete Armytage who

owns the land said she was afraid trespassers would find the grave so we agreed to keep it secret" [62].

Lady Armytage's ongoing intransigence led to further lobbying of official bodies by the YRHS. At their first annual general meeting, held at the *Three Nuns*, on 29th April 1989 they resolved to continue pressuring local authorities, despite a recent dismissal from the Tourism Development Officer of Kirklees Metropolitan Council citing "limited interest in many of the sites" [63]. The Society also attempted to take their campaign to parliament. Calder Valley MP, Sir Donald Thompson, had already proved unhelpful but they persisted, contacting the Labour MP for Dewsbury, Ann Taylor, who at that time was Opposition Spokesman for the Environment [64].

Ann Taylor initially appeared to be more cooperative and on April 27th the following year, she attended the Society's AGM at the *Three Nuns* to receive a petition from YRHS members, many of whom were in medieval costume [65]. The petition, calling for restoration of the historical sites in Kirklees Park and subsequent public access, had been signed by over five hundred people. The names included Richard Carpenter, writer of the popular 1980s television series *Robin of Sherwood,* and three of its stars, Clive Mantle, Robert Addie and Jeremy Bulloch, collected at a fan convention in Middlesex [66].

However, the YRHS were later disappointed to receive a letter from the MP baldly stating, "Lady Armytage informed me that the public do have access to the grave by appointment" [67]. This response inevitably seemed disingenuous to them when their members had so often been refused such permission, despite numerous requests. Meanwhile, an article in the *Spenborough Guardian* reported that Lady Armytage had "no particular reaction" to the petition. It went on to quote her as saying, "As far as I am concerned there are no plans for its (the grave's) future" [68]. Quite a retreat from the guarded optimism she displayed in 1987.

The 1990 meeting at the *Three Nuns* also marked an important watershed in the activities of the YRHS. Hitherto they had confined their campaign, largely through the local press and public events, to raising awareness of the Robin Hood sites at Kirklees and the need for access. But now they added a new string to their bow and began to embark on unofficial visits to the grave, with Barbara Green guiding many members who had been denied permission by Lady Armytage.

On this first occasion, they were scarcely subtle. Incited by a reporter from the radical (and now defunct) *Leeds Other Paper*, a large party comprised of YRHS members alongside medieval re-enactors from the Company of the White Boar, made their way across the fields behind the *Three Nuns* to the gravesite [69]. The group, many of whom were in costume, negotiated barbed wire, nettles, rhododendrons and brambles in their quest to find the ruinous monument. Surprisingly, despite their conspicuousness, they did not attract the attention of the gamekeepers.

Over the next two decades Barbara Green would trespass on the Kirklees Park estate a number of times to show the grave to those who had been fobbed off by Lady Armytage, although the visits were typically less blatant than the first. It is a pursuit that has proved highly controversial, even amongst those who believe in securing greater public access to the grave. Trespass is, of course, a civil offence and some critics have argued that by encouraging such behaviour, the YRHS harmed their own case, further antagonising Lady Armytage and making her ever more determined to keep the public off the estate.

However, trespassing to see the grave had been a common pastime amongst local people for decades before the YRHS started to indulge in it. In 1974, the *Huddersfield Examiner* had published an article entitled "Forgotten tomb of Robin Hood needs repair" which noted extensive vandalism at the site, including graffiti and damage to the stonework [70]. Meanwhile, Lady Armytage told the *Brighouse Echo* in 1987:

> "We've had so many problems with trespassers trampling all over it. There were times when my husband and I would clear up the mess only to return the next day to find it vandalised once again" [71].

Of course, whilst the trespasses of the YRHS were conducted in a rather more innocent spirit of genuine enthusiasm for the site, such activity could not help but align them with the vandals in the minds of their opponents. But as Barbara Green pointed out in her rebuttal to Lady Armytage, once again invoking the vandalism issue in the *Spenborough Guardian*:

> "How is stopping everyone else seeing the grave going to solve the problem with the vandals? Perhaps if the grave were less isolated and hidden, the vandals would have less chance of operating. Hidden away beneath a thick shrubbery of laurel bushes, surely it is an attraction for wrongful purposes" [72].

Although the efforts of the YRHS to secure public access to the grave continued to be frustrated, their efforts to publicise the Kirklees sites and Robin Hood's Yorkshire connections finally met with some success when Barbara's Green's non-fiction book, *The Outlaw Robin Hood: His Yorkshire Legend,* was finally published in 1991. Having previously been rejected by several local authorities including Calderdale, Bradford and Wakefield, it had eventually been taken on by Kirklees Metropolitan Council's Leisure Services [73]. A launch party took place on July 25th at the Showcase Cinema in Birstall, to coincide with the release of the film *Robin Hood: Prince of Thieves* [74].

Once again, this prompted extensive local press coverage for the Society. One article in the *Halifax Evening Courier* took Calderdale Council to task for their failure to publish a book dealing with historical sites within their boundaries, with an article entitled ""Council shunned a legend". The authority's director of Leisure Services, Paul Sheean, responded:

> "It was felt inappropriate to commit resources to the project because the only link to Calderdale was the alleged siting of the grave. After consulting with the owner of the land it was decided that the council could not encourage people to visit the grave against the landowner's wishes" [75].

Despite this minor achievement in their campaign, the YRHS was placed on hiatus as an active organisation in 1993. Barbara Green places the blame, not on lack of public interest or continued obstruction by their opponents, but on her own health issues and personal conflict amongst the core members of the group [76]. Nonetheless, Green was still regularly contacted for comment by the local press on matters pertaining to Robin Hood, such as in 1996 when Nottingham City Council considered distancing themselves from their Robin Hood connections, fearing that the image discouraged potential business investment. Inevitably, this led to renewed calls for Calderdale Council to cash in on the tourist potential of the Kirklees sites instead [77].

Nonetheless, Lady Armytage remained steadfast in her determination to keep the public away from the grave. She told the *Bradford and Pennine News*:

> "Urban people do not understand this place, they don't know the difference between grass and barley. It is nothing to do with snobbery. It is just not practical" [78].

She also denied that she had ever suggested access to the grave would be considered following the sale of Kirklees Hall in 1987, whilst reiterating that people could view the grave by appointment, despite evidence of many being refused.

For instance, during the mid-1990s Barbara Green was contacted by a disabled lady who she refers to as Rita Haley. Haley told Green she had recently contacted Lady Armytage to inquire if she could visit the grave, as she was composing an article on the subject for her adult education writing class. Lady Armytage demanded to see the piece before she could reach a decision, but despite the relative innocence of the content, she ultimately refused the request through her solicitors [79].

When Barbara Green returned to the fold in 1997 it was not with the Yorkshire Robin Hood Society, but an organisation called Gravewatch. Although they continued the campaign for access, Gravewatch were born out of a local parapsychology group, and press coverage focused primarily on their intention to investigate alleged paranormal activity around the gravesite [80]. However, it was also in these reports that the suggestion of a deliberate, and extensive conspiracy to deter public knowledge of Robin Hood's grave first appeared.

These suggestions were prompted by the experiences of Michael Hartley, one of the founding members of Gravewatch, and a freelance film producer. In 1996, a couple of years prior to his involvement with Gravewatch, he had been working on a promotional film about Brighouse and Clifton, the research for which predictably led him to the Robin Hood connections. Realising that this would make a suitable topic for a film in its own right, and undeterred by suggestions that Lady Armytage might prove uncooperative, he teamed up with two media students at Dewsbury College to produce a documentary on "The Life and Times of Robin Hood" [81].

Yet only a short time into the project the two Dewsbury students suddenly withdrew their support. When Hartley inquired as to their reasons for this decision, he found them reluctant to discuss the matter. Eventually, however, he was able to wheedle an explanation out of them.

> "Both revealed that someone had visited them late at night and told them
> to have nothing to do with the Robin Hood film. If they did it would affect
> their future careers, and the consequences could be even more serious if
> they continued to be associated with it" (82).

Barbara Green also suspected a campaign of deliberate misinformation when she discovered a leaflet in Brighouse Library titled "A Visit to the Historic Village of Clifton – Robin Hood Country". The information contained within proved to be entirely mistaken. Most egregiously, it claimed that the ruins of Kirklees Priory and the Gatehouse were "in the grounds of the Old Corn Mill". The leaflet had been produced by the Clifton Neighbourhood Council and, convinced that no local person could have made such a mistake, Green thought it significant that several employees of the Kirklees Estate were regular attendees at the Council's meetings [83].

The emergence of Gravewatch certainly occurred at an opportune moment, just as Kirklees Hall had been sold yet again. An editorial in the *Brighouse Echo* around that time was quite vociferous in its criticism of Lady Armytage's failure to make the most of her assets:

> "The recent history of the Kirklees Estate is a catalogue of lost opportunities...
> We're not looking at a theme park and all the tat that would involve but
> a thoughtful, carefully designed development taking in perhaps a Robin
> Hood trail and visitor centre."

However, it was no more sympathetic to the remit of Gravewatch, arguing that such a scheme:

> "...might also put paid to the rather sinister ministrations of the band of
> fanatics who are convinced evil lurks within those walls" [84].

In the face of such public derision, Gravewatch proved a short-lived venture, folding after only a year [85]. But with the advent of the internet, Barbara Green found it far easier to promote her campaign globally and so the name of the Yorkshire Robin Hood Society was eventually revived, albeit on a more informal basis. She also kept her efforts in the public eye with a number of books, including the novel *Spirit of the Greenwood* [86] and a history of the YRHS and the Kirklees controversy titled *Secrets of the Grave*. Both were self-published.

There can be no doubt that by the end of the 1990s, Barbara Green's rhetoric had grown ever more strident. Upon the foundation of Gravewatch in 1997, she told the *Brighouse Echo* that they aimed "to expose the sinister secrets hidden at Kirklees" and that "most people who wish to see the sites are left with no option but to trespass" [87]. Meanwhile, *Secrets of the Grave,* is littered with references to local officials "cap-doffing" and criticism of "overwhelming deference to someone who simply had an aristocratic title, which, at the end of the day, she had married into" [88]. Such language probably did her campaign very few favours, although by that time, it was already abundantly clear that Lady Armytage had little interest in appeasing her.

However, at the dawn of the new millennium, Lady Armytage's attitude towards public access to the grave seemed to be mellowing slightly. Sadly, this had little to do with the years of campaigning by the YRHS, who remained left out in the cold. Lady Armytage's change of approach seems to have been largely prompted by growing academic interest in the site, which she doubtless perceived as more "respectable" than a society of local enthusiasts with some decidedly eccentric convictions.

In 2000, historian David Hepworth completed his doctoral thesis on the subject of Kirklees Priory, and - following the International Robin Hood Conference in Nottingham - showed a number of eminent Robin Hood scholars, including Professors J.C. Holt, Stephen Knight and Barry Dobson, around the Kirklees Estate [89]. Hepworth later came to live on the estate as co-director of Kirklees Medical Ltd [90], a position that also allowed him to continue his researches into the history of the area. Barbara Green accused such academics of "jumping on the bandwagon" [91].

Nonetheless, Hepworth's influence led to Lady Armytage finally relenting and allowing very limited, managed access to the grave, and other sites of historical interest at Kirklees. The first guided tour was held as the climax of the Calderdale Walking Festival on 7th October 2001 [92] and such opportunities have since continued bi-annually under the name of the "Outlaws and Nuns" tour, operated by the independent organisation, Calderdale Heritage Walks [93]. Places tend to be very limited and the YRHS has criticised the arrangements as ultimately inadequate.

Refused permission to sell their wares on the estate during the tours, the YRHS have often picketed the gates at these events, with a makeshift stall and placards. The Society rather dramatically claimed they had been "barred" from the walks. However, as the *Halifax Evening Courier* noted:

> "Robin Hood enthusiasts were allowed on the walk provided they had pre-booked tickets. But Mrs. Green said 'There would be no point in us buying tickets because we would have just been shunted around on one of the walks'" [94].

It was not only on the question of access that Lady Armytage softened her views in the last decade. She also appeared to be growing more amenable to media publicity and allowed at least two television programmes to film at the grave, apparently without any restrictions on revealing its location. Quite why she should have suddenly performed such a volte-face is uncertain. Perhaps, as she had promised in the late 1980s, having finally secured a sympathetic future for Kirklees Hall and got the agricultural business running smoothly, she now had more time to devote to the grave? Or perhaps she was finally realising the financial potential of the site?

Certainly, the first of the two television programmes suggested the latter interpretation. It was broadcast on 12th November 2002 as part of the Living TV *Scream Team* series, a rather tawdry, youth-orientated take on the *Most Haunted* sub-genre of reality television. The episode featured the eponymous team conducting a vigil at the graveside with the help of celebrity "psychic", Ronnie Buckingham, and a historical tour of the estate led by David Nortcliffe. Throughout proceedings, references are repeatedly made to the fact that the grave is on private land, and that Lady Armytage demanded a substantial fee for permission to film there.

The second documentary was a far more high-profile affair, transmitted at prime-time on Channel 4 on 18th October 2003. *Fact or Fiction: Robin Hood* was presented by Tony Robinson (who had once starred as the Sheriff of Nottingham in the popular 1990s children's comedy series *Maid Marion and Her Merry Men*) and gave a great deal of emphasis to the Robert Hood of Wakefield hypothesis, even though the programme ultimately cast doubt on its viability.

Scream Team included footage of Barbara Green describing her experiences at the grave, but the filming took place in *The Black Horse* pub at Clifton rather than on the estate. However, the YRHS were not consulted for the filming of *Fact or Fiction* at all, despite their role in promoting the Wakefield theory for over twenty years. Green claims she subsequently contacted somebody from the production company, and was told that they were warned by certain sources to avoid the YRHS as they were "dodgy" [95].

Meanwhile, smaller production companies found it much harder to breach the hallowed portals of the Kirklees Estate. In 2004, Barbara Green was approached by Red Monkey Films, an independent company based in Rotherham, who primarily specialise in "creative video solutions" (or corporate videos, as they might more commonly be called). They were looking to make a film called *The Tale of the Death of Robin Hood of Yorkshire*, offering to "rip the lid from the myth and expose a dark tale of murder, betrayal, graveside apparitions and conspiracy theories" [96]. Green cooperated with the production, allowing herself to be interviewed for the documentary, whilst providing extensive research material and local knowledge [97].

Then, on the night of 20th April 2005, she invited the filmmakers to a vigil at the grave along with herself, new YRHS patron David Farrant, "exorcist" Gareth Medway and YRHS secretary, Catherine Fearnley [98]. Fearnley had a letter from Lady Armytage authorising her to visit the grave as and when she wished, although it did not specify whether or not other people were allowed to accompany her [99]. Red Monkey successfully shot footage of the event with the intention of including it in their forthcoming film, and there was a flurry of local press coverage over the next few weeks.

These articles, however, incurred an extremely hostile reaction from those associated with Lady Armytage. Christiaan Hohenzollern, a tenant on the estate and co-director of Kirklees Medical Ltd, wrote in a letter to the *Brighouse Echo*:

> "I had thought that the *Echo* was above such scurrilous reporting. I know for a fact that Lady Armytage never gave permission for such an activity which by your reporting of the event means that you condone trespass. Furthermore the members of the so-called Robin Hood Society were denied permission to enter the park and to do so... just goes to show what little respect the society has for other people's property" [100].

A short while later, David Hepworth launched a scathing attack on Barbara Green on the internet forums of the Worldwide Robin Hood Society, in which he insisted that Red Monkey would never be able to use the footage they shot.

> "Injunctions will be taken out to prevent their sale of the programme material to broadcasters globally, as will legal statements of what will happen to any broadcaster who does transmit any material showing the Kirklees estate or any building on it based on such materials in the possession of the company, their successors, licensees or agents. This remains copyright material that as far as Red Monkey are concerned still remains unlicensed and will remain so" [101].

It is scarcely surprising, therefore, that five years later when the Red Monkey film had still not appeared, Barbara Green believed the powers-that-be at Kirklees had successfully thwarted its release. She began to weave this speculation into her conspiracy narrative, which found new life when it was reported in the *Halifax Evening Courier* as "MI5 cover-up claim over Robin Hood in Yorkshire." In the article, Green accused the authorities of deliberately suppressing Yorkshire's connections with Robin Hood to protect the Nottinghamshire tourist industry. She goes on to assert that "film projects have been sabotaged" and "It has even been suggested that MI5 were involved" [102].

These claims emerged again in an American publication called *Paranoia: The Conspiracy Reader* [103], despite the source of the information having fiercely denied ever making such allegations. He says the subject arose during a conversation with some former MI5 film technicians, who denied that MI5 would have any interest in such matters. This is quite the opposite of what was reported in the *Evening Courier* and the source attempted to secure a retraction on several occasions but was unsuccessful [104].

Ultimately, following much discussion on internet forums, a spokesman for Red Monkey was forced to state:

> "Although Lady Armytage initially refused permission to film she did view an early edit and granted us a release to use footage filmed on her estate."

He also said:

> "As it stands we currently have a very strong, interesting and engaging 60 minute edit. However, this is a speculative venture. It brings in no revenue throughout production. We are at a stage, and have been for some time, where we require some funding and a substantial production window to complete. Funding issues aside, the time required is not currently available due to other commitments" [105].

Like so many disappointments connected with Robin Hood's grave, Red Monkey's ongoing failure to release a documentary shot six years ago, is as much the result of logistical obstacles and sheer inertia as any malicious act of obstruction by the Kirklees camp. Following David Hepworth's online attack on the project, and the producers' lack of communication prior to late 2010, it is understandable that some believed there had been a deliberate attempt to scupper it, but to weave into a narrative involving a widespread "cover-up" of the existence of the grave is, in this instance, to impute agency where there is none.

Conspiracy theories are not inherently irrational. The Watergate scandal alone is enough to demonstrate this fact and to remind us that a citizenry must be ever on guard against abuses of power by the authorities. The difficulty lies in trying to determine which conspiracy theories are justified and which are not [106]. There is no *prima facie* test for this but here it is a simple question of proportionality. Whilst the Robin Hood association is undoubtedly important to Nottinghamshire's economy, the idea that the East Midlands Tourist Board would commission MI5 to prevent Calderdale Council and local media from promoting Robin Hood's grave is patently absurd.

It is perhaps instructive that conspiracy theories typically emerge amongst the disenfranchised. Some academics have suggested that one motivation for holding such ideas is to create a satisfying causal explanation for the continued frustration of a desire [107], despite the amount of effort expended in the pursuit of that goal: If you don't succeed after sustained endeavour, then it's because "They" must be against you. Yet the truth is in most cases, it is simply the regrettable result of a wide array of structural and contingent factors.

For the few surviving members of the YRHS, it is clearly a source of alienation that they have spent twenty-five years attempting to secure access to the Robin Hood sites on the Kirklees estate, only to meet continual opposition and see their organisation ostracised. Convinced by the righteousness of their cause, they find it hard to accept that their campaign would not be more successful had only more people been aware of it. A high-level conspiracy to suppress the knowledge therefore becomes a much more palatable explanation than a nebulous combination of public apathy, a local authority's indifference, and the obdurate hostility of a minor aristocrat.

However, even if it marginally subsided in her later years, Lady Armytage's relentless refusal to engage in a public debate concerning access to the grave was demonstrably unreasonable behaviour. To an extent, her attitude was born out of an admirable desire to preserve the tranquil atmosphere of the Kirklees estate. She told the *Spenborough Guardian*:

> "There may not be much left of the original estate but it is an oasis I am trying to protect... You can't have bus loads of people walking through a working farm. Opening up to tourists would be a total change of business and would alter the whole character of the place" [108].

Yet Lady Armytage was clearly overestimating what people wanted from her. As the *Brighouse Echo* editorial quoted earlier stressed, nobody was seeking to turn the grave into the centre-piece of some tacky Robin Hood theme park. They were simply hoping for something along the lines of a woodland trail which passed the site [109]. Whilst initial tourist interest would undoubtedly be high, it would eventually settle down to a manageable level. Across Britain there are hundreds of ancient monuments, which can only be accessed by passing through working farms (often on well-established rights-of-way) and those farms seem to cope without any great difficulty. A well-fenced route would certainly negate the possibility of damage to crops or livestock.

Equally, her other objections seem largely spurious. The complaint about vandalism is, as Barbara Green points out, completely self-defeating. It is the very isolation of the location that currently allows wilful damage to go unnoticed. Again, there are hundreds of ancient monuments the length and breadth of the country, which survive public access without vandalism ever placing them at serious risk. Moreover, there would be plenty of volunteers willing to act as guardians of the grave. Indeed, one of the YRHS's original offers was to raise money for its conservation.

The logistical claims are also suspect. In his public attack on Barbara Green, David Hepworth insisted:

> "As I have repeatedly explained, there are no toilet or adequate parking provisions and the costs of such an infrastructure are prohibitive at the moment. Also any visits have to be accompanied for insurance purposes..." [110].

Doubtless this is true if the grave remained on entirely private land without a public right of access. However, if a right-of-way, or even just a permissive path, was established from the side of the A644, it is doubtful that such requirements would be necessary.

In light of such considerations, it is tempting to conclude that these objections are just a smoke screen for the Armytages' desire to preserve their anachronistic feudal privileges and keep the "hoi-polloi" as far from their door as possible. David Hepworth has asserted:

> "The owners for the last 440 years are still fully entitled to please themselves as to what they choose to do – it is their prerogative" [111].

Yet many would argue that where such antiquities are concerned, it is very much *not* the landowner's prerogative. To deny that access to historical monuments is a legitimate matter of public interest is an absurdly arrogant position.

Some in the Kirklees camp have also suggested that the actions of Barbara Green and the YRHS have actually had a detrimental effect on securing public access. David Hepworth has insisted:

> "There have been many occasions that very detailed plans have been agreed to provide more access, but every time, without exception, you have routed the press/media again... If you want to bring about a curtailment of access to the grave to the wider public, then I would suggest you continue your quest and let the natural progress occur" [112].

It is not clear what these unrealised access schemes amounted to, but it is uncertain that the question of access would ever have arisen had it not been for the efforts of the YRHS in the first place. Prior to Green's interest in 1984, there had not been a mention of the grave in the

Brighouse Echo for over twenty years. Many local people were not even aware of its existence. There is no evidence to suggest that the custodians of the Kirklees estate would have done anything to alter that situation without the awareness stirred up by the YRHS in the media.

Meanwhile, Green has been accused of conducting a personal vendetta against Lady Armytage. For instance, a relative by the name of John Armytage claimed on the forum of the Worldwide Robin Hood Society:

> "When she (Green) began her disgruntled campaign about my family, including, but not limited to the national tabloid press, there was a restriction put on her access to the grave" [113].

More pointedly, Hepworth had written:

> "You were fully aware of how distressed Lady A was during his (Sir John's) illness and would be aware of the terrific sadness she had at his death... Yet in this time of great personal strain to her, you began your campaign relentlessly" [114].

It is certainly true that in later years, the language of the YRHS could be particularly immoderate and vitriolic, especially on the internet, an environment that consistently encourages inappropriate stridency. However, the suggestion that Lady Armytage's antagonism only arose as a consequence of this vendetta, or that Green exploited Lady Armytage's grief, is disingenuous in the extreme. It is quite clear that Green did not begin her campaign for access in earnest until 1987; five years after Sir John Armytage had died. Media coverage of the YRHS prior to 1987 focuses almost exclusively on their promotion of the Robert Hode of Wakefield hypothesis and the supposed Yorkshire/Nottinghamshire rivalry.

In fact, Green's crusade was provoked by two very simple factors. The first was the sale of Kirklees Hall, which was surely a natural juncture for a debate about access to the historical monuments on the estate; a debate instigated by local newspapers such as the *Brighouse Echo* as much as by Barbara Green herself. The second was the fact that Lady Armytage had consistently refused to permit visits by members of the Society, despite her insistence in the press that the public could visit the grave by appointment. At this time, the YRHS had yet to make any claims regarding paranormal phenomena, or attack the Armytage family in public. They were little more than a harmless society of local enthusiasts with a penchant for medieval costume.

The question of trespass did not arise until 1990 and Green argues that they had been forced into such a course of action because their requests for legitimate access had been repeatedly rebuffed. Arguably, however, it was still remarkably imprudent to advertise this fact in the press quite so often, and did very little for diplomatic relations. Sadly, it is inescapable truism that in the eyes of the law-abiding majority, criminal actions undermine sympathy for a cause, no matter how justified that cause might be.

Nonetheless, it is necessary to put the "crime" in perspective. For one thing, unless damage to property can be proven, trespass is a civil rather than criminal offence. Injunctions can be taken out to prevent repeat offenders, which make the penalties far more serious, but in the first instance, the law regards trespass as a relatively trivial matter. Indeed, legislation in Scotland is considerably more liberal in this area and many would argue that such a common-sense policy should also be adopted in England.

It is also dubious to suggest that trespassing to see the grave represented an invasion of Lady Armytage's privacy. Access was typically effected from the side of the A644 on the far flank of Castle Hill, whilst the monument is located in dense woodland almost half-a-mile from any of the residential buildings on the Kirklees estate. Conversely, millions of people in Britain live in houses which can be seen into by passers-by on the street. Such people may well perceive the claim that Lady Armytage's privacy was unacceptably compromised as insufferably fatuous.

With Lady Armytage's death in 2008, and the question of inheritance still unresolved in the public sphere, the question of public access to the grave is inevitably suspended. The Outlaws & Nuns tours operated by Calderdale Heritage Walks still go ahead twice a year, but whether there is any wider arrangement on the horizon remains uncertain. The preceding chapters have emphasised that the grave is an important historical monument, regardless of its indeterminate authenticity. The inability of the public to enjoy such a site over the last century has been a demonstrable scandal, and the current provisions seem little more than a grudgingly yielded sop. For now, the struggle continues.

CHAPTER SIX

Vampire Blues

Access is not the only controversial issue with which Robin Hood's grave has become associated in the last twenty-five years. It has also been the focus for a glut of paranormal speculation, with one notion in particular stubbornly attaching itself to the site thanks to a media frenzy in the late 1980s, and subsequent uncritical repetition in a number of tomes on the supernatural. That notion is the Kirklees Vampire, a title which has subsequently been disowned by the orchestrators of the flap [1], leading to a frenzy of claim and counter-claim which continues to spill over countless internet message boards today.

However, to understand fully the genesis of the Kirklees Vampire saga and the bitterness of the ensuing recriminations it is necessary to take a diversion to discuss an even more famous example of modern legend making, which similarly continues to generate an excessive degree of heat. The events at the centre of the Highgate Vampire affair occurred forty years ago and over one hundred and fifty miles from Kirklees, but their repercussions are still felt in an interminable feud between sympathisers of the protagonists, David Farrant and Séan Manchester. It is a maelstrom, into which the issue of Robin Hood's grave has regrettably been dragged.

It is almost impossible to present an accurate record of the Highgate Vampire drama because - in the opinion of this author, at least - the two principal players have consistently proved to be unreliable witnesses, repeatedly altering or embellishing their recollection of events, often in an attempt to undermine each other's credibility. Fortunately, it is possible to reconstruct a basic chronology from the public record, even if the precise origin of both the occurrences and the feud remains bitterly contested.

At the centre of the story is Highgate Cemetery, a sprawling Victorian burial ground in north London, and probably the most famous in Britain. It is composed of two sections, divided by a thoroughfare known as Swains Lane. The west side, known for its array of imposing mausoleums, was opened in 1839 and contains the tombs of the Pre-Raphaelite luminaries, Christina Rossetti and Elizabeth Siddall. Meanwhile, the far airier east side was consecrated in 1854 and is home to the cemetery's most illustrious burial, the political philosopher Karl Marx [2].

Unsurprisingly, given its almost stereotypically Gothic architecture, the events connected with the Highgate Vampire were primarily focused on the west cemetery. Even today, following extensive restoration, it is a gloomy and forbidding place. In 1970 it would have been positively chilling. Many of the mausoleums were in a dilapidated state and open to the elements following bomb damage in World War II [3], whilst the whole site was engulfed by cuckoo grass, brambles and ivy. It is hardly surprising that such a location attracted stories in the public imagination, especially in the local oral tradition.

As the folklorist Bill Ellis notes, it is also significant that events took place against the background of at least three emerging cultural phenomena. Firstly, the 1960s saw an increase in the vandalism of graveyards, often simply as an act of adolescent rebellion against authority by embracing social taboos. This profoundly shocked an older, more conservative generation for whom such acts of desecration were incomprehensible and, therefore, were often perceived to be in the service of some more sinister agenda [4]. Such vandalism had been observed in Highgate Cemetery in the late 1960s, by which time the gates were sufficiently ruinous to allow access at night, allowing it to become a haven for curious youths, amorous lovers, after-hours drinkers, and the homeless [5].

Secondly, there was the phenomenal success of Hammer Films' Gothic horror features, particularly movies such as *Dracula: Prince of Darkness* and *The Devil Rides Out,* which firmly established occult tropes in the mass consciousness of a generation [6]. *Taste the Blood of Dracula* even used Highgate Cemetery as a shooting location in 1969, and whilst the film was not released at cinemas until after the Highgate Vampire flap had erupted, local residents must surely have noticed the production activity. It has led many to wonder if the whole affair was not an example of life imitating art.

The final factor identified by Ellis, was increasing experimentation with alternative religions, including budding neo-pagan traditions such as Wicca. Although Wicca employs symbolism borrowed from ritual magic systems established during the Victorian occult revival, it did not emerge until codified by Gerald Gardner in the 1940s, and despite what some adherents claim, owes little to any genuine historical tradition of witchcraft [7]. Nonetheless, it provoked a number of hysterical exposés in the tabloid press, who often erroneously associated such practices with black magic and Satanism [8].

The first public catalyst for the Highgate Vampire affair was a letter published in the *Hampstead & Highgate Express* on 6th February 1970, titled 'Ghostly walks in Highgate'. In this, a twenty-four year old by the name of David Farrant reported three sightings of a mysterious "grey figure" through the gates of Highgate Cemetery as he walked home via Swains Lane at night. He concludes:

> "I can think of no other explanation than this apparition being supernatu-
> ral. I have no knowledge in this field and would be interested to hear if
> any other readers have seen anything of this nature" [9].

The letter provoked quite a remarkable response, ostensibly confirming the existence of an authentic local tradition connecting the cemetery with the supernatural. Four letters were published in the following week's edition of the *Hampstead & Highgate Express*, including one that described:

> "...a tall man in a hat who walks across Swains Lane and just disappears through a wall into the cemetery... The bells in the old disused chapel inside the cemetery toll mysteriously whenever he walks."

Another added that the ghost manifested for several nights at regular monthly intervals. [10]

Another five letters were printed on 20th February, along with a front-page appeal for further correspondence, leading to six letters on 27th February, with the flow finally drying up after 20th March. These letters included additional accounts of a shadowy figure moving around the cemetery, along with a spectral bicyclist who chased women down Swains Lane, a figure disappearing mysteriously into a pond, and two sightings of a white lady [11].

It has been observed that, although all these apparitions have analogues in British folklore, there is very little consistency between the sightings. Prior to the media establishing the 'Highgate Vampire' brand, there was no dominant narrative [12]. However, whilst some commentators believe these letters prove that there was a genuine local tradition of ghost sightings around the cemetery even prior to the media frenzy, there is also evidence to suggest that at least some of the letters were fabrications, sent by associates of the interested parties [13].

The vampire myth began to take shape on 27th February, when the *Hampstead & Highgate Express* ran an article titled 'Does a wampyr walk in Highgate?' This introduced the speculations of twenty-five year old Séan Manchester, styled as President of the British Occult Society. Following the correspondence regarding the Highgate haunting, Manchester wished to reveal that his ongoing investigations into supernatural activity around Highgate indicated that it might be actually vampiric in nature.

He went on to assert that in the 18th Century, a 'King Vampire from Wallachia' had been brought to England by his followers, and installed in a house on the site that later became Highgate Cemetery. Manchester also suggested that modern occultists were attempting to raise the vampire for their own diabolical purposes.

> "Now that there is so much desecration of graves... I'm convinced that this has been happening in Highgate Cemetery in an attempt by a body of Satanists to resurrect the King Vampire" [14].

Today, Manchester insists that the term 'King Vampire' was a sensationalist embellishment on the part of the journalist [15].

Manchester also planted the seed for what would escalate into the infamous Highgate Cemetery vampire hunt when he said:

> "We would like to exorcise the vampire by the traditional and approved manner – drive a stake through his heart with one blow just after dawn between Friday and Saturday".

David Farrant appeared to agree with Manchester when on 6th March, the newspaper quoted him as saying:

> "Much remains unexplained, but all points to the vampire theory being the most likely answer. Should this be so, I for one am prepared to pursue it, taking whatever means might be necessary so that we can all rest" (16).

The 6th March article, titled 'Why do the foxes die', focused on the number of fox carcasses sighted by Farrant in the vicinity of the cemetery "with no outward sign of how they died". Manchester commented "These incidents are just more inexplicable events that seem to compliment my theory about a vampire." However, in later writings Manchester claimed to have seen the bodies of foxes with throat lacerations and drained of blood [17]. Such reports tend to be a common feature of his "evidence" for vampiric activity [18]. In the same article, a cemetery groundskeeper denied having seen dead foxes in the area.

The 6th March article is also the first public record of a meeting between Manchester and Farrant, who are pictured together in the cemetery on the previous weekend. Manchester continues to claim that he did not meet Farrant until around the time of the press coverage in 1970 and more importantly, that Farrant had never been a member of the British Occult Society [19], even though he would later refer to himself as its 'High Priest'.

According to Manchester, this organisation had been formed in 1860 and he'd succeeded to the position of President in 1967 [20]. However, no documentary evidence of the Society's existence before 1970 has ever been produced. Conversely, David Farrant contends that the British Occult Society (which he later renamed the British Psychic and Occult Society) was formed in the mid-1960s by a group of North London youths interested in paranormal phenomena, following his initiation as a Wiccan priest [21]. On Farrant's account, Manchester joined the Society briefly in 1969, but was subsequently expelled for bringing the organisation into disrepute [22].

Due to an absence of independent evidence, it is difficult to ascertain whose versions of events is accurate, and it is precisely such disputes which continue to fan the flames of their mutual animosity forty years after the original events. Nonetheless, it is perhaps instructive that the name of the British Occult Society does not appear in print until 27th February 1970, with Manchester described as its President. Farrant is not mentioned in connection with the Society until much later.

It is clear that few people took the speculation of either Manchester or Farrant particularly seriously in the early stages of the press coverage. Gerald Isaaman, editor of the *Hampstead & Highgate Express* at the time, would later recall that he initially regarded the affair as "a real hoot and we played the story for laughs. The rapid escalation of media coverage... turned a small local event into a major flap. It was the TV coverage that did the real damage" [23].

This wider media interest took off on Friday 13th March when Thames Television interviewed both Séan Manchester and David Farrant on Swains Lane for a programme called *Today,* broadcast at 18:00 that evening [24]. Rumour had spread that both parties were intending to lead a 'vampire hunt' in the cemetery that night and within two hours of transmission of *Today,* several hundred people had congregated around the gates of Highgate Cemetery, in a scene one witness described as reminiscent of a 'football crowd' [25]. The assembly proved too large for the local constabulary to control and at least one hundred people, many armed with rudimentary stakes, managed to access the cemetery, pursued by police officers with searchlights [26].

In a later account of these events, written many years after the fact, Séan Manchester claims that he was amongst those who penetrated the cemetery interior. Along with three companions, he made his way to an edifice known as the columbarium and upon gaining entry, discovered three mysteriously empty coffins. They anointed the coffins with garlic and proceeded to encircle them with salt, after which Manchester writes that a booming vibration started up, suggesting some supernatural presence [27].

The Highgate Cemetery vampire hunt was sensationally reported the following day as "Satan Riddle of Open Tomb" by the London-wide *Evening News* [28], whilst the next issue of the *Hampstead & Highgate Express* on 20th March quoted Manchester claiming he'd found evidence of practices connected with black magic [29]. As Bill Ellis observes, although many residents of the area may not have believed in vampires, the idea of Satanic cults who *did* believe in vampires indulging in ritual desecration seemed perfectly credible [30]. Consequently, public concern over the events at Highgate escalated.

The issue flared up again in early August 1970 when three teenage girls discovered a headless corpse dragged from one of the vaults, leading Manchester to inform the *Hampstead & Highgate Express* that stealing the skull of the corpse was a crucial step in the Satanists' plan to resurrect the King Vampire [31]. Whether such speculation was taken seriously or not, as a result of this macabre discovery and growing public anxiety about ritual desecration in the cemetery, police patrols in the area were increased at night [32].

It was one such patrol that, on the night of 17th August, discovered David Farrant trying to gain access to the cemetery from the adjacent churchyard of St. Michael's, carrying a crucifix and wooden stake [33]. He was arrested for being in an enclosed space for an unlawful purpose, and bailed at Clerkenwell Magistrates Court the following morning. National newspaper, *The Sun,* reported Farrant telling the magistrates "My intention was to search out the supernatural being and destroy it by plunging the stake in its heart" [34]. The case was adjourned until 30th September, and Farrant bailed.

With Farrant getting the lion's share of the exposure for his vampire hunting activities, Manchester took advantage of his rival's temporary exclusion from such pursuits by conducting a Catholic rite of exorcism in one of the vaults, near where the headless corpse had been discovered [35]. In later writings, Manchester describes opening one of the coffins and discovering a hardly decomposed corpse with trace of blood around its mouth [36]. However, it is notable that no such details are included in the *Hornsey Journal's* report of the ritual on 28th August. Again, this is typical of the revisionism and exaggeration that has infected so many accounts of the Highgate Vampire over the years.

Meanwhile, Gillian Bradish, the wife of the man who had put up Farrant's bail, claimed to have received a telephone call shortly afterwards from a man she believed to be Séan Manchester, threatening "Do you believe in black magic? Unless Bradish gives up bail for Farrant, something odd will happen to you and your children" [37]. Manchester strenuously denies making such a call and the Bradishes later came to accept this [38]. However, the damage was done. Once Farrant's friends heard of it, they paid a visit to Manchester's flat and a scuffle ensued, as a result of which Manchester was hospitalised and bound over to keep the peace.

When Farrant's case finally came to trial, he was discharged after his lawyer successfully argued that hunting a vampire was not in itself unlawful and that a cemetery did not satisfy the legal definition of an enclosed space [39]. Following his acquittal, Farrant made his intention to continue hunting the vampire perfectly clear. The ensuing blaze of publicity saw him holding a nocturnal vigil in the cemetery, accompanied by a reporter from the *Evening News*. The article was published on 16th October under the headline "Midnight date with Highgate's Vampire", alongside photographs of Farrant wielding a cross and stake [40].

The previous day, the BBC had broadcast a segment on events at the cemetery as part of their flagship current affairs programme, *24 Hours*. It featured reconstructions of both Manchester's exorcism in the vault and Farrant's fateful vampire hunt of 17th August, in which he is once again seen brandishing a cross and stake [41]. Only two weeks later, on Hallowe'en, police once again had to control a crowd converging on Swains Lane, many of whom were trying to access the cemetery [42].

Such problems continued throughout the following year and the police arrested several youths armed with stakes prowling the area after dark. David Farrant was once again caught in the cemetery on the night of 8th October 1971, along with his girlfriend, Martine de Sacy. They claimed to have found evidence of Satanic desecration in an open mausoleum, and were performing a ritual to cleanse its taint [43]. Farrant also took a series of photographs following the ceremony, including one of de Sacy naked in the vault, although he later suggested that these were posed for publicity, following an offer from an American magazine [44].

By this time, Farrant was increasingly associating himself with occult practices and carving out his niche as a "Wiccan High Priest" to contrast with Séan Manchester's portrayal of an exorcist in the tradition of Montague Summers. Indeed, Ellis notes that Farrant's activities were perceived by many as dangerously analogous to the rites of the very Satanists he repeatedly claimed he was attempting to combat [45]. Such adverse publicity was certainly to the chagrin of Manchester, who had already fulminated in the press against "amateurs" compromising his investigation [46].

Thus, in *The Sun* on 23 November 1972, Manchester is quoted as suggesting that the only way of putting Farrant's occult powers to the test would be a public demonstration in front of objective observers [47]. Shortly after this article was published, flyers began to appear on underground stations across north London advertising a "magical duel" between Manchester and Farrant, due to take place on Parliament Hill at midnight on Friday 13th April 1973. In the event, Farrant failed to appear, claiming that he feared a lynch mob, whilst Manchester contented himself with performing an exorcism ritual for the benefit of the assembled crowd [48].

Following this publicity, Manchester claimed to have founded Ordo Sancti Graal, a religious sect steeped in mystical Christianity, Holy Grail lore especially [49]. He announced his new organisation in the pages in the *Hampstead & Highgate Express* on 4th May 1973 and declared that he was about to embark on a pilgrimage from Hampstead Heath to north Africa, along with twelve disciples, carrying as few worldly goods as possible [50]. It is not recorded as to whether they ever reached their destination.

Meanwhile, Farrant's occult reputation continued to grow unabated. On 31st August 1973, the *Hornsey Journal* published an exposé of his activities, including the claim that he had sacrificed a stray cat in Highgate Woods [51]. This led to a public outcry with a local RSPCA officer and others calling for Farrant's conviction for animal cruelty in the letters page of the newspaper [52]. In addition, the R&B artist and Highgate resident, Long John Baldry, threatened Farrant with a private prosecution, believing it to have been his missing cat which Farrant had supposedly sacrificed [53]. Today, Farrant insists that the press misrepresented his activities and that he never killed any cats, pointing out that John Baldry's pet returned safely home after several weeks [54].

However, Farrant's response at the time was to send his accusers 'voodoo' dolls, along with a rhyming curse [55]. He posted similar items to two police detectives accused of 'roughing up' his fellow occultist John Pope (later John Pope de Locksley), following Pope's arrest on a charge of indecent assault [56]. Baldry was particularly unnerved by the receipt of these effigies, leading him to ask fellow musician and occultist Graham Bond to perform a ritual to negate their efficacy. Bond died after falling beneath the wheels of train in mysterious circumstances several months afterwards, an event which Baldry always attributed to the malign influence of Farrant's curse [57].

Later that year, the *Hornsey Journal* added further fuel to the fire when it reported finding evidence of Satanic rituals in a notorious derelict mansion house, located on Avenue Road, Crouch End [58]. Only six nights later, on December 13th, the police discovered David Farrant and John Pope in the house performing an occult ceremony, naked, around the embers of a fire. They explained they were dedicating the house as their "Temple of Pan" [59]. The pair were charged with arson but later acquitted [60]. Coincidentally, this is the house in which Séan Manchester would later claim to have finally exorcised the Highgate Vampire [61].

Whilst Farrant escaped penalty on that occasion, vandalism was proving an ongoing problem in Highgate Cemetery, and the police were growing increasingly tired of his shenanigans. Hence, when another headless corpse was discovered on Swains Lane on 12th January 1974, Farrant's residence was their first port of call [62]. In his flat, they found numerous photographs showing desecrated vaults, including those including the naked Martine de Sacey, which they used to build a case against the self-styled Wiccan High Priest.

Farrant was tried at the Old Bailey on 10th June 1974 on charges of bodysnatching and desecrating graves. This was in addition to separate counts of stealing items from Barnet Hospital where he had briefly worked as a porter, illegally possessing a firearm, and attempting to pervert the course of justice; the last of which was in relation to the material he had sent to the detectives investigating the case against John Pope [63]. Farrant conducted his own defence, arguing that the desecration had been committed prior to his discovery of it and the photographs were only a record of his findings. However, he was unable to produce his ex-girlfriend Martine de Sacy to corroborate his story [64].

The most serious charge of bodysnatching was dropped after a local youth took responsibility for the crime [65], but Farrant was convicted on all others counts and sentenced to a surprisingly harsh four years and eight months imprisonment. Following this fall from grace, he was rapidly denounced in the press as a 'phoney witch', although some newspapers commented on the disproportionate severity of his jail term [66]. He was later refused the right to appeal, despite having finally located Martine de Sacy, and persuading her to testify on his behalf [67].

Press coverage of the trial frequently referred to Farrant as the High Priest of the British Occult Society, although Séan Manchester has repeatedly claimed over the years that Farrant's title was fraudulently adopted [68]. Nonetheless, there is contested evidence that Manchester corresponded with Farrant during his prison term [69] and over the course of 1975, they both contributed articles on occult topics to a short-lived journal called *New Witchcraft*.

The first appearance of the Highgate Vampire story in a mass-market volume also occurred in 1975, in the form of a chapter contributed by Séan Manchester to *The Vampire's Bedside Companion* by renowned parapsychologist, Peter Underwood. In a narrative that has been successively embroidered over the years, Manchester attempted to emphasise his own role in the affair by dating his involvement back to late 1967, when he had been introduced to a teenage girl named Elizabeth Wojdyla.

He claims she had told him that, whilst walking home down Swains Lane one night with a friend, they had both witnessed "graves opening up and the people rising" through the gates of the cemetery. Manchester allegedly met her again in 1969, still traumatised by her experience on Swains Lane and suffering from a mysterious malady, which he immediately identified as evidence of vampiric influence, and successfully exorcised [70]. The 1975 account also introduces the character of 'Lusia' whose possessed sleepwalking supposedly led Manchester to the vault that he had exorcised in August 1970 [71].

Despite Manchester's repetition of these accounts, he has never produced Elizabeth Wojdyla or 'Luisa' to independently confirm their veracity. Wojdyla's former boyfriend Keith MacClean has done so, but he has gone on to become a close associate of Manchester as a member of Ordo Sancti Graal. Photographs of both women also exist, in which they purportedly exhibit the signs of vampiric attack, but a number of contradictory assertions have been made over the years, including that the photographs were posed reconstructions [72].

The exact identity, and ultimate fate, of 'Lusia' has been a consistent source of speculation, as

Manchester would later claim that seven years after her death from leukaemia, her reanimated corpse, in the guise of a giant spider, attacked him at her grave in the Great North London Cemetery [73]. In a 1986 article, the magazine *City Limits* claimed to have identified 'Lusia' as one of Manchester's former paramours, but no evidence of her death in the mid-Seventies, or burial in the Great North London Cemetery, has ever been found [74].

But whilst Manchester's fanciful narratives ostensibly appear amusing, his next major appearance in the media took on a more sinister hue. An article titled 'The New Nazis' appeared in the *Borehamwood Post* on 29th September 1977, during a period of high racial tension in the country. Credited to Manchester, it professed to uncover a neo-Nazi cell known as the League of Imperial Fascists, who were planning anti-Semitic attacks in a predominantly Jewish area of London [75]. It was accompanied by photographs of members of the supposed group in SS uniform, including one of the 'Commander', with his identity obscured by a black strip over the eyes.

However, just over a week later on 9th October, the *Sunday People* published an article exposing the *Borehamwood Post* article as a fabrication. They claimed to have spoken to David Farrant's old associate, John Pope, who told them that he had been persuaded to pose as a Nazi in a photograph, taken by Manchester, for undisclosed purposes. The article also pointed out that if the black strip was removed from the eyes of the 'Commander', he bore a striking resemblance to none other than Séan Manchester [76]. Manchester has subsequently denounced the whole affair as a plot to discredit him, masterminded by David Farrant [77].

Farrant had been released on parole in 1976 and despite evidence of collusion with Manchester in this period, their public feud was far from over. In the summer of 1978, posters began to appear around the Highgate area, announcing:

> "A DUEL. A matter of honour will be resolved at dawn on 18 August 1978,
> Queens Wood, Highgate, between SEAN MANCHESTER and DAVID FARRANT,
> COMBAT WITH SWORDS. To the death or exhaustion" [78].

The *Hornsey Journal* reported on the advertisements on 28th July 1978, generating police attention and forcing the participants to relocate the proposed duel to Citadelle de Montreuil-Sur-Mer in France [79].

The *Hornsey Journal* would later report on 1st September that they had received a letter from a representative of the British Occult Society claiming that their President, Séan Manchester, had expired in France from a fatal wound sustained in the duel. Farrant was represented as confirming this statement, whilst Manchester himself could not be contacted [80]. Yet only six months later in April 1979, the supposedly deceased vampire-hunter was being interviewed for *LBC Radio*, and the local press, on the subject of mysterious animal deaths in Finchley [81]. He later insisted that his remarkable resurrection could be attributed to the fact that he had, in fact, only received minor injuries in the duel.

Meanwhile, on 30th June 1978, the *Hornsey Journal* had announced Farrant's intention to stand as a candidate for an organisation he dubbed the Wicca Workers Party, in the next General

Election [82]. The article revealed that, if elected, he would campaign for renewable energy, the abolition of public decency laws, alternative medicine being made available on the NHS, an exit from the European Common Market, plus reform of the prison system and police force - a subject no doubt very close to his heart at the time.

As the 1979 General Election drew near, a new spate of posters purportedly promoting the Wicca Workers' Party began to appear. However, their design had been doctored to contain several examples of popular far-right iconography [83]. Indeed, they appeared to explicitly associate the Party with posters that had allegedly once been used by the League of Imperial Fascists, the group Séan Manchester claimed to have unmasked operating in Borehamwood in 1977. It should be noted that the question of whether the League of Imperial Fascists ever truly existed has never been resolved.

When Farrant was forced to withdraw his candidacy due to his criminal convictions, a letter dated 25th April 1979 was sent to the editor of the *News of the World* claiming to be from David Farrant, advising his supporters to switch their vote to the National Front. Farrant has consistently denied any links with the far-right and the letter was later publicly exposed as a forgery [84]. It has never been conclusively established who was responsible for this hoax, or for producing the doctored posters, although predictable accusations have been made.

Having learnt his lesson regarding dabbling in the murky world of fringe politics and investigative journalism, through the 1980s Séan Manchester returned to what he knew best, staging elaborate ceremonies for publicity. In 1984, he advertised something called the Great Invocation of the Full Moon, to take place on Parliament Hill on Friday 13th July. *City Limits* reported this as another duel to settle the leadership of the British Occult Society, featuring a photograph of Manchester and Farrant side-by-side [85]. When Greater London Council heard of this event, they immediately took out an injunction against it, causing Manchester to complain of religious persecution to the *Hampstead & Highgate Express* on 15th June [86].

Manchester attempted to proceed with the Invocation anyway and he appeared on *LBC Radio* on the morning of the 13th July describing how he would perform a ritual to welcome five 'Sisters of the Moon' into the ranks of the British Occult Society. Sadly, when Manchester arrived at Parliament Hill carrying his ceremonial sword, the police were waiting for him, and he was duly arrested for possessing an offensive weapon [87].

In 1985, Manchester published the first edition of *The Highgate Vampire,* supposedly his definitive account of his role in the affair. It was expanded (primarily by the indulgent use of purple prose) from his chapter in *The Vampire's Bedside Companion,* and once again greatly elaborates on the part he played, going far beyond what was publicly recorded at the time in the press. Perhaps surprisingly, it is relatively sympathetic towards David Farrant, agreeing with the defence in the 1974 court case that the desecration at Highgate Cemetery had been carried out by Satanists, prior to Farrant's discovery of it [88].

By the late 1980s, Manchester was styling himself 'Lord' Manchester, whilst claiming to be descended from an illegitimate child of the Romantic poet, Lord Byron. In 1988, he finally wrapped up the British Occult Society, and instead concentrated on an offshoot, the International Society for the Advancement of Irreproducible Vampire & Lyncanthropy Research [89], today simply titled the Vampire Research Society. It was also during this period that he first showed an interest in the Robin Hood legend, agreeing to act as patron to both John Pope's London Robin Hood Society and Barbara Green's Yorkshire outfit.

Whilst Manchester was in contact with both Pope and, apparently, Farrant at various points during the 1980s, the détente did not last. Farrant publicly questioned Manchester's version of events from *The Highgate Vampire* and began to deny that the supernatural phenomenon witnessed at Highgate Cemetery in the early 1970s had ever been a 'vampire' in the first place [90]. Moreover, Farrant now denied that he had *ever* believed it to be a vampire, despite having frequently told the press at the time that he was hunting such a creature, and being regularly photographed flaunting a cross and stake. Today, he insists that such posturing was entirely for the benefit of the media, who had adopted the vampire narrative with such enthusiasm [91].

In describing the haunting as a "psychic entity" Farrant adopted the ontology of parapsychology and modern occultism, thus giving his speculation a veneer of credibility compared to Manchester's lurid vampire-hunting exploits. It has often been observed that Manchester's own accounts of his deeds bear little resemblance to either Catholic, or folkloric vampire traditions, instead appearing to have been stitched together from a combination of Bram Stoker's *Dracula,* the occult novels of Dennis Wheatley, and various Hammer horror films [92].

However, Manchester's Gothic predilections were increasingly secondary to his more messianic aspirations. Whilst his brand of Christianity had previously been of a liberal variety, and saw little danger in flirting with more esoteric teachings, his theology grew increasingly conservative at some point around this time. Although he continued to operate the Ordo Sancti Graal, it was increasingly associated with the Old Catholic Church, a loose denomination formed in the late 19th Century, when a number of bishops seceded from the Roman Catholic Church over the issue of papal infallibility.

Having previously claimed to have belonged to the minor order of exorcists since 1973 [93], Manchester was ordained as a priest of the Old Catholic Church on 13th April 1990. He was subsequently consecrated as a bishop on 4th October 1991 [94] and now refers to himself as 'the Right Reverend Séan Manchester, Founder of the Sacerdotal Society of the Precious Blood, Superior General of the Ordo Sancti Graal, Presiding Bishop of the traditionalist British Old Catholic Church, Old Catholic Bishop of Glastonbury and Primate of Ecclesia Apostolica Jesu Christi.'

Following his ordination, Manchester rapidly began to disassociate himself from his former activities and associates. Although vampire hunting was still very much on the agenda, he denounced all occultism as a gateway to Satanism. When confronted with evidence of his own involvement with the occult, such as the articles he wrote for *New Witchcraft,* or the aborted Great Invocation of the Full Moon, he insists that he was operating undercover in an effort to expose the diabolists in society's midst. His church claims to offer 'outreach' to all those ensnared by Satanism, for which all brands of occultism are regarded as a mask [95].

Yet despite Manchester's desperate attempts to distance himself from his past involvement with the occult, he nonetheless is the man who wrote in the first edition of *The Highgate Vampire:*

> "The set of symbols I work with are predominantly Christian, yet you will find in the text that I cast a circle, what some might call a Magic Circle. While I am not a witch in any sense of the word, I suppose as a secular person handling consecrated material against hostile psychic forces, I am practising 'white' magic" [96]

However, in 1991, Manchester published a revised edition of *The Highgate Vampire.* In addition to giving the narrative a decidedly more Christian hue, it omits all favourable references to Farrant, now dismissed as a publicity-seeker who jumped on the Highgate Vampire bandwagon. As for Farrant's occult pursuits, at best Manchester portrays them as the work of a self-promoting charlatan, and at worst as evidence of genuine Satanic worship [97]. Meanwhile, Manchester's sympathisers run a blog called *Friends of Bishop Séan Manchester,* which specialises in character assassinations of anybody who criticises the bishop.[*]

For his part, Farrant continues to mock Manchester's vampire-hunting antics and inconsistent public statements, whilst maintaining that he himself never believed in vampires, despite all evidence to the contrary. Farrant also frequently questions Manchester's religious credentials, which has proved a decidedly contentious issue. Whilst it appears that Manchester can demonstrate apostolic succession, the Old Catholic constituency in Britain must be very small indeed. It is impossible to find any references to the British Old Catholic Church on the internet that cannot be traced back to Manchester, and it is not in communion with any Old Catholic organisations worldwide.

Manchester is known to be very sensitive to commentators who express doubts over his piety, and threatens libel action against all those who question his claims. Whilst he has never successfully prosecuted anybody in a court of a law, he has made numerous complaints to Ofcom and the Press Complaints Commission regarding misrepresentation in the media. Some of these have been upheld, yet Ofcom ruled that it was perfectly acceptable for a Channel 4 documentary to have described him as a "1970s weirdo" [98]. It is instructive that whilst Manchester insists he feels "an aversion to superfluous and sensationalist publicity" [99], he also boasts that he has "contributed to countless television documentaries and studio debates" [100].

Today, the ongoing feud between Séan Manchester and David Farrant, along with continuing speculation as to what actually happened in Highgate Cemetery in the early 1970s, is practically a cottage industry. It has produced countless books, documentaries, comic-strips, even T-shirts and mugs. For all their claims to be at the cutting edge of modern psychical research, defending their own reputations in relation to an obscure episode in social history that took place some forty years ago has essentially become their full-time career.

---

[*] As of the time of going to press (autumn 2011) David Farrant and friends run an equally vitriolic Facebook group entitled *The Séan Manchester Hateblog.*

Nor does their animosity towards each other show any signs of abating. Indeed, with the advent of the internet, millions of words have been expended in an endless flame-war, which is sure to reignite whenever and wherever the Highgate Vampire is mentioned. Any quest for truth is immediately smothered by the endless struggle between these two eccentric cults of personality. Neither party can be regarded as a reliable source, as both frequently and flagrantly rewrite the past to suit their agenda. Similarly, each emphasises their own role at the expense of the other, representing anything that does not fit their personal interpretation of being a hoax, seemingly unaware that by doing so they further undermine the credibility of the whole case.

Meanwhile, although the pair might have provided the local community with a great deal of amusement over the years, the custodians of Highgate Cemetery have never forgiven Manchester or Farrant. In 1973, the cemetery was closed to all but relatives of those interred there, and in 1975 the Friends of Highgate Cemetery was established to protect and restore the site. Fifteen years later it was finally opened to the public once again. However, whilst visitors to the east cemetery enjoy open access, entrance to the west cemetery is only permitted on guided tours. The Highgate Vampire is conspicuously never mentioned.

The north front of the 17th Century Kirklees Hall, now converted into luxury flats
(David and Carol Whitehead)

(ABOVE) Members of the Yorkshire Robin Hood Society with their patron Sean Manchester (centre) and others at the Barnet Carnival in 1988 (Barbara Green)
(BELOW) Founder member of the Yorkshire Robin Hood Society, Ruth Harrington, with future patron John Pope de Locksley at the Barnet Carnival in 1988 (Barbara Green)

(ABOVE) A gritstone outcrop on Blackstone Edge known as Robin Hood's Bed, where the outlaw is supposed to have once rested (Author)

(BELOW) The spurious 18th Century epitaph set into the monument at Robin Hood's grave (John Billingsley)

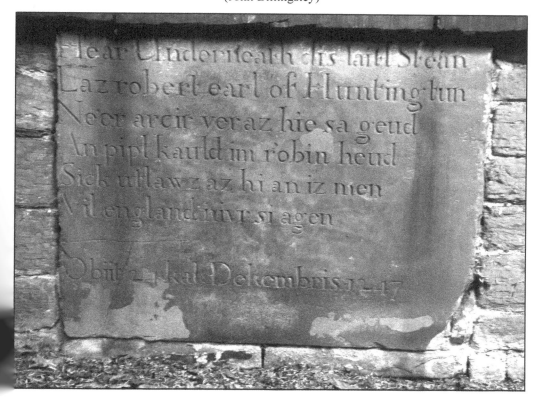

(ABOVE) The dilapidated building known as the "gatehouse" of Kirklees Priory, in which Robin is supposed to have died (John Billingsley)
(BELOW) The deplorable condition of the monument at Robin Hood's grave today (John Billingsley)

(ABOVE) Nathaniel Johnston's 1669's sketch of the stone at Robin Hood's grave with possible embellishments by William Stukeley, copied by Gertrude Harris Fleming St. John (West Yorkshire Archive Service)

(BELOW) Looking over a tract of Kirklees Park from Hartshead. Robin Hood's grave is located in the woods along the ridge in the centre of the photograph (Author)

(ABOVE) An old graveslab in the churchyard at St. Peter's, Hartshead, believed by some to be the original stone from Robin Hood's grave (Author)
(BELOW) The Church of St. Peter at Hartshead (Author)

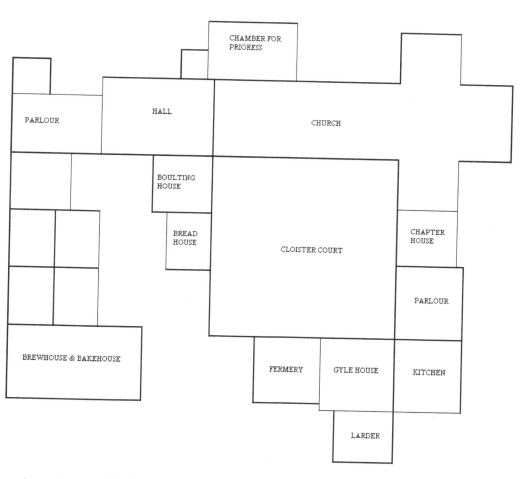

A rough plan of Kirklees Priory at the time of the Dissolution of the Monasteries (Author)

The obelisk known as the Dumb Steeple at Cooper Bridge, on the edge of the Kirklees estate (Author)

(ABOVE) The *Three Nuns* pub at Cooper Bridge, on the edge of the Kirklees estate, focus of many supernatural reports (Author)

(BELOW) Evelyn Friend (left) and Barbara Green (right) promoting the Yorkshire Robin Hood Society at an event in the late 1980s (Barbara Green)

(ABOVE) A dead yew tree in the churchyard at St. Peter's, Hartshead, from which Robin is supposed to have cut is final arrow (Author)

(BELOW) Rev. Jospeh Ismay's second sketch of the detail on the stone at Robin Hood's grave made in 1759

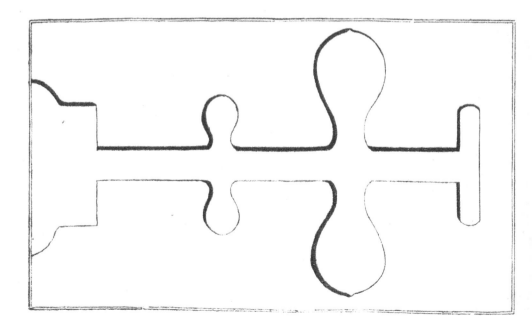

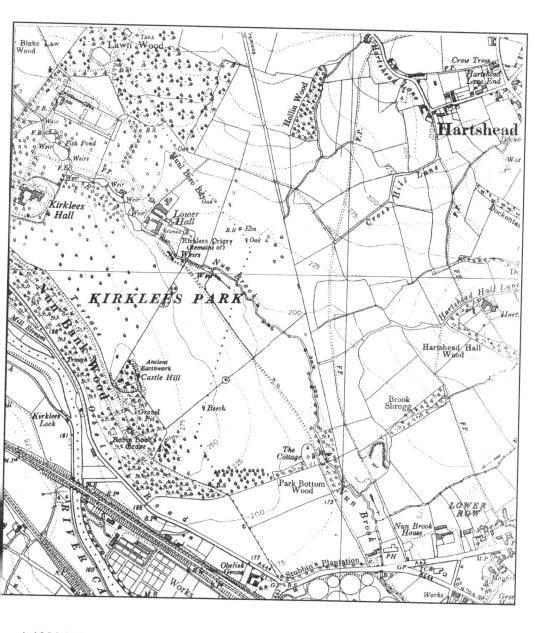

A 1956 Ordnance Survey map of the Kirklees estate, showing the relative positions of the various sites

THE ROOM ROBIN HOOD DIED IN

KIRKLEES PRIORY WHERE ROBIN HOOD DIED

(ABOVE) The monument at Robin Hood's grave in happier times when it was still the show-piece of Kirklees Park (Unknown)

(OPPOSITE ABOVE) The upper room in the gatehouse, in which Robin is supposed to have died (Unknown)

(OPPOSITE BELOW) The building known as the "gatehouse" of Kirklees Priory, in better condition (Unknown)

THE MOST FAMOUS ENGLISH OUTLAW ON THE STAGE:
MR. WALLER AS ROBIN HOOD.

MR. LEWIS WALLER AS ROBIN HOOD, AND MISS EVELYN MILLARD AS MAID MARIAN.

DRAWN BY JOHN CAMERON.

On the evening of October 11, Mr. Lewis Waller arranged to produce at the Lyric Theatre the romantic drama "Robin Hood," by Mr. Henry Hamilton and Mr. William Devereux. The piece had already been seen in the provinces.

CHAPTER SEVEN

Ain't No Grave Gonna Keep My Body Down

The first association between Robin Hood's grave and the supernatural is the story related in Thomas Gent's work of 1730, *The Ancient and Modern History of the Famous City of York,* quoted in full in Chapter 3 [1]. It describes how a local knight attempted to remove the grave-slab to use as his hearthstone, only to find it persistently moved by mysterious forces whilst he slept. These occurrences, reminiscent of what would now be called poltergeist phenomena, ultimately forced him to replace the stone in its original location. Significantly, it took far less effort to return than it had to take away.

Unlike many of the later stories concerning the grave, this tale ascribes supernatural properties to the stone itself rather than the historical drama connected to the site. It features several motifs common in megalith lore across Britian, the significance of which will be discussed more extensively in Chapter 9. Indeed, the story is typically folkloric in that it when Gent recorded it, it appeared to exist abstractly in the oral tradition of the region, but the events could not be connected with any specific individual or date. It is an early equivalent of the modern 'friend-of-a-friend' story.

With the advent of the Romantic tradition in the mid-18th Century, the supernatural became a common feature of the cultural environment. With its penchant for the picturesque and all its inherent superstitions, Romanticism frequently drew on supernatural imagery in its narratives. Ghosts served many functions in Romantic art, communicating a sense of the immanent past, and acting as a personification of the numinous natural world. The supernatural could also act as a metaphor for emotional concepts, particularly the Romantic concept of the Sublime, with its compelling fusion of dread and wonder.

Hence, it is not surprising to find the supernatural invoked in the various Romantic eulogies to Robin Hood's grave and Kirklees Park. The 1760 poem *Kirk-Leas*, written as an elegy for Sir John Armytage following his death in the Seven Years' War, contains the following lines in relation to the outlaw's resting place:

> "But now, at Ease, the fallow Deer / Feed round his tomb devoid of fear. / Perhaps he views them with delight, / The Does and Fawns amuse his sight! / Approach, thou Spirit! – hover round - / Delight to haunt this sacred ground" [2].

The sentiments expressed by this unremarkable doggerel cannot be regarded as anything more than poetic license, certainly not evidence of a supernatural tradition. However, it does emphasise that even two hundred and fifty years ago, the gravesite was provoking such imagery in the psyche of visitors. The precise nature of that imagery seems to reflect the state of the grave itself. Whilst today the supernatural phenomena connected with the site is perceived as shadowy and corrupt, in the 18th Century, when the grave was a showpiece folly set amidst rolling parkland, the associated spectres were regarded as pastoral and benign.

The transition can be seen in Charlotte Brontë's 1847 novel, *Shirley*. Again, whilst there is no direct reference to any overt supernatural tradition, the language used is instructive. Kirklees Park, disguised as Nunnely, is referred to as "one of Robin Hood *haunts*" [3] in Chapter 12. Later, in Chapter 29, the reluctance of a melancholy character to travel to dine at Nunnely one evening is described in the following terms:

> "The tutor would much sooner have made an appointment with the ghost of the Earl of Huntingdon to meet him, and a shadowy ring of his merry men, under the canopy of the thickest, blackest, oldest oak in Nunnely Forest. Yes, he would rather have appointed tryst with a phantom abbess, or mist-pale nun, among the wet and weedy relics of that ruined sanctuary of theirs, mouldering in the core of the wood" [4].

Despite the grave's familiar reputation for supernatural phenomena today, the first published reference to such matters in the modern period does not appear until 1986 in a book called *Land of Lost Content: The Luddit Revolt 1812* by Robert Reid. He writes:

> "The Armytage family lived over the brow of a hill on a splendid site once occupied by Benedictine (Cistercian) nuns. It was called Kirklees. There was more than an insularity about it which local people only reluctantly tried to penetrate. The mystery was helped physically by the thick shroud of trees that surrounded the place, and was sustained by local tales of ghosts of prioresses and nuns and of the death of Robin Hood whose grave is so imperturbably marked as lying with Kirklees grounds" [5].

Some sources have mistaken the title of this book to mean that it was *published* in 1812 [6] and taken the relevant passage as evidence of an extensive supernatural tradition. It is questionable how anybody with a basic grasp of history could have made such a blunder given that the Luddite rebellion only occurred in 1812, and it is hardly likely that in the early 19th Century a book on the subject would have been published in the same year. Moreover, the phrase "land of lost content" did not enter the English language until 1896, from A.E. Housman's poem, *A Shropshire Lad*.

Given the egregiousness of this error, it is not unreasonable to suggest that a mischievous author may have deliberately attributed Reid's book to 1812, in an attempt to fabricate evidence for an older supernatural tradition than actually existed at Kirklees. This was then compounded by subsequent authors, who failed to check the provenance of the original source. The passage is frequently quoted in discussions of the supernatural phenomena at Robin Hood's grave, and still often erroneously dated to 1812.

Nonetheless, the quote should not be dismissed entirely. Robert Reid was a local author and it is entirely possible that he was familiar with a genuine tradition concerning spectral nuns and prioresses at Kirklees. Certainly, first hand recollections of such sightings emerged later, as we shall see. However, it is curious that the only published reference to the ghosts of nuns prior to 1986 is the metaphorical passage from Charlotte Brontë's fictional work, *Shirley*.

It is certain that Barbara Green read Reid's book, as she has used the passage frequently in both her published work[7] and YRHS newsletters. It is not clear exactly how long after the volume's publication she became familiar with the quote, but it does seem to have profoundly influenced her perception of the site. Phantom ladies and the veil of secrecy shrouding Kirklees are recurrent themes in much of her writing on the subject after the late 1980s, especially the material in *Secrets of the Grave*, which she modifies and repeats across numerous sources.

However, Green's interest in the supernatural character of the gravesite began quite innocently with the Yorkshire Robin Hood Society's visit to Barnet Carnival in 1987. It was here that she first encountered Séan Manchester [8]. He was introduced to her by his former rival John Pope, who by that time had become obsessed with the Robin Hood legend, and was claiming descent from the legendary outlaw, changing his name to John Pope de Locksley to emphasise this fact [9]. As President of the London Robin Hood Club, Pope had invited the YRHS to Barnet Carnival and been broadly supportive of Green's campaign, despite his own attempts to prove that the Barnsdale of the ballads was actually Barnet Vale [10].

At the time, Manchester was referring to himself as 'Lord' Manchester, despite apparently having no legitimate claim to such a title[11] and pursuing a career as a photographer. Barbara Green recalls:

> "I noticed a Lord Lichfield type of person roaming round with an enormous zoom lens poised at the ready. He came over to us and organised Ruth, Locksley and myself into a huddle and took some pictures... Séan offered to be our patron and his offer was readily accepted" [12].

Although Green engaged in a great deal of correspondence with Manchester over several years, the only other time they met was again at the Barnet Carnival in 1988 [13]. Green was obviously smitten with the figure, who - prior to his ordination in 1990 - was still presenting himself as a dashing and chivalric figure in the mould of his supposed ancestor, Lord Byron. She writes:

> "I was fascinated by him, both by his flamboyance and his claim to be

Britain's leading vampirologist... It was not long before we were debating
the vampire theory surrounding Robin Hood" [14].

From their letters, it appears that whilst it was enthusiastically received by Manchester, the vampire theory was actually first suggested by Barbara Green [15]. Perhaps she initially mooted it in an attempt to impress their glamorous new patron, or perhaps she hoped that such speculation might lead to a blaze of publicity for the grave at Kirklees as it had done for Highgate Cemetery. If the latter is true, then the strategy backfired spectacularly. Publicity was indeed forthcoming, but it only undermined the credibility of the YRHS and thereby the campaign for access. Indeed, it handed their opponents a stick with which to beat them. One local publication would opine:

"The Society, quite frankly, comes across as eccentric. Their associated
with the International Society of Vampirists would not convince people
that they were soundly based" [16].

The first mention of the matter in the press came in an article for the *Huddersfield Daily Examiner* on 13th June 1988. Titled "Is there a curse of Kirklees?" it reported on the litany of disappointments suffered by the YRHS in their quest for recognition, whilst hinting at darker reasons for these failures. The "curse" itself was supposed to have been uttered by Little John as his master lay dying, although this appears to be an exaggeration of John's request to burn the nunnery down in *Robin Hood's Death*. This conjecture came from Evelyn Friend, an increasingly active member of the YRHS, who also claimed to be a 'Christian psychic' [17].

The article wonders:

"Does all this ill luck have a sinister aspect? The Society believes the troubles
stem back to a malediction uttered upon the nunnery and the vampiric
prioress who is said to have bled Robin Hood to death. Since then, says
the Society, the area has been the scene of murders, fatal accidents and
black magic rites. It cites the bloodshed of the Luddite revolt, the tragedy
of the Brontë family and the death of Sir John Armytage near the famed
grave in a horse riding accident in 1677 as three examples of the curse at
work" [18].

The vampire theory began as nothing but speculation based on an idiosyncratic reading of the narrative of Robin Hood's death. According to this interpretation, the actions of the Prioress are a manifestation of vampire folklore. This is why she bled Robin to death [19], an unconventional method of despatch, which does not have a known analogue in any other medieval ballad [20]. Whilst the Prioress is the source of the evil, there is also the insinuation that Robin himself became a vampire, as the curse is typically transmitted to their victims.

In *Secrets of the Grave,* Barbara Green writes;

"I was interviewed many times by the press about my views about Robin
Hood being a vampire. What I said and still do, is that Robin's death was
vampiric, as he was bled to death" (21).

However, such caution is less in evidence only a few pages later when she writes:

> "Was the wicked prioress of Kirklees a Lamia, the female demon of classical mythology who sucked blood from her victims?... If vampires exist, then undoubtedly the prioress fits into the concept of one" [22].

However, more committed vampire enthusiasts took the hypothesis much further. In his 1997 work *The Vampire Hunter's Handbook*, Séan Manchester approvingly quotes Rob Brautigan in the fanzine *International Vampire* arguing that Robin himself could have been a vampire. This is suggested on the grounds that Robin was a criminal who met a violent death, only to be buried in unconsecrated ground without receiving the last rites. All these factors feature in folklore as qualifications for the curse of vampirism [23]. Manchester also found it interesting that when Sir Samuel Armytage excavated the grave, no remains had been discovered, which he thought might represent evidence that the outlaw's body was not at rest [24].

The International Society for the Advancement of Irreproducible Vampire and Lycanthropy Research (ISAIVLR), of which Manchester was the President, were sufficiently intrigued by the possibility of vampiric activity at Robin Hood's grave to investigate further. On 29th November 1988, the ISAIVLR sent a letter to Lady Armytage requesting permission for one of their 'executives' to visit the grave. They also asked if she would:

> "...consider the possibility of examining the contents, if any, of the grave should the necessary permission be obtained"

And:

> "...allow an accredited investigator from our society to keep vigil nocturnally near the grave for several nights?" [25].

Unsurprisingly, Lady Armytage was not remotely impressed by this communication. Her response, dated 15th December 1988, simply reads:

> "Thank you for your letter dated November 29th. I am afraid I cannot give any consideration to your requests" [26].

Manchester immediately relayed this curt dismissal to Barbara Green, informing her that "it's action stations now!" In this letter, apparently signed by Manchester himself, he goes on to suggest that she send a copy of both ISAIVLR's original request and Lady Armytage's reply to the local press and various tabloid newspapers, including the *Sunday Sport* and the *News of the World* [27]. He now claims that this correspondence is a forgery [28].

Manchester's advice to Green at the time certainly contradicts a statement made many years later by a representative of the Vampire Research Society on their weblog:

> "(In the case of) the Kirklees mystery... matters were taken out of the

Vampire Research Society's hands by others in 1989 when reports of the ensuing investigation started to appear in local and national newspapers and even on some television and radio programmes. The Society could hardly deny that an investigation was in progress but this certainly put us at odds with the owner of the suspect site which is on private land" [29].

However, if the letter really was written by Manchester and he is now seeking to disown it, it is worth emphasising that the reason the Society could not deny an investigation was taking place was because their own President had suggested informing the press about it in the first place. It was not taken out of their hands by others, it was a deliberate policy designed to generate media attention, even if Manchester did delegate responsibility for his dirty work to Barbara Green. It is certainly far from the "aversion to superfluous and sensationalist publicity" he insists he feels [30].

Today, Green is equally coy about the matter, innocently writing that:

> "...inevitably the press got hold of the story and muddled it up, saying we wanted to exhume Robin and vampires were running amok round Brighouse and Clifton" [31].

Again, the only reason the newspapers made such a claim is because she sent them a copy of ISAIVLR's letter to Lady Armytage, in which the Society clearly request that Lady Armytage allow them to "examine the contents, if any, of the grave should the necessary permission be obtained."

Of course, a media storm did descend upon them, especially as the story broke in early January when real news is typically scarce. A flood of stories appeared between 5th and 7th January 1989, across the newspaper spectrum. Practically all the local outlets covered it, as did tabloids such as the *Daily Express* and the *News of the World*, who ran with the typically lurid headline "Robin Blood Killed By Vampire" [32]. The story was even featured by more respectable titles such as *The Independent*, and those as far away as the *Saturday Star* in South Africa [33].

All the reports carried some basic information, including speculation regarding the vampiric nature of Robin's death, and Lady Armytage's refusal to allow ISAIVLR permission to investigate the site of the grave. Many also featured reaction quotes from Lady Armytage herself. She told several sources:

> "I have sought legal advice and want nothing to do with these people. Would you? They want to dig him up and hold vigils over the grave" [34].

Meanwhile, the *Daily Star* quoted a "friend" of the Kirklees landowner as saying:

> "Lady Armytage is annoyed and upset – the request is macabre whether it is serious or not" [35].

In the *Yorkshire Post*, Barbara Green feigned surprise that anybody could possibly regard such a request as outlandish.

> "The legend may be rooted in vampire folklore and the ISAIVLR are the right people to research it. Why are the researchers being denied access? I don't think they are cranks. It does have a vampiric atmosphere about it" [36].

However, the same newspaper referred to the ISAIVLR as a "shadowy organisation", whilst the *Brighouse Echo* dwelled on the fact that the society used as PO Box number as their address [37]. Manchester's group were made out to be as sinister as the entities they purported to investigate.

The matter flared up again following a YRHS press statement describing an ISAIVLR investigation sometime between 21st and 23rd January.

> "A cursory inspection of Robin Hood's grave at Kirklees has been made by Ruthwen Glenarvon, editor of the society's vampire research journal. Although no major discovery has been unearthed at the site or in the surrounding area, his report indicates that further investigation is warranted due to a number of perforations in the earth above the tomb. These are described as being of finger width and of an indeterminate depth" [38].

The question of the exact identity of 'Ruthwen Glenarvon' is uncertain. It is patently a pseudonym; "Ruthwen" is a name taken from John Polidori's 1819 novel *The Vampyre*, whilst *Glenarvon* is the title of an 1816 novel by Lady Caroline Lamb, a lover of Lord Byron. The name was adopted extensively by the editor of the ISAIVLR private newsletter, *The Cross and the Stake* [39], and it was used to sign the December 1988 request to Lady Armytage. As the person in question was evidently a Doctor of Psychology [40], an assumed name was no doubt a necessary precaution to protect his reputation.

The January 1989 investigation naturally provoked an angry response from Lady Armytage. She told the *Yorkshire Post*:

> "Someone must have trespassed to do this research and I'm not pleased. They are definitely cranks and if this persists, I might have to inform the police" [41].

Meanwhile, Séan Manchester privately expressed doubts regarding the "perforations" around the grave in a letter to Barbara Green. He claimed to have no idea what they might signify and were possibly evidence of nothing more exciting than worms [42].

Disappointed by the hostile press response so far, Barbara Green contacted the Anglican vicar, Rev. John Flack, who at that time was Team Rector for the Brighouse parish. Flack was already a rising star within the Church of England hierarchy. He would go on to become Bishop of

Huntingdon and later, the Archbishop of Canterbury's envoy to the Holy See in Rome. As such, it is doubtful that he recalls his involvement with the YRHS as a shining moment in his illustrious career, as it rapidly turned into a public relations disaster for all concerned.

Green wrote to Flack in early 1989 to inquire about the possibility of holding a blessing ceremony at Robin Hood's grave, and for the Church of England's support in campaigning for the restoration of the monument [43]. Flack was initially cooperative. He insisted he could not conduct a ritual at the graveside without the landowner's permission, but was willing to hold a prayer service for the outlaw at St. Martin's Church in Brighouse. In a classic display of Anglican diplomacy, he claimed that he was "not qualified to make any judgment on vampiric infestation" [44].

It was not long before the prayer service story was picked up in the press, yielding headlines such as "Vicar forgives legendary bandit vampire victim" [45], along with the suggestion that he was seeking to perform the blessing at the grave itself. Nonetheless, Flack made it quite clear in the *Yorkshire Post*:

> "I am not sure though whether we will be able to consecrate the grave. Firstly, we would have to be sure there were some remains there and that has been in some doubt. Secondly, we would need the permission of the estate owner, Lady Armytage, to go near the grave" [46].

Needless to say that despite the YRHS's polite representations to Lady Armytage [47], the requisite permission was not forthcoming. Indeed, following the first spate of press reports, Flack was fielding media inquiries from across the world and it was not long before he was contacted by the Bishop of Wakefield, and Lady Armytage herself, expressing displeasure at these developments [48]. Not only was Flack forced to repeatedly deny that he had said he was going to consecrate the grave, he was forced to abandon the prayer service idea altogether.

The media narrative rapidly changed to "Church of England refuses to bless Robin Hood's grave", giving the ISAIVLR more fuel for their vampiric fire. Flack told the *Yorkshire Post*:

> "I was totally misrepresented by the press and television. I said I would not go anywhere near the grave, which is on private property. What I offered to do was say prayers for Robin. Now I have withdrawn any offer I made. I certainly would not do anything with the full glare of press and media attention" [49].

Meanwhile, the *Halifax Evening Courier* reported Barbara Green exclaiming, "You would think we were asking to hold a Black Mass at the graveside the way things have developed" [50]. She vowed to fight on undeterred and her next option was to contact Father Matthew Dwyer, priest at St. Joseph's Roman Catholic Church in Brighouse. Father Dwyer also refused to involve himself, arguing:

> "The ability to discern in such cases is not within my competence... not knowing the answer, it would be out of order for me to proceed publicly

in such a manner as to suggest that I did" [51].

Meanwhile, the Church of England referred the YRHS to Bishop Anselm Gelders, formerly Bishop of Bermuda, but now resident at the House of the Resurrection, an Anglican monastic community in nearby Mirfield. As part his previous role, Genders had performed a public ritual of exorcism for the Bermuda Triangle in 1978, and - doubtless to the church hierarchy - he seemed like the ideal person to resolve the Kirklees controversy as tactfully as possible [52].

Genders initially repeated Flack's assertion that without knowing if there really was a body interred in Robin Hood's grave, it would be inappropriate to proceed with a blessing at the site. However, quickly realising that this was not the answer the YRHS wanted to hear, he informed them that if their concern truly was the salvation of Robin's soul, then the distance from his grave would not affect the efficacy of prayer, which could be performed anywhere [53]. He was forced to concede that to exorcise an evil *place* required proximity, but pragmatically pointed out that following the grisly outcome of the exorcism of schizophrenic Michael Taylor in 1974, the Church of England were uncomfortable about proceeding with such ceremonies in the public eye [54].

All these rebuttals have since entered the narrative as evidence of dark forces holding sway over Kirklees, impervious even to the sanctity of the church. Manchester even tried to suggest it was significant that two years later Flack's church, St. Martin's, was the scene of "ritualistic" desecration [55]. It is true that none of the churchmen consulted by the YRHS were themselves prepared to ask Lady Armytage if they could perform a blessing ceremony at the grave and arguably, this was rather gutless. However, once again, it is less evidence of a conspiracy or malign supernatural influence, than of institutional politics and official indifference to the YRHS's cause.

In the late summer of 1989, Barbara Green's suspicions regarding occult activity at Kirklees were exacerbated. She recalls:

> "Around this time I received several frightening letters from a person who signed himself the King of the Witches, threatening me that the Yorkshire Robin Hood was being hexed. I burned these incriminating missives and pulverised the ashes of the 'spells' to a paste with holy water. They were just so chilling and scary I felt I had to destroy them immediately in order to nullify any power they might possess".

This further convinced Green that sinister forces were working against her Society and attacking the sanctity of Robin Hood's grave itself.

However, Séan Manchester suspected that the missives actually came from William Binding, the uncle of John Pope (de Locksley) [57]. Whether Séan Manchester's accusations were true, it is the first sign that the Highgate feud was beginning to infect matters concerning Kirklees. It will be recalled that John Pope was an associate of David Farrant in the 1970s, and they participated in occult rituals together. He had evidently reached a temporary rapprochement with Séan Manchester during the mid-1980s, but these harmonious relations had broken down by 1989 when Manchester started petitioning Barbara Green to expel Pope from the YRHS, once more denouncing him as a Satanist. Although Green ultimately refused to accede to Manchester's request, she did challenge Pope regarding his alleged Satanism [58].

Meanwhile, William Binding, who passed away in 2007, was a very dubious character indeed. He came to national prominence in 2001 when Conservative leader, Iain Duncan Smith, was forced to expel him from the party. This was following revelations that Binding had belonged to a number of white supremacist organisations, including the British branch of the Ku Klux Klan, the pro-apartheid Springbok Club and the British National Party, for whom he'd stood as a parliamentary candidate in the 1997 general election [59]. It should be noted that occultism is a popular interest amongst radical far-right groups.

Manchester counselled Barbara Green to ignore the material she was receiving in the post, as the spells had no efficacy [60]. Despite these assurances, Green and her associates were evidently spooked and began to believe that a malevolent presence was targetting them. Interestingly, it seems that the catalyst for this apprehension came not from Green herself, but from her lodger, simply referred to as Jayne, who allegedly had no interest in the speculation surrounding Robin Hood's grave.

> "All of a sudden Jayne refused to sleep in this room. She said 'something' had come in through the window and scared her. She insisted on camping out on the floor of my bedroom... Whatever it was then came into my room and put the wind up the pair of us... I felt a definitive sense of evil taking me over and for several nights I hardly slept" [61].

Green was once again forced to call on the services of her parish priest, Rev. John Flack. He advised her that she had been right to destroy the offending letters and proceeded to bless each room in her house, sprinkling them with holy water. After this, "the gremlins left" [62].

With evidence of supernatural activity apparently mounting and the official church still refusing to acknowledge the problem, Séan Manchester claims that on Sunday 22nd April 1990, he was forced to tackle the potential vampiric activity around Robin Hood's grave himself [63]. An account of his alleged actions that night first appeared in 1992, contained within the pages of a magazine called *The Unexplained,* and was subsequently expanded for a chapter in Manchester's 1997 publication *The Vampire Hunter's Handbook.* These remain amongst the most famous accounts of the phenomenon unequivocally dubbed 'The Kirklees Vampire'.

Manchester describes how he arrived at Kirklees with two researchers, but after penetrating the woodland on foot, one was overcome with dread, and returned to their vehicle. Manchester and his remaining assistant pressed on to inspect the building supposed to have been the Priory Gatehouse, and claimed to have discovered a number of occult symbols carved in the vicinity [64]. The pair then proceeded to the grave itself. Manchester writes:

> "My armoury of vampire repellent included crucifixes, holy water, garlic

and small container wherein the Host is kept. I also brought a clutch of stakes" [65].

The vampire-hunter claims their first encounter came as soon as they arrived at the grave and, "a terrible scream filled the night air and caused us to start" [66]. Retiring into the trees, they began their vigil and for three hours, nothing stirred.

> "Then we heard it. First of all, it wafted faintly on the night air, like the discordant sound sometimes made by the wind in the trees. But then it grew louder still – and closer – and we recognised it to be more akin to a dreadful wailing. Something was approaching. I quickly lit a candelabrum stuffed with five candles, grabbed the largest crucifix available and stepped into the path of the unearthly groaning. 'Behold the Light! The brief exorcism caused the wailing the cease abruptly" [67].

Manchester claims he then discovered his assistant entangled in a thicket of brambles, having witnessed the source of the wailing sound. He described the apparition as "a darkly-clad woman who at first appeared serene – then rapidly manifested into a wraith with red eyes, staring and horrible" [68]. Following this encounter, they beat a hasty retreat, after first sprinkling holy water and planting garlic around the graves of both Robin Hood and the prioress, Elizabeth de Staynton [69].

Despite its fame, there are a substantial number of problems with Manchester's account of his vigil at the graveside. To begin with, any sceptical reader will find the evidence he offers as cause for the investigation distinctly problematic. He cites the discovery of the finger-width holes around the grave by Ruthwen Glenarvon in January 1989 and, "nearby villagers... obliged to call in priests to exorcise their homes of a malignant force" [70], clearly referring to Barbara Green's experiences in autumn 1989. Manchester writes as if these facts were brought to his attention by independent witnesses. They were not. Instead, they were presented by observers already predisposed to believe in the existence of vampiric activity. It is a classic case of confirmation bias, an inclination to pay more attention to data that supports a hypothesis.

Manchester also fudges the chronology. He claims that Glenarvon's discovery had taken place "in the winter of 1987" and claims that "animals drained of blood had been discovered in the immediate vicinity" [71]. Yet the first mention of such carcasses appears to be from a YRHS newsletter reporting their first organised trespass to the grave on 27th April 1990 [72], a whole five days after Manchester claims he held the vigil! He also says, "these were by no means the first incidents to come to my attention" before relating an experience which did not actually emerge until 1994 [73].

A further problem with Manchester's account is his insistence that they visited both the Gatehouse and the grave of the Prioress. Unlike Robin Hood's grave, both these edifices are within extreme proximity to the residential buildings on the estate. Indeed, the de Staynton grave is situated in Lady Armytage's back garden! It seems incredible that they could have made nocturnal visits to these sites without anybody noticing. Considering that Lady Armytage subsequently denied that permission to inspect the estate had ever been given to any vampire hunter [74], it is difficult to see how they could have accomplished such a feat without being detected and expelled.

Manchester writes that he "made the discovery of several occult symbols, some identified as being Satanic, etched into the priory garden wall and the building itself. These ancient signs were another indication of diabolism all those centuries ago" (75). However, Manchester is clearly referring to the medieval mason's marks which can be found across the Kirklees estate. Moreover, he did not "discover" them; they were first mentioned to him in late 1989 in a letter from Barbara Green [76] and are referred to in numerous academic studies of Kirklees Priory.

Whilst Manchester associates these marks with Freemasonry, which he regards as part of the "Left Hand Path" [77], there is simply no connection. The Freemasons did not emerge until the 18th Century and the marks at Kirklees are nothing more than the signatures of medieval stone-masons. Manchester now argues that he was referring to his discovery of more recent chalked symbols on the gatehouse [78], but this is demonstrably not what he originally claimed, and he has been unable to supply convincing evidence of this graffiti.

Perhaps most damning problem, however, is that fact that there is no reference to Manchester's Kirklees vigil in any correspondence with Barbara Green around that time. Indeed, in a letter dated 10th July 1990 and apparently signed by Manchester, he maintains he could not possibly conduct an exorcism at Robin Hood's grave because until he is ordained as a bishop, he does not have the authority [79]. Subsequently, in a letter of 28th May 1992, he discusses a projected visit to Kirklees in language that suggests he has never been to the area before [80].

From all these inconsistencies it seems reasonable to conclude that Manchester has a number of questions to answer if he wishes his story to be taken seriously. The date is particularly suspicious, as it is so close to the YHRS's first organised trespass to the grave from the *Three Nuns*. As Paul Weatherhead comments in *Weird Calderdale*:

> "It is remarkable that neither party visited the grave for the first six years *(sic)* of the Yorkshire Robin Hood Society's existence and then both visited independently within days of each other!" [81]

For the next few years, the situation went quiet. A number of pieces were published regarding the Kirklees Vampire, including a chapter in Rosemary Ellen Guliey's 1991 book, *Vampires Among Us,* and Séan Manchester's article for *The Unexplained.* This raised public awareness, but following press hostility to the vampire theory, Barbara Green had returned to focusing on more historical matters, such as the triumphant publication of her book *The Outlaw Robin Hood: His Yorkshire Legend.*

Séan Manchester was also beginning to express doubts regarding the validity of the vampire theory. In a letter to Barbara Green, he revealed that he had received information suggesting that the grave was not authentic [82]. Since then, he has always stressed that he never conclusively identified the supernatural phenomena at Kirklees as vampiric, or that it was connected to Robin Hood. In *The Vampire Hunter's Handbook* he is careful to note:

"The real question, sure, should have been whether or not the grave's occupant was the cause of vampiric hauntings; not the particular name attributed to the tomb" [83].

The Yorkshire Robin Hood Society finally folded in 1993 due to Green's ill-health, and dwindling interest amongst members following so many setbacks to their campaign. However, the following year Green's interest was rekindled, following her encounter with Roger Williams, a musician living in the nearby village of Bradley [84]. Williams told her of his two ghostly encounters in the vicinity of the grave many years earlier, which not only seemed to confirm many of Green's suspicions about supernatural activity at the site, but has since become one of the most frequently referenced experiences in discussions of the Kirklees haunting.

Williams recalls:

"The first (experience) was in the early Sixties while walking up there with a friend. It was the first time I had seen the grave and as we were walking away from it, I saw a figure standing about twenty years away to the left of the grave-site... This figure started to move towards us and I saw it was a woman. I say move because she seemed to kind of glide towards us and there wasn't any noise of feet walking over dry fallen leaves, twigs and dry bracken on the ground. As she came within five yards of us we saw her very clearly. Her eyes seemed very dark and she looked mad, annoyed at us. Then she moved on past us, didn't look back and then she was gone. We realised that what we had just seen wasn't a real person at all and it shook us up a lot. It was 2:30pm and it was a bright, sunny afternoon.

The second time I saw the apparition was in 1972, again in the autumn. I am a musician and my bass guitarist, Phil Marsden, asked me if I knew where Robin Hood's grave was and would I take him up there to see it. It was Saturday afternoon. The day was chilly but nice. As we were coming away from the grave I bent down to fix my shoelace. Then Phil said 'Hey, Roger, there's a woman coming'. As I looked up I saw the exact same thing I had seen that day in 1963, except this time she stopped not six feet from us. I'll never forget the experience. She wore a long off-white dress, kind of squarish round the neck with long sleeves. But again it was her eyes I remember most, dark, mad, set in her pale face. She looked at me and then at Phil, so close I could have touched the hem of her dress... Then she moved right past us and was gone.

Both times I saw this apparition things started to happen in my house. Noises, banging and a feeling like I was being watched. And the lad I was up there with in 1963 got just the same and so did Phil Marsden. So you see, I really would advise people to be careful. Better still not to go up there till the site has been blessed. Wild horses wouldn't drag me up there again" [85].

Both Barbara Green and Séan Manchester have associated the spectre seen by Roger Williams with the ghost of the 'wicked Prioress' [86]. The experience is also significant in that it occurred long before any speculation regarding the ghost of the Prioress had appeared in the press. However, Williams never refers to the figure as the 'Prioress' himself. Nor does he make it clear if he was familiar with the story of Robin Hood's death prior to his first encounter, or that Kirklees Park had once been the site of a nunnery.

Indeed, Williams himself has subsequently cast doubt on the association of the spectre with the Prioress. He told Séan Manchester in 2005:

> "Although some people have suggested she might be the prioress who killed Robin Hood she certainly did not look like a nun. What is more, not only was she *not* wearing a nun's habit, but the style of dress does not even fit the time of Robin Hood. My sister-in-law, Sandra, recently drew a sketch of the apparition based on my description and checked it against illustrations in her mother's collection of books on ladies costume through the ages... She found that this type of dress was very fashionable for one short period in history... around the late 1400s to the early 1500s, during the reign of Henry Tudor" [87].

Curiously, the apparition could be said to fall into a category of apparitions seen across Britain throughout the ages, known as 'White Ladies'. Indeed, it is one of the most common ghost traditions in the country, and perhaps it is evidence not of the spirit of the Prioress, but another manifestation of this universal folkloric motif? It is significant that in various local traditions such 'white lady' apparitions are regarded as the tutelary guardians of sacred sites, including graveyards and other ancient burial sites [88].

Either way, Barbara Green found her interest in the grave revitalised by these new revelations. Following the traumatic break-up of a love affair, Barbara Green had not concerned herself with matters connected to Robin Hood for some time [89]. But after her encounter with Williams she found herself drawn to the grave once more, and decided to guide three curious young men to the monument one frosty, starlit night. Whilst on her previous unofficial visit, she had approached the site across the fields from the *Three Nuns* pub, on this occasion she chose to clamber over the wall running adjacent to the A644 and proceed through the bramble-choked woods up the flank of Castle Hill - no mean feat in the darkness.

Although Green had not partaken herself, her companions were reputedly in various states of intoxication and her account suggests that a contact high, combined with adrenaline of the experience was colouring her perception.

> "I felt a great wave of exhilaration as we trekked up the wooded hillside, and felt almost as if we were back in the days of Robin and his merry band, laughing in the face of authority and risking all in the cause of justice... I was as high as a kite from the sheer excitement of it all... By the time we arrived at the grave, I was hysterical with laughter at the antics of the three young men and caution had been thrown to the winds" [90].

At the graveside, they continued to lark about, whilst Green took photographs and scattered some palm crosses across the enclosure by way of a blessing. It was clearly not sufficient, however, because Barbara Green was about to experience the haunting at Robin Hood's grave firsthand. Although the account of Roger Williams was no doubt at the forefront of her mind at the time, it was not the Prioress she believed she encountered, but a character which had so far been overlooked in discussions of supernatural activity at Kirklees.

Green had remained in the vicinity of the monument to place the palm crosses whilst the others explored the surrounding woodland, and in her own words:

> "..while I was so occupied on my own I became aware of a presence. I became very anxious... restless and increasingly agitated. I felt the hair on my head begin to rise, almost as though I had been plugged into an electric socket. My mouth went bone dry and I felt as though I would choke on my tongue. I looked desperately around for the others and tried to shout for them but found I could neither shout nor move."

> A horrible, panicky feeling swept over me and from the surrounding trees I saw, and felt, streams of evil pouring forth and washing over me. I felt, in that instant, that I was going to die on the spot. Then, even more terrifyingly, I saw materialising before me a person I knew well. Hideous, sneering and hateful, surrounded by tongues of flaming red hair, I was looking into the freezing grey eyes of my ex-lover, yet as I recognised that foul and malevolent visage, I was sat the same time aware that I was seeing the spectre of the wicked prioress's paramour, Red Roger of Doncaster" [91].

This version was taken from *Secrets of the Grave*, published in 2001, and Green continues to maintain that this represents her definitive account [92]. However, a somewhat different description of events appeared closer to the time.

> "I saw them, at first as flittering, amorphous forms merging with the murky mists coiled ever thicker and malevolently round the trees. Two distinct forms that I had no trouble recognising as the Prioress of Kirklees and her lover, Red Roger of Doncaster... Like a bat she hung there for what seemed an eternity, her black nun's robes flapping eerily while her eyes flashed red and venomous and her teeth bared sharp and white between snarling blood red lips" [93].

This initially appeared in an issue of *International Vampire,* a journal self-published by the Dutch vampire researcher Rob Brautigam, and has subsequently been quoted in several more reputable sources including *Ten Yorkshire Mysteries* by Len Markham. Today, Barbara Green insists that the narrative published in *International Vampire* was designed as a semi-fictional account of her experiences, which has subsequently been uncritically repeated without reference to its original context [94].

However, several years after the publication of *Secrets of the Grave*, the embellished version reappeared in the *Daily Mirror*, under the headline, "I was haunted by Robin Hood's killer". Here Green is directly quoted as saying:

> "His face was contorted in anger, it was horrible and he came rushing towards me. He was wearing a black cloak and was about 5ft 11 and his feet weren't touching the ground! Then a black shape appeared behind him, it had an outline of a woman" [95].

The article also implies that Green's experience prompted her interest in the Robin Hood legend, rather than the other way round.

In *Secrets of the Grave*, Green is quite open to the possibility that the experience was a result of her state of mind at the time.

> "I still wonder whether it was supernatural or related to drug withdrawal on my part, for I had been sent to a psychiatrist by the Occupational Health Department of my work because of my sick leave... She prescribed me some tablets, saying that they would cure me. I could not see how tablets could cure my personal muddle but took them for about a week before binning them. Could this have caused my experience or hallucination?" [96].

The question of reliable witness accounts of the phenomena at Robin Hood's grave is always vexed. Even Barbara Green acknowledges that her own experience may have been influenced by both her medical condition and her preconceptions about the sight. The testimony of Séan Manchester is similarly troublesome for the reasons discussed above, and because again, he is already disposed to believe in the paranormal. Hence, confirmation bias is always a danger. So far, Roger Williams is the only independent witness but given the interval between the actual experience and his written account of it, his reliability is uncertain.

Fortunately, a new report emerged in 1995, published only a short time after the events themselves and from a seemingly credible witness. Journalist Judith Broadbent, and photographer Sue Ellis, visited the grave with the rare permission of Lady Armytage in November 1995. This was in preparation for a feature on Robin Hood of Yorkshire for *Yorkshire Life* magazine. The article was published in the January 1996 issue, and from the content it is clear that Broadbent had come across the grave's supernatural reputation whilst researching the story, but she insisted elsewhere that, "I'd always been sceptical about ghosts, ghouls and apparitions."

Yet in the *Spenborough Guardian* on 29th December 1995, she described her 'spooky encounter' at the grave.

> "My colleague and I visited the grave to take photographs. We both had cameras, but mine jammed so I wandered off to the edge of the copse. Hearing heavy footsteps approaching from behind me, I turned around. No-one was there. My bag and camera were both slung over my shoulder. They began to feel really heavy as if something tried to pull them from

me. We then left the area to take pictures of the estate. When I tried my camera again, it worked perfectly!" [97].

Judith Broadbent later informed Barbara Green that following their visit to the grave, Sue Ellis fell "seriously ill a week later and was taken into Pinderfields with a mystery illness – akin to meningitis. She was paralysed from neck down for two weeks" (98). Green inquired if Broadbent thought the supernatural force at Kirklees could've been responsible for the photographer's sudden malady. She replied, "There could possibly be a connection as she's usually so fit and healthy" (99).

However, the accounts of Séan Manchester, Roger Williams, Barbara Green and Judith Broadbent stand in stark contrast to those of Edith Ellis, an elderly lady from Dewsbury who had contacted Barbara Green in the late 1980s to relate an experience from her childhood. Edith wrote:

> "My cousin Alice lived in an old cottage at Littlethorpe Hill near Hartshead Church. My cousin always said when she tended her window box of snowdrops she had heard Robin calling for Maid Marian... I once stayed for the weekend and I looked out of the window. It was a clear, moonlit night. Suddenly, over by Kirklees Hall, a light flashed in the fields. Next day Alice and I walked over and we found an arrow embedded in the wall" [100].

Ellis describes a considerably more benign manifestation of supernatural phenomena at Kirklees than the aforementioned encounters, and it suggests that the tradition was not as unified as some commentators have tried to make out. It is also the first time the ghost of Robin Hood himself has been associated with Kirklees and represents a completely divergent body of belief from the 'wicked Prioress' theory propagated by the YRHS and ISAIRVL over the last thirty years.

This tradition was later confirmed by Steve Hill, who passed on a family story to Paul Weatherhead for publication in *Weird Calderdale*. It refers to Steve's father, John Hill, who in 1924 not only worked as a tenant farmer on the Kirklees estate, but lived in the Gatehouse itself.

> "The encounter... was on his way home from the *Three Nuns*. He was walking home through the woods when something fell out of a tree and knocked him to the ground. When he got up he could see the old Gatehouse and in the window he could see a man with a bow. We always said it was the drink, but he was adamant it was Robin Hood's ghost" [101].

It is notable that in the first half of the 20th Century when these experiences supposedly took place, the Kirklees estate was still predominantly scenic parkland, whilst the grave and Gatehouse were still in a good state of repair and regularly open to visitors. The incongruity between these earlier sightings, and those recorded in the second half of the century, seems to confirm the notion that the haunting reflects the atmosphere of the site. When it is airy and picturesque, it is the ghost of the noble outlaw that is witnessed. Conversely, when the area is decaying and apparently shrouded in secrecy, it is the spectre of his treacherous killer. Whether this reflects the perspective of the observer or the nature of some external phenomena is contentious.

Nonetheless, with more and more supernatural experiences at Kirklees coming to light, Barbara Green believed that the issue deserved further investigation. Although she had disbanded the YRHS in 1993 feeling that she'd reached something of a dead-end, with fresh avenues to pursue and new blood showing an interest in the case, it seemed like the opportune moment to move forward [102]. Thus, she united with local film producer Michael Hartley, and Mark Gibbons of the British Earth and Air Mysteries Society, to form Gravewatch, again under the patronage of Séan Manchester [103]. Their self-declared remit was to conduct a proper para-psychological investigation into the Kirklees haunting.

Paranormal TV drama *The X Files* took off in Britain in 1997, and the programme provided lazy journalists with an excellent narrative in which to fit stories such as these. Hence, the launch of Gravewatch was greeted in the local press with typically crass headlines such as "X marks the spot as Hood file opens" [104], and "Ghostbusters open the Hood X-file" [105]. Several newspapers quoted Barbara Green saying:

> "With the founding of Gravewatch a determined effort is about to be launched using modern equipment in the hands of a group of intrepid investigators, which it is hoped will expose the sinister secrets hidden at Kirklees" [106].

Meanwhile, Lady Armytage told the *Evening Courier*, "I have lived here for fifty years and never seen a ghost" [107].

Two nights after their inaugural meeting, several members of Gravewatch led by Barbara Green made a clandestine nocturnal visit to the grave. Although they followed a route Green had taken before from the side of the A644, on this occasion, she managed to get seriously lost amongst the dense undergrowth of the Kirklees woodland. Fearful of using torches lest they attract the attention of gamekeepers, they pressed on through the rhododendrons, growing increasingly entangled and confused [108].

Suddenly Mark Gibbons shouted, "Can you see it? It's there, over there in the trees." At the time members of the team believed that he was referring to the grave which they found almost immediately afterwards. However, he later revealed that he'd seen an apparition amongst the trees.

> "I was overcome with fear and panic, both at the sight of the spectre or whatever it was and the way I felt it was watching us. It was dressed in a kind of white robe but I couldn't its face. I could hear footsteps coming from behind me, but nobody could see anything. I also felt that it was trying to communicate with us, trying to tell us where the grave was".
> [109]

Again, Gibbons' reliability as witness is open to question. He was a confirmed believer in the paranormal [110] and the circumstances of experience were arguably particularly conducive to misinterpretation. Nonetheless, the detail of the apparition indicating the whereabouts of the grave is interesting. In one account, Gibbons explicitly claims, "I saw the apparition lift its arm and point and I knew that it was telling me where the grave was" [111]. This is another characteristic feature of 'white lady' lore across the country. Such figures are often believed to gesture towards sites of significance, including buried treasure and scenes of tragedy.

It is also significant that despite his faith in the supernatural, Mark Gibbons was quite determined that he "didn't want anything to do with vampires". He wrote:

> "I don't believe in them. It's a simple matter of logic as I see it – if people keep vampiring each other and turning their victims into vampires, they would soon run out of people to vampire, because we'd all be vampires!" [112].

Perhaps thanks to his influence, Barbara Green also grew considerably more guarded about mentioning the 'V-word' in the press.

Gibbons' disbelief notwithstanding, Séan Manchester still retained a connection with Gravewatch. Following the *Brighouse Echo's* reference to "the rather sinister ministrations of the band of fanatics who are convinced evil lurks within… (the Kirklees Estate's) walls" [113], Manchester wrote a strongly worded letter to the newspaper denying that their actions could be described in such terms. Displaying something of a lack of self-awareness, he directed readers to his account of his vigil at Kirklees in *The Vampire Hunter's Handbook* to see the folly of the *Echo's* accusations [114].

Mark Gibbons was not the only one to have strange experiences following his membership of Gravewatch. Shortly after the media focused on the group's founding, Michael Hartley found himself plagued by a string of misfortunes, including ailing health and a sudden dearth of commissions. Meanwhile, he was ostracised by his local community in Clifton. The villagers began to refer to him as a 'gravedigger', and he was berated in the street by the vicar of St. John's Church, a close friend of Lady Armytage, who inevitably disapproved of his involvement in such a venture [115].

Fearing that his professional standing was being undermined by his involvement with Gravewatch, Hartley decided to withdraw publicly from the organisation, and in February 1998 issued a press release which was quoted briefly in the *Brighouse Echo* [116]. However, the remaining members felt the newspaper had confused their facts somewhat, and so another statement was released, this time by Mark Gibbons stating the various convictions of the organisation. This once again precipitated a media feeding-frenzy, with numerous press sources reviving the vampire story and reporting that Gravewatch had disbanded due to internal disagreements [117].

Tired of the media's hypocritical interest in the topic of Robin Hood's grave, which flared up only when controversy was involved, whilst remaining disappointingly indifferent to supporting the long-term campaign for access, Barbara Green decided to run with the story of the group's dissolution. She told the *Brighouse Echo*:

> "I just got totally fed up with trying to get somewhere but always getting knocked back. After 15 years we are still in the same situation."

She added elsewhere:

> "I still think its important but I don't think local people are all that bothered... We are going to see whether there's any reaction to the fact that we have disbanded". [118]

For a time, Barbara Green once more turned her attention away from Kirklees, focusing instead on a new venture with Gibbons and Hartley, dubbed the British Parapsychological Research Centre, which aimed to investigate a variety of paranormal cases in the area [119]. But, despite her claim in *Secrets of the Grave* that she "thought it might be better for the Robin Hood situation if we did in fact let it fizzle out for the time being instead of being confrontational" [120], it was not long before Green returned to the fold.

Whilst through Mark Gibbons' influence with Gravewatch, Green had distanced herself for a vampiric interpretation of the supernatural phenomena at Kirklees, she had maintained a number of contacts in the world of vampire research, including Rob Brautigam, the editor of *International Vampire* [121]. Although Brautigam had originally been a correspondent of Séan Manchester, and applied to join the Vampire Research Society, he eventually found himself drawn towards the camp of Manchester's arch-nemesis, David Farrant.

When Brautigam met Barbara Green in London in the late 1990s, he introduced her to David Farrant (who was also of course an associate of her old acquaintance John Pope de Locksley) and the two struck up a correspondence regarding the paranormal aspects of the Kirklees case [122]. Despite evidence that he followed Manchester's activities assiduously over the years, Farrant claims that he had no knowledge of the controversy surrounding Robin Hood's grave, or even of the monument's existence, until he had met Rob Brautigam and Barbara Green [123].

Inevitably, news of such an alliance reached Séan Manchester, as his attitude towards Barbara Green rapidly turned sour. Following the demise of Gravewatch, Barbara Green had begun to prepare an autobiographical account of her connection with Robin Hood's grave over the years, which was eventually self-published as *Secrets of the Grave* in 2001. However, her submittal of the proofs to Séan Manchester for comment provoked a furious response directed through her solicitor. He accused the book of being "sordid" and "highly defamatory and inaccurate", and resented being mentioned in the same context as Farrant and Pope de Locksley. As a result, he withdrew permission to reproduce any copyright material belonging to him in the final publication [124].

This led to a schism between Manchester and Green, which has persisted until this day, despite Green's best efforts to repair it, in the early stages at least. She made it very clear in the published manuscript of *Secrets of the Grave* that she wished Manchester no ill-will.

"There has certainly been no intention by the author to misrepresent Bishop Manchester or to undermine his dignity and it is difficult to understand why he has chosen to disown his part in the story... Bishop Manchester has played a legitimate and honourable role both as patron of the Yorkshire Robin Hood Society (from which he has now resigned) and as investigator into the Kirklees mystery and we are sad that he has chosen to sever his links with the case" [125].

However, her efforts were to little avail. Manchester's animosity towards Farrant was such that he still refuses to cooperate with any project that mentions Farrant's name in conjunction with his own [126]. It could only be seen as a calculate snub, therefore, when in February 2004 Barbara Green appointed David Farrant as the new President of the Yorkshire Robin Hood Society [127]. By this time he had been corresponding with Green on the subject of Kirklees for several years and in the same period, became romantically involved with Catherine Fearnley, the secretary of the YRHS.

Since his decision to distance himself from the claims made by Manchester and his former self regarding the nature of the supernatural phenomena reported around Highgate Cemetery, David Farrant has grown very scathing of any talk pertaining to vampires. As such, his interpretation of people's supernatural experiences connected with Kirklees displays quite a different hue to much of what has been written before. He regards it as genuine "psychic phenomena" [sic] which "materialises spasmodically in the vicinity", but does not believe that it is possible to comment on the origin of that phenomena or say that it definitely emanates from any remains which may lie buried beneath the monument marked as Robin Hood's grave [128].

In other contexts, meanwhile, Farrant has even expressed doubt regarding the authenticity of the monument.

"The grave is supposed to contain the mortal remains of Robin Hood, due to a plaque on the site of it stating that this is the case. There is absolutely no more evidence than this and even this is considerably weakened by the fact that the whole thing itself is a Victorian folly. There exists absolutely no substantial proof that this is really the grave of the legendary Robin Hood" [128].

As such, Farrant arguably made an odd choice of patron for a society whose stated remit is to promote the outlaw's burial site at Kirklees. It would not be unreasonable to suggest that the appointment had less to do with the Yorkshire Robin Hood legend than with the supernatural traditions of the site, and a desire to antagonise Séan Manchester. It is also somewhat ironic that Farrant distances himself from claims that the grave contains the mortal remains of a possible historical figure, yet is quite happy to affirm the existence of paranormal entities.

As a result of his new status and growing interest in the alleged supernatural phenomena at Robin Hood's grave, in April 2005, Farrant paid a visit to the region of Kirklees along with Gareth J. Medway, an occultist and social historian responsible for a definitive exposure of the late-1980s 'Satanic child-abuse' scare titled *Lure of the Sinister*. Whilst in the area, they planned to conduct parapsychological investigations into any presence at Kirkless and perform a blessing ceremony at the graveside. Prior to their expedition, they spoke to Roger Williams, who told them in no uncertain terms not to visit the monument at night. "It is an evil place. All your crucifixes won't protect you" [129]. Nonetheless, they proceeded undeterred, allowing Red Monkey Films to record their activities as part of the company's documentary on the mystery surrounding Robin Hood's grave [130].

Farrant and Medway, along with Barbara Green and Catherine Fearnley, plus two members of the Red Monkey film crew, met at the grave at seven o' clock on the evening of 20th April 2005, approaching from different directions so as not to attract attention [131]. The legitimacy of their presence on the Kirkless estate has been continually disputed. Although Catherine Fearnley possessed a letter from Lady Armytage authorising her to visit the grave at her convenience, it did not make any stipulations for an entire entourage, including a camera crew. Needless to say many voices connected to the estate later insisted the party had thus technically trespassed [132], an accusation that was taken up enthusiastically by Séan Manchester's sympathisers [133].

Farrant recalls that he felt:

> "...an atmosphere of timelessness around the grave and its immediate vicinity... Interestingly, general bird calls were noticeably absent, and the one that was drawn to our attention was a blackbird that appeared to be 'making an alarm call', as these birds do when they are frightened".

He also reports:

> "All observed a distinct 'coldness' that seemed to encompass the actual grave within an area of two feet or more. Thermal readings confirmed this, but compass alignments reacted unpredictably" [134].

The ceremony itself was conducted by Gareth J. Medway, in his capacity as a Hierophant of the Fellowship of Isis, an international pluralist spiritual organisation founded in the 1970s. In a ritual lasting approximately two hours, he recited hymns to three ancient Greek goddesses; Athena, to banish evil; Hecate, to guide restless spirits 'into the light'; and to Themis, to bring peace to the site. He then perambulated the area with a wand, imported specially for the purpose from the Himalayas, in order to banish lingering malign energies [135].

Diagnoses of the efficacy of the blessing have varied. Catherine Fearnley told the *Huddersfield Examiner* on 2nd May 2005 that it was "completely successful in that the powers of darkness at the grave have now been fully dispersed" [136]. Others have been more circumspect. Gareth Medway writes that:

> "There is little evidence as to whether this ritual was successful... no-one lives anywhere near the grave so there is nothing to go by."

However, he does believe it significant that during the ceremony, he stumbled over the words of the hymn to Hecate, at which point Barbara Green felt a distinct chill "implying that there was some occult force resisting what I was attempting to do" [137].

The ceremony prompted a spate of articles in the local press, in which it was frequently described as an "exorcism". Upon hearing of the affair, Kirklees Estate resident Christiaan Hohenzollern wrote his angry letter to the *Brighouse Echo*, accusing the newspaper of condoning trespass by reporting such an episode. Several weeks later, David Farrant replied:

> "The grave was left in better condition than when we found it. By this I mean it was necessary to clear the grave slab of a certain amount of foliage and rubble... For the record I do not personally believe that any of us did anything untoward or 'wrong' indeed, we visited an extremely isolated area (which accordingly interfered with no one) and really I would have thought that our critics might have taken it into account, indeed, even acknowledged our good intentions" [138].

Despite his rush to defend their actions, Farrant's involvement with Kirklees and the YRHS has proved tumultuous to say the least. His relationship with YRHS secretary Catherine Fearnley broke down in mid-2007 following her conversion to Roman Catholicism, and subsequent tentative contact with Séan Manchester [139]. This led Farrant to sever his connections with the Society and withdraw his services as patron. In a number of blog posts from late 2007, he is openly critical of the aims of the YRHS, writing, "I find the whole saga of Robin Hood's ghost extremely tedious" [140].

With Barbara Green similarly disowning Fearnley, Farrant was later reinstated the following year. The détente was to prove short-lived, however. In late 2010, Green dismissed Farrant for failing to publicly support her contention that the continued non-appearance of the Red Monkey film project was the result of a conspiracy against it [141]. Farrant insists:

> "I am unable to accept this, having seen no evidence of it whatsoever. I am aware of the many difficulties small independent film companies face with getting budgets to support their projects. I have since personally been in touch with the producer, and he assured me this had been the case" [142].

Farrant's role as patron of the YRHS was taken over by John Pope de Locksley, but the society exists in little more than name nowadays [143]. Meanwhile, David Farrant is not finished with the Kirklees controversy, stating:

> "Although I am no longer active patron of the YRHS, I am still very much interested in the Robin Hood case. Hopefully, I shall be returning to the area in the near future to conduct a vigil with others at the gravesite, to attempt to see if the blessing ceremony we performed there had the intended effect" [144].

Since Farrant usurped his place in connection with investigation of supernatural phenomena at Kirklees, Séan Manchester has been keen to distance himself from the topic and Barbara Green, who he insists he regrets ever meeting [145]. Today, he repeatedly asserts that he never conclusively identified the haunting at Robin Hood's grave as 'vampiric', and whilst this much is true, it was arguably unwise to include a chapter titled 'The Kirklees Vampire' (without so much as a question mark to append it) in a publication called *The Vampire Hunter's Handbook*. Nor was it wise to boast in the chapter of performing a "short exorcism" at the site whilst equipped with "an armoury of vampire repellents."

The Vampire Research Society publicly states:

> "Though there is undoubtedly a mystery at Kirklees, which might or might not be vampiric in origin, the VRS and its founder now accept that the urgency was partly manufactured by the claims of a tiny number of people who had their own agenda; an agenda, moreover, that the Society does not share. With hindsight the VRS does not believe it would investigate any further without proper consent should these circumstances once again prevail... It also deeply regrets any anxiety that might have been caused at the time when a certain local Robin Hood society leaked the goings-on and attendant phenomena to the press. This left Séan Manchester no alternative but to set the record straight in a specialist magazine and book" [146].

Once again, it is worth reiterating that the "urgency partly manufactured by a tiny number of people" included Séan Manchester himself, who on all the evidence instructed Barbara Green to inform the press of the activities of the International Society for the Advancement of Irreproducible Vampire and Lycanthropy Research (as the Vampire Research Society was calling itself at the time). Nor was he forced to "set the record straight" in subsequent publications; these efforts only muddied the waters further by conflating the chronology of events and raising the spectre of outright falsehood.

Moreover, it is far truer to say that the agenda of the Yorkshire Robin Hood Society was changed to that of the ISAIVLR rather than the other way round. Whilst it was clear that Barbara Green was hoping the publicity from such involvement would focus attention on the grave's deplorable state of repair and the lack of public access, it actually served only to further prejudice critics of the YRHS against the group. Whether it genuinely set back the campaign for greater access to the grave is now a moot point, but it certainly allowed Kirklees to be dragged into an intractable and vitriolic feud, which discredits all those involved through association.

CHAPTER EIGHT

Maps And Legends

Read any discussion of the supernatural phenomena associated with Robin Hood's grave and it will not be long before the topic of 'ley lines' receives its first mention, along with the suggestion that the grave lies at a convergence of such lines. Often this assertion is dealt with uncritically, as if the concept of a ley line is now such an established component of the paranormalist's lexicon that it requires no further elaboration. However, ley lines, especially their meaning in this context, are every bit as controversial as the supernatural itself, and to argue that one is evidence of the other is circular reasoning of the most vicious kind.

The idea of a 'ley' ('ley line' is actually a tautology) was originally developed by Herefordshire amateur antiquarian Alfred Watkins. They were first mooted in his 1922 work *Early British Trackways,* but received a fuller exegesis three years later in *The Old Straight Track,* which is still regarded as a classic in the field of alternative archaeology. Although the academic establishment was hostile from the very beginning [1], it led to the formation of the Old Straight Track Club and from 1927 to 1935 [2] this group of enthusiastic amateurs devoted their energies to scouring the countryside for evidence of potential leys.

Whilst leys have become associated with a variety of New Age speculation, Watkins' original conception was purely archaeological. Touring his home county, he had noticed that many significant ancient monuments seemed to form linear alignments across the landscape. Intrigued, he conducted a survey of these apparent alignments and concluded that what he dubbed a 'ley' was formed wherever four or more such sites appeared together in a straight line [3]. There was nothing mystical about these alignments. Rather, Watkins simply believed that the monuments had been deliberately placed in these arrangements to act as the ancient equivalent of sighting posts along prehistoric track-ways [4].

The variety of sites eligible for inclusion in a ley was always nebulous. Prehistoric monuments were regarded as the key feature, a category that included stone circles, menhirs, barrows and other miscellaneous earthworks, but the remit also extended to incorporate sites of topographic significance such as hilltops and even certain place-names [5]. More controversially, sites of lesser demonstrable antiquity such as medieval churches and holy wells were also included. Watkins argued that often these were built on much older sacred sites, but it has typically proved impossible to assess the validity of such a claim (6).

The Second World War seriously curtailed the activities of county antiquarians in Britain, and for three decades the idea of leys was largely forgotten. It was subsequently revived by the polymath and counterculture icon John Michell in his 1969 underground classic *The View Over Atlantis*. However, the ley had now taken on quite a different character. Synthesising Watkins' archaeological hypothesis with the various occult and geomantic speculation that had been so embraced by the baby-boomer generation, Michell posited that leys were much more than alignments in the landscape. They were in fact the visible markers of currents of "earth-energy" coursing imperceptibly through our environment [7].

Michell's model gave birth to a whole new fringe discipline loosely labelled 'Earth Mysteries' which aimed to explore the connection between antiquities and the possible existence of these mysterious 'earth-energies'. Underground magazines such as *The Ley Hunter* were established as a forum for discussion and whilst the archaeological orthodoxy was quick to condemn these new approaches [8], many involved in such research aspired to an admirable degree of academic rigour, and a refreshing multidisciplinary approach that encompassed archaeology, earth sciences, landscape history, anthropology, folkloristics and spirituality.

Earth mysterians suggested that ancient sacred sites such as stone circles, burial chambers, holy wells and churches were built atop lines of earth-energy because our ancestors were far more 'sensitive' to such energy, and recognised its value for human consciousness, perhaps as a means by which to tap into an animistic conception of the natural world [9]. Many modern dowsers claim to be able to replicate this sensitivity and attempt to discover leys even where visible signs on the ground no longer survive.

The connection between ancient sites and folklore grew particularly significant. It has long been observed that many such places are associated in the folk memory with hauntings, fairies and, increasingly, UFO sightings [10]. A sceptical observer might suggest that this was just a consequence of uneducated communities attempting to project meaning on to the inscrutable remains of their forebears. However, these manifestations were now interpreted both as a product of the conduits of earth-energy on which antiquities were situated, and further evidence of the existence of such conduits [11].

For the more cautious earth mysterians, the implication was that earth-energies created anomalous physical phenomena (such as earthlights) or altered states of consciousness, which were then interpreted in supernatural terms by witnesses [12]. But as the ideas of Earth Mysteries were co-opted by more credulous New Age philosophies, leys and paranormal phenomena became conflated to the extent that leys are now often regarded as intrinsically paranormal.

Indeed, the lines themselves became the dominant area of interest. This was a long way from

Watkins' original conception, in which the alignments were a secondary feature of the monuments and had no existence in their absence. According to the modern conception, leys do not require the proximity of antiquities. *Anything* can be sited on a ley, from a medieval grave to a modern haunted house, as long as it has some sacred or supernatural significance. The consequence of this slackness of definition is that there are now an almost infinite number of sites eligible to be considered on a ley, and - accordingly - an almost infinite number of potential leys. The concept has lost all meaning.

Sadly, it is this interpretation of a ley to which Robin Hood's grave has become attached. Today, David Farrant still cites the ley hypothesis as a possible source for the paranormal experiences at Kirklees.

> "On the question of causes for these various phenomena, it is an interesting point that Robin Hood's grave appears to lie on a major ley line; or indeed, at a point where two ley lines cross or converge. I have often said in my capacity as a psychic investigator that ley lines themselves might be conducive to attracting, even 'replaying', psychic phenomena" [13].

Leys were first mentioned in connection with the grave around 1990, when Barbara Green first became interested in the topic through a correspondent who introduced her to the ideas of psychic-quester, and bestselling author, Andy Collins [14]. His books *The Seventh Sword* and *The Black Alchemist* enjoyed a great deal of currency amongst certain sections of the New Age movement in the late 1980s and early 1990s, and whilst they are scarcely credible as allegedly factual accounts, they undoubtedly make compelling fictions.

In these tomes, Collins wove a Byzantine narrative in which malign occultists were attempting to manipulate the country's ley network for their own nefarious purposes.

> "The People of Hexe are attempting to take control of the entire energy matrix in Great Britain… conducting sinister rites at important power sites such as stone circles, barrows, holy wells, hill forts and Christian shrines" [15].

It was all based around "evidence" discovered as a result of his own "psychic quests", which to the casual observer may resemble a curiously sincere form of live-action roleplaying.

Green's correspondent, meanwhile, believed that "a site of considerable value, such as Robin Hood's grave, already situated on a black, poisoned ley node, would be an ideal site for a cult of the shadow" [16]. He also suggested that the People of Hexe were attempting to:

> "…raise the archetypes and energies of British cult heroes and corrupt those energies to their own evil ends… (Robin Hood) could destroy his own legend by 'reliving' it under the forces of darkness. It wouldn't bear thinking about!" [17].

Rather than dismiss these theories as somewhat fanciful to say the least, Barbara Green and Evelyn Friend adopted them wholeheartedly. In *Secrets of the Grave,* she recalls:

> "We mapped out the ley lines on an Ordnance Survey map, finding that as well as the straight line... running between Hartshead Church and Castle Hill (an ancient hillfort at Almondbury), another straight line crossed through them from an ancient holy well, Alegar Well, in Brighouse which was now concreted over, to the famous *Three Nuns* Inn on the edge of the Kirklees estate. Robin Hood's grave was in the centre of these four lines of force" [18].

Clearly, these only fit a very loose conception of a ley. Neither of the lines cited include four or more locations, the original criterion set by Alfred Watkins, and all contain sites of such wildly diverse provenance that they can only be regarded as representing leys according to the 'earth-energy' account. Nonetheless, it is worth commenting on these various ley 'nodes' to understand why they were regarded as significant in connection to Robin Hood's grave, and see if anything can be salvaged from the interpretation so far.

The alignment between St. Peter's Church, Hartshead and Castle Hill is the most interesting of the two proposed lines, as it most closely conforms to Watkins' original hypothesis and had been observed prior to Barbara Green's interest [19]. Confusingly, Castle Hill refers not to the rather gentle rise at the south edge of the Kirklees estate on which Robin Hood's grave is situated, but a much more imposing top at Almondbury above Huddersfield, some five miles away. To avoid future confusion, one will be referred to as Castle Hill (Kirklees) and the other, Castle Hill (Almondbury).

Today, Castle Hill (Almondbury) is conspicuously topped by the Victoria Tower, built between 1897 and 1899 to commemorate Queen Victoria's Diamond Jubilee, and designed to bring the total height of the hill to exactly 1,000 feet [20]. Even without the tower, the summit possesses a significant degree of what geographers call topographic prominence, and is a dominant landmark visible throughout this swathe of the South Pennines. Such a commanding elevation is doubtless what recommended its use as an Iron Age hill-fort over two-thousand years ago. In its time, the hill has also been the site of a Norman motte-and-bailey, a 14th Century village, an Armada beacon, Chartist rallies and a World War II anti-aircraft battery [21].

Excavations have suggested that the Iron Age hill-fort was constructed around 550 BCE and endured until at least 45 CE, when the fortifications were extended (22). This hill-fort may well provide a genuine connection with the Kirklees estate. If the earthworks on Castle Hill (Kirklees) are indeed Iron Age and for a defensive purpose, as much of the most recent archaeological thinking suggests, then it is not unreasonable to think that the site may have been associated with the larger structure at Almondbury. Castle Hill (Almondbury) is also highly visible from the vicinity of Kirklees, including St. Peter's Church, Hartshead, meaning that an alignment between the two would closely fit Watkin's understanding of a ley as evidence of an ancient trackway.

Conveniently for proponents of the paranormal ley, Castle Hill (Almondbury) is also steeped in folklore. Most famously, it is where the Devil landed following a great leap from Scar Top at Netherton almost two miles away, only to get lost in the labyrinth of tunnels that supposedly lie beneath the hill [23]. A dragon was also thought to have made its lair amongst these tunnels, a tradition reinforced by a nearby plot of land referred to as Wormcliffe in medieval sources (probably derived from "wyrm", the Anglo-Saxon term for a dragon). Legend holds that this creature guards a horde of treasure, including a mysterious 'Golden Cradle', thought to be buried in one of the surviving earthworks on the north-eastern side of the hill [24].

The dragon motif is especially significant as John Michell suggested that, as conduits of terrestrial force, leys should often be found associated with dragon symbolism. He believed that leys worked on the same principle as the Chinese geomantic system of *feng-shui*, which holds that the environment is crisscrossed by flows of energy roughly translated as the 'dragon's breath'. Michell went on to suggest that in pagan societies, the dragon originally represented the power of earth energies, and that sites with dragon legends were - therefore - where our ancestors had recognised these energies to be at their strongest [25].

As a result, it may also be worth noting that the parish of Hartshead-cum-Clifton possibly had its own dragon legend. In his history of the area, Rev. H.N. Pobjoy recalls:

> "...in the late Twenties, I was told that the little wood on the rise to the north of Blakelaw had once been the home of a dragon that terrified the neighbourhood. How far back this story went my informants could not say, but 'it was a right long time'..."

Pobjoy suggests that the name Blakelaw may have been derived from "dracanh lawe", Old English for "mound of the dragon" [26]. This exact location no longer exists, having been erased by the construction of the M62, but it was certainly in the vicinity of St. Peter's Church.

St. Peter's Church at Hartshead lies six miles slightly north-west of Castle Hill (Almondbury) and certainly has no shortage of associations with Kirklees Park. Until 1886, it was the local parish church, and an Armytage family vault was established there by Sir Samuel Armytage in the 18th Century. Joseph Ismay, a close friend of Sir Samuel, served as a curate at the church in 1738 [27], although its most famous incumbent was Patrick Brontë who did as stint as curate between 1810 and 1815 during the Luddite uprisings [28].

The church itself is one of the most venerable in the region. Although much of the fabric of the current building is the product of extensive restoration work carried out in 1881, a church is first recorded on the site in 1120 when the Earl of Warren granted it to the Priory of Lewes. The west tower, south door and chancel arch are all surviving remnants of this 12th Century Norman structure [29]. Many have speculated that a church may actually have stood on the site since the Saxon period, due to the proximity of the Walton Cross [30], the decorated base of a 10th Century preaching cross, referred to as the Wagestan in ancient documents (including the foundation charter of Kirklees Priory). This stood fifteen feet high as late as the 18th Century.

In deciding that early churches were eligible as points on a ley, Alfred Watkins reasoned that such buildings were often built on top of much earlier sacred sites in order to ease the transition from early religions to Christianity [31]. There is certainly a degree of evidence to support such continuity of tradition in the early Christian period, including a famous 7th Century letter from Pope Gregory I to Mellitus, the third Archbishop of Canterbury, recommending such a course of action [32]. The potential Saxon heritage of St. Peter's Church suggests that it may be a candidate for such a site.

This supposition is reinforced by the nearby presence of the Lady Well, a holy well dedicated to the Virgin Mary, now almost entirely lost beneath hawthorn bushes. Wells dedicated to the Blessed Mother were often used for baptism in the earliest period of Christianity in England, and H.N. Pobjoy wondered if Paulinus himself, the first Christian missionary to proselytise in the north, once conducted services here [33]. Holy wells are also often regarded as evidence of pre-Christian worship, as water sources were considered sacred by many of the pagan religions of the British Isles. Many consider a holy well in proximity to an ancient church as possible evidence of worship at the site over thousands of years.

A dead yew tree in the churchyard also adds credence to such speculation, as yew trees have been associated with burial grounds for millennia, and are another common feature of Christianised pagan sites. This particular yew tree has now been dead for over a century, apparently felled by a lightning strike, but its remains are left standing thanks to an entrenched local tradition that Robin Hood cut his final arrow from its branches before proceeding to his death at Kirklees Priory. There is also a belief that arrows fired at the Battle of Agincourt were taken from it (34).

It is also worth mentioning that Philip Ahier mentions St. Peter's as a favoured location for the rather macabre custom of porch-watching. He recalls the people of Hartshead would gather:

> "...to watch in the porch of this Church on St. Mark's Eve (April 24th) from 11:00pm till 1:00am on St. Mark's Day, April 25th. The third year (for this 'watching' had to be done three years in succession) the 'watchers' were supposed to see the ghosts of all those who were to die the next year pass by into the Church. When anyone sickened who was thought to have been seen in this manner, it was soon whispered that he would not recover... This absurd and cruel superstition was so strongly believed that if those who were ill heard of it, they despaired of recovery. Many are said to have actually died by their imaginary fears" [35].

Perhaps ironically, that very porch was used by the Yorkshire Robin Hood Society as the backdrop to a tableaux of Robin Hood's death, filmed for a documentary by German television station, Zweites Deutsches Fernsehen, in 1992 [36]. Nonetheless, it seems unlikely that there are still any lingering spirits at St. Peter's. Nearly all who visit the church today comment on its air of serenity. Even that persistent scourge of burial grounds, David Farrant, was moved to comment, "The atmosphere around the church did seem peaceful" when he surveyed the area following his blessing of Robin Hood's grave in 2005 [37].

Given the undisputed provenance of Castle Hill (Almondbury) and possible antiquity of St. Peter's Church, Hartshead, it is arguable that the north-south alignment running between them is a contender for a genuine ley, especially as each site is visible from the other. The problem is that it is possible to draw a straight line between any two sites in the country. In order to qualify as a ley, it requires to pass through at least four significant monuments [38]. Depending on where the line is drawn to meet the broad summit of Castle Hill (Almondbury), it also potentially crosses the site of Kirklees Priory and the Iron Age earthworks on Castle Hill (Kirklees). The latter may be eligible for inclusion, but the former is very dubious indeed.

Still more debatable is the second supposed ley, which Barbara Green worked out herself, running from Alegar Well in the east, to the *Three Nuns* Inn in the west. However, not only is the origin of these sites far less demonstrably ancient, their exact location is ambiguous. The *Three Nuns* was rebuilt adjacent to its original foundations, and the Alegar Well was destroyed in the early half of the 20th Century. Equally, there is no compelling reason for a ley to exist between these two sites. They are not monuments in any significant sense and there is no line of sight between them. This alignment could only be regarded as a ley if you accept the 'earth energy' conception.

The only memorial of the Alegar Well today is a short, steep street bearing the same name running between Clifton Common and Wakefield Road (A644). As it is located near the roundabout where traffic enters Brighouse from Junction 25 of the M62, most local residents only know the name as a notorious rat-run and have rarely pondered on its origin. In fact, it is a probably a corruption of 'helly carr', Old English for 'holy slope'. As such, the well may have been quite old indeed, but it is impossible to confirm [39].

During the Victorian period, it was the practice for young men and women from across the area to gather at the well on the morning of Palm Sunday. They would have with them a corked bottle containing Spanish liquorice, which they would fill with water from the spring and shake up to create a concoction known as Popololli, probably to disguise the astringent taste of the minerals in the water. The tradition was renown as an opportunity to encounter members of the opposite sex, and couples who met there would 'plight their troth' by drinking from each other's bottle [40]. It has been suggested that this custom was a corrupted remembrance of much older rituals, from the early period of Christianity when such wells were believed to possess healing powers, or even earlier still.

Today, the Alegar Well is wholly obliterated, and even its exact whereabouts are unknown. We can assume that it was somewhere in the vicinity of Alegar Street, and Barbara Green spoke to an elderly Brighouse resident who claims the spot now lies beneath the forecourt of a petrol station on Wakefield Road [41]. Green believed the well:

> "...would have become a poisoned ley node, or black line, when it was blocked up, further adding to the malevolent influences flowing towards Robin's grave" [42].

Of course, for proponents of the paranormal ley, the eastern point of this "black line" is by far the most interesting. Situated on the very border of the Kirklees estate itself, the *Three Nuns* inn has a colourful history, and - in recent years - its fair share of supernatural phenomena. Having said that, the mock Tudor edifice seen today is not the original building. Its predecessor was demolished in 1939, and the foundations lie beneath the modern car park. The new structure retains many of the original fixtures and fittings, however, including much of the oak panelling [43].

The original hostelry began life in 1497 as a guesthouse for travellers run by the sisters of Kirklees Priory, and gained its name shortly after, when three nuns by the names of Cecilia Topcliffe, Joan Leventhorpe and Katherine Grice took up residence there following the Dissolution of the Priory in 1539 [44]. Whilst Leventhorpe and Topcliffe (a former Prioress) were both in their dotage by this point, Grice was only a twenty-five year old novice [45]. A local legend claims that, following an ill-fated affair with one of Henry VIII's commissioners - whose duty it was to survey the Priory holdings for the Crown - Grice found herself with child, and subsequently committed suicide in Nun Brook [46]. Sadly, corroborating evidence of this tale is hard to come by.

Throughout its life, the *Three Nuns* remained a popular coaching inn. It has been suggested that Oliver Cromwell stayed there on his way to the Battle of Marston Moor in 1644, whilst it was definitely a favoured meeting place for Luddites during the 1812 uprising. A whole panoply of Luddite relics, including swords and hammers, was discovered concealed in a ceiling at the inn in 1920 [47]. It was a reminder of one defining moment in the tragic history of the cause in which the surrounding area played an important role.

Only three hundred yards from the *Three Nuns*, at the busy junction of the A644 and A62 stands a curious finial-topped obelisk called the Dumb Steeple. The exact history and etymology of this monument has been hotly disputed. Local historian J. Horsfall Turner believed the name to be a corruption of 'doom steeple', so called because it originally marked the boundary of Kirklees Priory's lands, outside which the laws of sanctuary no longer applied for a wanted man [48].

However, whilst this interpretation has often been repeated, it does not stand up to examination. The laws of sanctuary only applied to the consecrated precincts of the religious house itself and - as a minor nunnery - it is unlikely that Kirklees could have claimed such rights anyway. An alternative and more credible explanation is that the monument was originally known simply as the 'Obelisk' and the name 'dumb man's steeple' was only attached to it following its role in such a disastrous episode in Luddite history [49].

The Luddite cause emerged, appropriately enough, in Nottinghamshire in 1811 as a response by textile workers to loss of employment due to increased mechanisation; this at a time of existing economic depression due to the effects of the Napoleonic Wars. Their name was taken from a late 18th Century icon in the region called 'Ned Ludd', who had allegedly destroyed two stocking frames in Leicestershire, despite the harsh penalties for such action. The name became a popular pseudonym for local organisers and following his example, the Luddites initiated attacks on the machines they perceived as disenfranchising them, and even the mill owners who had installed them.

Although the cause was violently opposed by both industrialists and the authorities, the Luddites enjoyed a significant amount of support amongst the working classes. It is no surprise that parallels were drawn with the activities of that icon of rebellion, Robin Hood. A popular rhyme of the period goes: "Chant no more your old rhymes about bold Robin Hood / ... I will sing of the achievements of General Ludd," whilst the North Midland Luddites signed their letter with the address "Ned Ludd's Office, Sherwood Forest" [50].

The movement spread to Yorkshire the following year, when Enoch Taylor of Huddersfield acquired the rights to manufacture cropping frames [51]. Previously, the job of cropper had been one of the most skilled and highly paid in the textiles industry, providing cloth with a high quality finish that could drastically increase its value. Despite the fact that the new machines could not replicate the finish of an experienced artisan, the new machines represented a serious threaten to the croppers' livelihoods, and this small class of worker were at the vanguard of Luddite activity in West Yorkshire.

Regular meetings began to take place at venues such as the *Shears Inn* at Liversedge, the *St. Crispin Inn* at Halifax and of course, the *Three Nuns*. At the peak of their activity, there were at least three hundred active Luddites in the region, all bound by an oath of secrecy and organised by twenty-two year old George Mellor, who was given the appellation 'King Ludd' by his followers [52]. Initially raids were carried out on mills in the Huddersfield area using blacksmiths' hammers known as 'Old Enoch', manufactured by the same man who created the hated cropping machines. A local saying ran "Old Enoch makes 'em and Old Enoch breaks 'em" [53].

The West Yorkshire authorities were initially taken unawares, but responded swiftly, calling in the military and enlisting special constables, whilst offering large rewards for information, and attempting to infiltrate Luddite cells. As a local worthy and former Sheriff of Yorkshire, it is scarcely surprising that Sir George Armytage IV was at the forefront of action against the movement. He had already commanded the Huddersfield Fusilier Volunteers during the 1794 food riots, and now he assembled the Upper Agbrigg Militia to mercilessly put down another popular rebellion [54].

One of the Luddites' most detested adversaries was William Cartwright, owner of a large mill at Rawfolds in Cleckheaton. He had been the first in the area to install cropping frames in 1809 and in April 1812, the local Luddites learned that he had just taken a new delivery of these machines [55]. Accordingly, they began to hatch a plot to destroy these arrivals before they could compromise the croppers' jobs, and to teach Cartwright the error of his ways.

The night of Saturday 11th April was chosen to carry out their plans, and to avoid detection they arranged to meet coming from different directions in a field between the Dumb Steeple and the *Three Nuns*. The location was chosen as it was a well-known landmark, which could be easily identified by those travelling from afar, with good access to the neighbouring Spen Valley, but isolated and - at three miles away - sufficiently removed from their target to avoid unwanted attention [56].

Perhaps in addition to these prosaic practical reasons, the site was chosen as a deliberate gesture of contempt, as the field in question was part of the Kirklees estate, the ancestral home of their enemy, Sir George Armytage. You also have to wonder if they were conscious of the fact that the grave of that legendary outlaw Robin Hood lay only half a mile away. It is certainly an interesting correspondence, and given how well-known the legend of his death at Kirklees was locally during the 18th and 19th Century, it is unlikely that the potent symbolism escaped them.

The host began to assemble at ten o' clock and by midnight, when they set off across Hartshead Moor to Cleckheaton, there were approximately one hundred and fifty present. As they proceeded towards Rawfolds, they were joined by Luddites from Leeds, to form a company at least three hundred strong [57]. Many were in disguise, including women's clothing, whilst they carried a vast arsenal of weaponry including hammers, hatchets, crowbars and pistols [58].

Sadly, despite their great number, the Luddites were routed. Cartwright had been expecting an attack and was sleeping at his premises, along with four trusted employees and five soldiers. Meanwhile, the mill had been extensively fortified in anticipation; the doors were barricaded, stairwells booby-trapped and a carboy full of acid stood in readiness on the roof. Although the attackers managed to overcome the sentries, they were corralled in the courtyard as Cartwright and allies were able to ring the mill bells to summon help, before opening fire from the upper floors [59].

Untrained in the use of weapons, the Luddites were easily overcome and forced to beat a hasty retreat, although not before two men had been killed and scores injured. Cartwright callously refused to offer medical assistance to the wounded until they revealed the names of their leaders. None cracked. A couple of nights later, Rev. Patrick Brontë saw several men surreptitiously burying their fallen comrades in the far corner of the churchyard at St. Peter's. It is said that as a mark of respect, that end of the cemetery has remained free of subsequent interments ever since [60].

In the aftermath of the Luddite assault on Rawfolds, and the assassination of Huddersfield mill owner William Horsfall a couple of weeks later, the authorities cracked down hard on the Luddites [61]. Both rewards for information - and penalties for involvement - were increased, but despite incentives, the Luddite fraternity held until the autumn, when Benjamin Walker finally gave up George Mellor and others. It is a mark of the local support the Luddites commanded that Walker was ostracised by the community for the remainder of his days [62].

The arrest of Mellor resulted in a show trial in York during January 1813, and whilst many of the participants were pardoned, their ringleaders were shown no mercy. The court handed down a record number of capital sentences and penal transportations. Fourteen were sentenced to death for their part in the attack on Cartwright Mill, charged with riot, burglary and robbery under the newly passed Frame Breaking Act. They were all sent to the gallows on 16th January 1813 in the largest hanging to take place in York [63]. Meanwhile, William Cartwright was awarded £3,000 by a conglomerate of his fellow mill-owners in recognition of his "heroic" actions [64].

The bloody fate of the Luddite conspirators, who met in the fields adjacent to the *Three Nun* that fateful night in April 1812, was cited by Evelyn Friend as further evidence of the "curse of Kirklees", first mooted in the *Huddersfield Examiner* article of 13th June 1988 [65]. Surprisingly, however, this aspect of the history of the south-eastern corner of the Kirklees estate has subsequently been largely overlooked by the YRHS, despite its clear resonance with the legend of Robin Hood. As ever, the historical significance of the site has been overlooked in favour of more occult speculation.

The supernatural reputation of the hostelry began with a report in the *Halifax Evening Courier* on 15th June 1985. The article describes various phenomena including "an apparition of a veiled woman, doors opening and closing, mysterious footsteps and an inexplicable chill," all experienced by workmen during renovation works. Of particular interest is the experience of a plumber, who - whilst working in the cellar: "told how a shadowy figure had brushed past him – a woman with a veil over her head" [66]. Some commentators have been quick to note the similarities between this phantom and that seen in the vicinity of Robin Hood's grave only half a mile away, whilst the figure has been associated with both Katherine Grice and even Elizabeth de Staynton [67].

Initially, the disturbances were connected to interference with one of the old wooden fittings. Site manager Ian Thompson claimed:

> "The trouble started when we removed one of the panels and found a carved ram's head on the other side... We leaned the panel against a wall and for the next few days until it was removed all sorts of strange things happened."

He described it as possessing "very strange eyes... almost human" and the carving does indeed have an unsettling visage [68].

The landlord, however, was sceptical about the story, saying:

> "My wife and I have lived here for nine months and we haven't seen or heard a thing. The theory is that it's all to do with the ram's head but as far as I know that was a motif used by Ramsdens (brewery) before the pub was taken over by Tetleys" [69].

Nonetheless, even with the ram's head carving replaced, the inn continued to accumulate accounts of supernatural experiences, including the apparition of a laughing, bearded man watching drinkers, and strange incidents associated with a painting of the eponymous nuns, taken from the original inn [70].

Despite the landlord's scepticism in 1985, by 1991 a new manager was forced to call in a medium to perform an exorcism [71]. Upon enquiring about the matter, Barbara Green was refused further information on the grounds that, "the *Three Nuns* is very sensitive to spirits etc. and I do not wish to disturb them" [72]. Visiting around the same time, Green definitely detected a malign atmosphere, describing the inn as "the most sinister and disturbing of the points on the ley line… This place reeked of evil" (73). Allegedly, when the pub was visited by a team of parapsychologists thirteen years later, the medium who had performed the 1991 exorcism contacted them out of the blue, and told them not to proceed with the investigation, or else it could undo all her work [74].

Returning to the original debate, for the purposes of Barbara Green's argument, this supposed ley between the "poisoned node" of the Alegar Well and the "sinister" *Three Nuns* is certainly the most important. Unfortunately, the designation is too flawed to bear scrutiny. The disparity in the provenance of the sites, the difficulty pinpointing the precise historical location of either "node" and the lack of topographical connection between the two is more than sufficient to disqualify it as a Watkins ley.

But even if it is regarded as a conduit for 'earth energy', how could this be proved? The only argument in its favour is the 'sanctity' of the Alegar Well and the paranormal phenomena connected with the *Three Nuns*. However, it is circular reasoning to suggest that a ley can be identified by the mysterious phenomena in its vicinity, and then assert the mysterious phenomena occurs at that location *because* it is on a ley. Dowsing might offer independent verification, but this would only satisfy existing believers and even so, this ley would be impossible to walk, as much of the land it passes through is private, or now bisected by the M62.

Amazingly, despite these many absurdities, even the Kirklees estate seemed to take the idea of leys passing through the estate seriously. In a post on the *Blue Boar Inn* message board dated 30th June 2005, David Hepworth claims that Lady Armytage had actually commissioned a 'ley line study' in the late 1990s. He does not specify exactly what evidence this 'study' examined, but he recalls it confirmed that a ley runs through the Iron Age earthworks on Castle Hill (Kirklees), which would've also passed through the chancel of the Priory church. Hepworth even suggests it is significant that Robin Hood's grave lies on the same "plane" as the earthwork [75].

Barbara Green had already suggested the grave lay close to the intersection of the two leys she'd identified and in the summer of 1991, following successive rebuttals by ministers of various Christian denominations, several members of the YRHS attempted to 'cleanse' the grave by performing a blessing at the "nodes" of the two leys [76]. On the advice of Bishop Anselm Genders, they read the Litany from the Common Book of Prayer and sprinkled holy water at each of the four sites. Amusingly, Séan Manchester refused to sanction the ritual, fearing that despite its Christian character, it was akin to occult practice [77].

Nonetheless, this extemporised blessing seemed to satisfy Barbara Green at the time, and it marked the end of her attempts to have the grave officially consecrated. Unfortunately, to suggest that the grave would have been in any way influenced by the leys running through Kirklees, only highlights further problems with the 'earth energy' concept of a ley. No matter how the lines are drawn, the monument only ever lies 'close' to the intersection. In which case, the sceptic could inquire exactly how close to a ley a place needs to be, to be affected by it? Given the sheer number of ancient, holy and haunted sites in Britain alone, surely any location you can name is 'close' to a ley? If so, then the whole concept is rendered trivial and collapses entirely.

The more restrained ideas of the Earth Mysteries movement have lately gained academic respectability as facets of 'phenomenological archaeology' but whilst there is still a lot of loose talk about leys in New Age circles, even their former advocates have disowned the 'earth energy' concept. As long ago as 1985, Paul Devereux, then editor of *The Ley Hunter,* invoked Bob Dylan to insist that "Those who think our understanding of ley hunting must stay as it was in the Sixties are simply 'one too many mornings and a thousand miles behind'" [78].

More pointedly, Devereux's occasional co-writer and veteran earth mysterian Nigel Pennick suggested:

"The function of much ley hunting today seems to serve the psychological need for participants to feel a sense of importance and control which is absent from the individual in the modern world. Like every other belief system it gives us the feeling that we are special because we are members of an elite than possesses a secret knowledge hidden from lesser humans" [79].

This tendency can be easily identified in the motives of Barbara Green and her associates. It is a similar impulse to that which generated the conspiracy theories and alternative historical narratives connected with Kirklees. Having been consistently ignored in the official discourse and excluded from any direct involvement with the fate of Robin Hood's grave, the idealised creation of patterns such as leys (which can be affected by something as simple as reading prayers at the cardinal points) restored a semblance of influence. It allowed Green the impression that the YRHS were achieving their aim to protect the grave. Moreover, they believed themselves to be doing so on a plane of which the 'powers that be' were dangerously unaware.

However, even if a mystical connection between the sites is refuted, something important can still be salvaged from the ley debate. Once the link between these various locations is uncoupled from an external source, and acknowledged as a construct of the human mind, it can be recognised as a fundamentally creative act. To dismiss this model purely because it lacks any material reality would be easy. But by drawing all these places together in an imaginative union, Barbara Green has transmuted her local landscape, investing it with significance to an extent that deeply enriches our experience of the topography.

To the millions who live their lives untroubled by an awareness of anything beyond the surface of the environment they inhabit, this might seem like a strange impulse. Yet it is a process that would be recognised by countless societies throughout world, and across the ages, for whom perceiving meaning in the landscape is an integral part of their psyche. Whilst many such societies believe that meaning to exist independently, it does not undermine these patterns to say they are projections. Indeed, it enhances them by revealing a symbiotic relationship between people and place as an elemental facet of human experience.

Even in the cynical western civilisation of the 21st Century, the imaginative construction of landscape is not nearly as alien as it might seem. Although we are accustomed to think of the landscapes we inhabit as merely an external physical environment, they are very much participatory phenomenon. Landscapes are mental as much as physical, 'mindscapes' manufactured through personal narratives rooted in our pre-existing ideologies and inclinations [80]. Each of us construct our own mental maps as we move through the world, in which various locations are endowed with personal significance. This need is replicated on a societal level, with publicly agreed narratives mapped onto the physical terrain.

The difference is that so many of these cognitive maps are primarily utilitarian, constructed in the interests of navigation and commerce. For instance, whilst the tourist and heritage trails so ubiquitous across modern Britain may offer to interpret the 'landscape' for the casual visitor, they are as much about generating tourism revenue than offering a genuine experience of place. The notion of constructing symbolic landscapes for spiritual reasons has largely been lost from our everyday awareness, which is why investing the topography around Robin Hood's grave with imaginative significance seems so strange to the purely functional mind.

This was not always the case. As already noted, ritual landscape are a characteristic feature of pre-modern societies worldwide. But, moreover, the term 'landscape' itself was originally introduced into our lexicon through the work of 16th Century Dutch painters, and subsequently reinforced by the Romantic movement [81]. Landscapes have always been about imaginative and aesthetic selection to create meaning. As such, the model of a mystical landscape around Kirklees constructed by Barbara Green and others is perfectly consistent. It may have more in common with art and religion than history or archaeology, but these paths are no less valuable to the human race.

Drawing the many resonances, correspondences and connections around Kirklees into a geographic unity may be an imaginative act, but these parallels nonetheless exist in the history of the region itself, even if they are not linked by anything as concrete as leys. As psychogeographer Merlin Coverley writes:

> "This sense of an eternal landscape underpinning our own has been termed the *genius loci* or spirit of place... a kind of historical consciousness that exposes the psychic connectivity of landscapes... imbued with a sense of the histories of previous inhabitants and the events that have been played out against them" [82].

In this tiny corner of West Yorkshire the same motifs seem to recur time and time again – thwarted rebellion and corrupted sanctity, phantom ladies and guardian dragons – all clustered around the powerfully symbolic locus of Robin Hood's grave. They can all be regarded as manifestations of the unique *genius loci* of Kirklees and whilst this 'spirit' may not have an existence independent of our own perception, our active creation of it results in a deepening awareness of the landscape, which should not be underestimated.

CHAPTER NINE
The Same Old Rock

Let us now return to review the story given by Thomas Gent, in his 1730 book, *The Ancient and Modern History of the Famous City of York*:

> "(Robin Hood's) tombstone, having his effigy thereon, was order'd, not many years ago, by a certain knight to be placed as a hearth-stone in his great hall. When it was laid over-night, the next morning it was 'surprisingly' removed one side; and so three times it was laid, and as successively turned aside. The knight, thinking he had done wrong to have brought it thither, order'd it should be drawn back again; which was performed by a pair of oxen and four horses, when twice the number could scarce do it before" [1].

This is the first record of any supernatural tradition associated with Robin Hood's grave, yet it has been almost entirely overlooked by the plethora of modern mythmakers who have turned their attention to the site. If the tale has been referenced, it has typically been used as confirmation of the hypothesis that the original gravestone was moved sometime during the 17th Century [2]. However, despite the lack of emphasis it has received in recent years, it is arguably the most authentic and instructive legend associated with the grave.

One scholar who did not ignore its potential significance was the folklorist Lewis Spence, who invokes the story in his 1947 essay, *The Supernatural Character of Robin Hood*. Spence is primarily interested in the narrative as support for his identification of Robin Hood with a figure derived from pre-Christian fairy traditions. Indeed, his argument is essentially an update of that first proposed by Thomas Wright and canonised by Sir Sidney Lee in the *National Dictionary of Biography*.

Spence writes:

> "Robin's burial under a great stone and, indeed, his general association

> with monoliths further connects him with Faerie. The list of fairies who haunt stones, have their dwelling places within them, or who are in some way identified with them is a long one... But what were fairies?... The main clue is unquestionably that which leads to the belief that they were spirits worshipped in connection with a very ancient cult of the dead – the souls of chiefs who were buried at the sites of the great stone circles and monoliths in Stone Age or Bronze Age times, and who came to be thought of as inhabiting or ensouling these stones" [3].

Meanwhile, with specific reference to Gent's story regarding Robin Hood's grave, Spence opines:

> "The facts that his traditional tomb was situated among a grove of trees and that it consisted of a standing stone which was capable of self-propulsion and miraculous motion, as is the case of many other stones at the sites of ancient British monoliths, bring him into line with those spirits who haunt such standing stones and were formerly worshipped at them. In a word, his gravestone behaves like a traditional fairy monolith, it "walks", turns or stirs" [4].

Although Spence's argument was somewhat more subtle than those offered by his contemporaries Lord Raglan or Margaret Murray, as Chapter 4 endeavoured to demonstrate, such identification has fallen out of academic fashion. The 'pagan survival' theory of folklore is largely discredited and there is very little evidence that Robin Hood was anything other than a literary invention of the Middle Ages. Nonetheless, we should not throw the folkloric baby out with the pagan bathwater, and whilst Spence may have been mistaken in one respect, it is quite possible that he was on to something in another.

Many 19th and early 20th Century folklorists attempted to identify Robin Hood with pre-Christian deities through the frequency with which the outlaw's name is found in toponyms, particularly those of stones and wells. Their fault lay in failing to ascertain when these places first became associated with Robin's name. Modern scholarship has shown that the earliest examples do not emerge until the 15th Century, and reflect the popularity of the ballads during the late medieval period rather than any connection between the hero and pre-Christian traditions [5].

However, it is clear that the outlaw's name was frequently grafted on to existing place legends, in much the same way that during the Middle Ages, the name of the Devil, King Arthur and others became attached to earlier folkloric sites [6]. Whilst the origins of Robin Hood may not have been mythological, he certainly became linked to older mythological beliefs following the growth of his legend. Thus, Spence's error was to regard Gent's story as evidence that Robin himself belonged to a more ancient tradition. But, he may have been correct to suggest that the gravesite was of some greater antiquity than is generally supposed, only becoming linked with the outlaw in the 15th Century, along with so many other monoliths.

In 1976, the archaeologist Leslie Grinsell published the results of a lifelong interest, a mammoth survey, which he called *Folklore of Prehistoric Sites In Britain*. In it, Grinsell identified a number of motifs that recur in legends associated with prehistoric remains throughout Britain. One of the most common tropes is "Immovability or Automatic Return" [7], whilst a closely related tradition is that of "Retribution for Disturbing an Antiquity" [8]. In the former, any attempt to relocate the monument meets with failure either because it cannot be shifted by normal means, or because it mysteriously and persistently returns to its original position. The latter includes narrative in which the monument is successfully moved, but such strange occurrences follow its displacement that it must eventually be returned.

Grinsell cites a number of examples in support of his taxonomy, and the correspondences between these legends, and Gent's story about Robin Hood's gravestone cannot be ignored. For instance, one example relates that "a farmer who took a standing stone from Pant-y-Maen barrow in Denbighshire to use as a gatepost was unable to make the stone stand upright as such and so he returned it to the barrow" [9]. Substitute 'gatepost' for 'hearthstone', and this tale echoes Gent's exactly.

Perhaps the most interesting and numerous similarities are with the King Stone, a weathered limestone monolith that forms part of a collective of prehistoric monuments known as the Rollright Stones near Long Compton in Warwickshire. Standing almost two and a half metres tall, the King Stone is the classic prehistoric standing stone (or 'menhir'), erected in the middle Bronze Age, either as an outlier for the Whispering Knights stone circle some seventy-five metres away, or as a cemetery marker [10].

There are two variations of the story connected to the King Stone. In the first, a local farmer by the name of Humphrey Boffin attempted to move the monolith to the courtyard of his house just before the outbreak of the English Civil Wars. However, following mysterious and cacophonous noises in the night, he was forced to return the stone to its original location. Whilst it had taken twenty-four horses to pull the stone to Boffin's courtyard, it only took two to take it back [11].

In the second version, a miller in nearby Long Compton thought the King Stone would be useful for damming his millpond and removed it for that purpose. Yet any water he successfully dammed during the day subsequently disappeared overnight. Fearing that this was supernatural retribution for moving the stone, the miller duly restored it to its rightful place. Once again, whilst three horses were required to uproot it, only one was needed to return the stone [12].

The similarities between these narratives and Gent's are obvious. In each case, an influential local attempts to move a significant stone for their own purposes, but this action results in unwelcome supernatural activity during the night which eventually forces them to replace it. Moreover, the effort required to remove the stone from its proper place is always significantly greater than the effort required to reinstate it.

Of course, comparable legends are associated with prehistoric monoliths throughout the British Isles. But the King Stone displays yet another parallel to Robin Hood's grave in that the monument was ultimately enclosed with iron railings to prevent locals taking chippings of the stone for luck [13]. The practice of taking chippings from prehistoric monoliths to ensure health or good fortune is another folkloric motif regularly connected to such sites identified by Grinsell [14].

Such correspondences are certainly curious. Why should Robin Hood's gravestone at Kirklees have sustained so many motifs more usually connected with prehistoric monoliths? A potential answer emerges when you begin to consider the number of demonstrably archaeological sites in Britain, which became associated with Robin Hood's name following the popularity of the legend in the late medieval period. Countless monoliths, cairns and other anomalous stone features were renamed after Robin, and given related legends pertaining to the outlaw to accompany their new title.

For instance, Grinsell refers to a group of prehistoric barrows in Somerset known as Robin Hood's Butts. Local tradition held that if any material was removed from these barrows, it would return of its own accord by the next day. It was also believed that Robin Hood and Little John used to use the barrows for target practice owing to a small indenture on the top of each barrow [15]. This is a clear example of a prehistoric site with folklore fitting the motif of 'Automatic Return' becoming associated with the outlaw at a later date.

The greatest concentration of such legends, however, occurs in the north Midlands and the South Pennines. There are multiple sites, which have been known at one time or another, as Robin Hood's Stone, Robin Hood's Butts, Robin Hood's Well, Robin Hood's Quoit, Robin Hood's Seat, Robin Hood's House, Robin Hood's Bower and so forth. As the 18th Century Halifax antiquarian, Rev. John Watson, commented, "The country people here attribute everything of the marvellous kind to Robin Hood" [16].

In the legends associated with these monolithic stone sites, Robin Hood and Little John frequently take on the attributes of giants. For example, large stones are typically said to have been thrown by the outlaws several miles from a prominent hilltop. This suggests that during the late medieval period Robin's name was often grafted on to much earlier giant lore relating to remarkable stones. Such a transmutation is quite understandable. Heroes such as Robin Hood and King Arthur are 'larger than life' individuals, and although their medieval legends might portray them as ordinary men, in vernacular superstition such magnified characteristics readily associated them with giants [17].

The Calder Valley is replete with such examples. On the summit of Blackstone Edge, approximately twelve miles south-west of Kirklees, there is a prominent gritstone outcrop known as Robin Hood's Bed. One local tale claims that, as its name suggest, the legendary outlaw slept beneath the rock whilst his band of merry men kept watch [18]. It is also possible that Robin Hood's Bed might once have represented another legendary site for the outlaw's resting place. In Welsh 'bedd' means grave and Celtic tradition survived long in the region the nearby village of Walsden translates as 'valley of the Welsh'.

The folklorist Jessica Lofthouse adds:

> "He (Robin) did find a sheltered hiding place in Robin Hood's Bed, able to
> see all movements on the Roman road and the ancient highway, to see

yet not be seen. I have been told... that here 'no winds ever blow, always a still calm. To while away waiting time in the Bed he took a large boulder from the giant's overspill at hand, threw it and watched its course. Six miles away on Monstone Edge that boulder dropped, a feat amazing, and has been called Robin Hood's Quoit ever after. The Quoit was there centuries before Robin" [19].

A similar legend is attached to a destroyed site formerly at Wainstalls, just under ten miles west of Kirklees, once known as Robin Hood's Penny Stone. It was first recorded by John Watson in 1775 as a large natural boulder topped by a rocking stone, which has since been broken up for building material. Watson also writes that Robin Hood "is said to have used this stone to pitch with at a mark for amusement; and to have thrown the standing stone in Sowerby off an adjoining hill with a spade as he was digging" [20]. Here we see Robin in the guise of a giant once again. The standing stone in question, Sowerby Lad, has also sadly been removed [21].

In 1837, John Crabtree referred to a tradition that there had once been a stone circle surrounding Robin Hood's Penny Stone, suggesting that it was a site of ritual importance in the prehistoric period [22]. Although the stone circle had clearly vanished even by the late 18th Century (or else one presumes Watson would've mentioned it), there is evidence of prehistoric activity in the surrounding area. In 1872, a fine example of a Neolithic axe-hammer was discovered nearby, which is now on display at Tolson Museum in Huddersfield [23].

There is another Robin Hood's Penny Stone on Midgley Moor, only a mile across the tributary valley of Luddenden Dean, at which the legendary outlaw is supposed to have once rested [24]. Again this is a natural erratic boulder, but it appears to be aligned with both a now-recumbent standing stone and the remains of a Bronze Age round barrow known as Miller's Grave, only two hundred yards away [25]. There is extensive evidence of prehistoric activity on Midgley Moor and a number of other stone monoliths of indeterminate date, including a stone perhaps instructively called the Greenwood Stone [26].

The name Robin Hood's Penny Stone was once thought to have denoted a plague stone, a point at the boundary between parishes where food and other essential items were exchanged for money during times of plague. This hypothesis was leant credence by the fact that there is a natural basin on the crown of Robin Hood's Penny Stone (Midgley Moor), in which it was once tradition to leave pennies (although this custom has since been transferred to a nearby standing stone known as Churn Milk Joan). It is thought this echoed the older practice of leaving payment for goods in natural basins filled with vinegar, which was once believed to act as a disinfectant [27].

Perhaps a more credible explanation, and one which better explains the association of these stones with Robin Hood, is that it refers to a local pastime popular in the 16th Century known as 'pennistone' in which stones were thrown at pennies balanced on a peg. For Robin Hood in his gigantic aspect, only large boulders were appropriate for use in such a game. The first reference to 'pennistone' in the Calder Valley appears in 1539, describing it as "an unlawful game" that "pulls down men's walls" [28]. Hence, it seems likely that the game was common as early as the 15th Century and the name of 'Robin Hood's Penny Stone' may have been applied to prominent boulders in the region around the same time.

Elsewhere in the country, we find giant legends that echo the narrative of Robin's death. For instance, a Sussex giant known as Bevis of Hampton is supposed to have selected the location of his own burial by throwing his sword Morglay from the battlements of Arundel Castle. Several sites claim to represent the spot at which the sword fell, including Bevis's Grave, Bevis's Thumb and Bevis's Tomb, all prehistoric long barrows [29]. Although the motif of Robin's final arrow did not appear in the ballads until the 18th Century, variations may have existed in local folklore long before it was written down.

The original giant legends into which the name of Robin Hood was inserted may well have emerged earlier than the medieval period. This is especially possible when such legends often pertain to sacred sites, which have endured since prehistory. It is indicative of a common pattern of transmission whereby anomalous stones, the original purposes of which have been long since forgotten by the local population, are credited with all manner of supernatural associations, from creation by giants to automatic return. In the late Middle Ages when the legend of Robin Hood became widespread, his name was increasingly connected to such stones because his persona conforms to earlier motifs associated with them.

It is not too great a leap of reasoning, therefore, to suggest that the site of Robin Hood's grave at Kirklees may not originally have been a gravestone at all. The possibility exists that it was the location of a much older stone monument, which became associated with the name of Robin Hood according to a process of folkloric transmission common across Calderdale, and northern England, in the 15th Century. That is to say, supernatural legends pertaining to a stone at Kirklees existed in the folk memory of the region some time before that stone became associated with Robin Hood.

The exact nature of such a stone is harder to hypothesise. It could perhaps have been a prehistoric standing stone or more probably, given the context, an early Christian wayside cross, waymarker or boundary stone. However, it may be significant that there is some evidence in the Calder Valley of stones utilised in prehistory being reused as boundary stones and waymarkers in the medieval period. For instance, whilst Churn Milk Joan on Midgley Moor was not erected as a standing stone until 1602, to mark the boundary between the Midgley and Wadsworth parishes [30], some crude examples of rock art on its east and south face indicate the stone was already significant in prehistory [31].

One point in favour of the waymarker theory is that early versions of the narrative of Robin's death all emphasise the grave was beside the highway. As W.B. Crump argued, the old road between Brighouse and Cooper Bridge running along the southern flank of Castle Hill adequately fulfils this criteria [32]. Prior to the construction of the Elland-Obelisk Turnpike in 1815, it was the primary route along the north bank of the River Calder and it is reasonable to suggest this road was of some antiquity. Highways in earlier centuries often tended to cleave to hillsides rather than attempt to navigate the boggy floodplains of the valley bottom.

A similar example of such prudence is the Long Causeway, a route which linked the Calder Valley with east Lancashire, running over the hills between Halifax and Burnley. Although its origins are prehistoric, it was used extensively throughout the medieval period and right up until the Industrial Revolution. Perhaps most significantly, a number of historically important wayside crosses survive on the stretch of the Long Causeway between Todmorden and Burnley.

The precise origin and purpose of these wayside crosses remains disputed. One theory is that they were erected by the monks of Whalley Abbey in Lancashire following its foundation in the 14th Century to act as guide posts for travellers on the Long Causeway in times of snow. Their concentration on the hills between Todmorden and Burnley, with five crosses in two miles, does support this suggestion. However, the topography in places is such that the crosses would not have been visible from certain treacherous stretches of the route, making them redundant as guide posts [33].

It has also been pointed out that many of the crosses are demonstrably older than the 14th Century, although they may have been reutilised by the Whalley monks. Local tradition in the 19th Century certainly believed they predated the Norman Conquest, and there is some evidence to confirm this. One possibility is that they were early Christian preaching crosses, perhaps even erected by Paulinus, the first Archbishop of York, who toured the region in the early 7th Century on his mission from Pope Gregory I to convert the pagan Anglo-Saxons to Christianity [34].

One of the most famous Long Causeway monuments is Mount Cross at Shore above Todmorden, although it no longer stands on the route of the old highway, having been moved sometime in the 19th Century [35]. It is a five-foot high shaft, terminating in a wheel cross head, with evidence of 10th or 11th Century vine scroll decoration on the faces [36]. As such, a medieval date (albeit pre-Conquest) seems certain but even comparatively recent stone monoliths can attract curious lore. Writing in 1911, the antiquarian Abraham Newell recorded a local belief that "the cross had been set up as a memorial to a popular robber who had been denied Christian burial" [37]. The parallel with the early narratives concerning Robin Hood's grave should be obvious.

Legends of significant interments at such sites seem to be a common feature of waymarkers throughout England. Herefordshire antiquarian Alfred Watkins documented a:

> "...fine old long stone... near Wern Derries, Michaelchurch Escley... The usual folklore legend that a great general is supposed to be buried there is attached to it and also... that a farmer in ploughing the field found it in the way so dug deeply all round it, and then hitched twelve horses to it in a vain attempt to uproot it" [38].

Here we find both the motif of a buried hero and immovability, whilst Watkins himself believed the stone could well have been prehistoric in origin.

It is also not uncommon to find tales of buried giants attached to Anglo-Saxon crosses. The most famous example is probably the Giant's Grave in the grounds of St. Andrew's Church in

Penrith, Cumbria. The monument itself is distinctly curious, consisting of four hogback Saxon gravestones bookended by two eleven foot high preaching crosses. Legend relates this to be the final resting place of Owen Caesarius, a famous 10th Century Cumbrian King, whose stature many tales have exaggerated to that of a giant [(39)].

Back on the Long Causeway, another monolith of interest is Stump Cross at Mereclough on the Lancashire stretch of the route. Today it is unrecognisable as a cross, having been defaced in earlier centuries and its general profile has led to suggestions that it may have been a reused prehistoric standing stone in the first place. Meanwhile, Newell notes that it was once known as Robin Cross and a number of extant sites in the vicinity recall this title such as Robin Cross Hall. He also speculates:

> "The personal name Robin... would appear to suggest that although other uses may have originated them, or become associated, a memorial character has become attached perpetuating the memory of some popular local hero" [(40)].

Robin Hood perhaps?

Legends of Robin Hood can certainly be found associated with old wayside crosses. Robin Hood's Picking Rods on Ludworth Moor in Derbyshire are one such example. This monument consists of two gritstone columns placed side by side, but it is thought these were once both part of the single shaft of a 9th Century Anglo-Saxon preaching-cross which came to be damaged at some point [(41)]. Local folklore claims that the outlaw and his men used these stones to bend their bows into shape. Later, Robin shot an arrow at this mark in order to win the freedom of a maiden held hostage by a local nobleman. Robin again takes on the character of a giant in this legend, as he subsequently throws a boulder from the top of Werneth Low into the River Tame [(42)].

A more local cross with an unambiguous connection to the legendary outlaw is Haigh Cross at Lindley, between four and five miles from Kirklees. A correspondent to *Yorkshire Notes & Queries* in 1890 recalled "There is a tradition that Robin Hood shot an arrow from Fixby to Haigh Cross, both near Huddersfield" [(43)]. Given how similar this story is to the later version of the narrative of Robin's death (Fixby to Haigh Cross is an improbable distance for an arrow flight), it is possible the story was transposed from Kirklees after that variation was popularised in the late 18th Century. However, it still illustrates how easily Robin's name became attached to stone monoliths in the region for many centuries.

The original purpose of Haigh Cross has been lost in the mists of time; the current monument is of no great antiquity and bears the legend "Re-erected by T&T 1808. After wilfully being pulled down". Nonetheless, it is clearly an entirely new cross, suggesting the original had been so defaced that it was beyond repair. Despite this, it is also marked "Quarmby's de Cres 1304". One prosaic theory is that it was first erected as a boundary cross to settle a dispute between the Manors of Quarmby and Lindley in 1219 [(44)].

More fancifully perhaps, the 19th Century local historian, J. Horsfall Turner observed that it stood along the route of a Roman road running to York from a 2nd Century Roman fort located two miles to the east of Haigh Cross at Slack. The road was still marked on the 1854 Ordnance Survey map. Turner believed this highway was used well into the Anglo-Saxon period, at which point wayside crosses were established along its course [45]. The Walton Cross at Hartshead would have been one such cross, and it is perhaps instructive that in order to traverse the land between these two markers, any Roman road would have passed directly through Kirklees.

Archaeological evidence of such a road has never been uncovered at Kirklees, although there is evidence of activity in the vicinity during the relevant timeframe. As Chapter 2 recounts, well-preserved Roman pottery has been excavated on the estate, and the earthworks on Castle Hill are believed to be the remains of an Iron Age defensive structure which may still have received use in the Romano-British period. Indeed, the possibility of a nearby Roman road was one of the reasons this feature was erroneously ascribed Roman origins by archaeologists in the early 20th Century [46].

Evidence has recently emerged to prove that some Roman roads may actually have followed the route of earlier prehistoric highways. However, as early as 1936, F.R. Pearson was suggesting in his book *Roman Yorkshire*: "It may be, of course, that the camps at Meltham and Kirklees mark the course of an old British trackway across the Pennines, in use long before the Romans came" [47]. If such a hypothesis was true, then it may lend credence to the vague possibility that the stone at Robin Hood's grave was originally a waymarker, or standing stone of substantial antiquity.

Alfred Watkins was certainly convinced that prehistoric trackways were marked by monoliths, which were reused in later periods. He writes:

> "The way was planted at intervals with stones, which by their size, shape or appearance, different from stray local ones, made assurance to the wayfarer that he was on the track... It is obvious that prehistoric ways must have been in use before the ownership of land existed and that as this later phase evolved trackways would naturally form boundaries and their waymarkers become boundary markers" [48].

The location of Robin Hood's grave certainly corresponds to an observable trend in the location of prehistoric standing stones in the South Pennines "just above the final break of slope, where the steep side... commences, such that from the stones there is a view both into and out of the basin" [49].

There is also some speculation that the Dumb Steeple monument at Cooper Bridge barely half a mile away, may also have had more venerable origins. Although the current structure was only erected in the 18th Century, Philip Ahier speculates that this might have replaced an earlier prehistoric standing stone.

He cites the work of the well-respected 19th Century Yorkshire antiquary, Harry Speight.

Although this attempt at toponymy is decidedly controversial, it is worth noting as yet another of the many correspondences and parallels which obtain in connection to Kirklees.

Speight wrote:

> "Conical stones and even huge rough blocks of stone became the expression of this religion in an idol form... In several place in the West Riding, there are, in my judgment, still existing monuments of this primitive worship. They are known by the not very enlightening name of Dumb Steeples. No legends or traditions appertain to them, nothing is known of their origin or history, and still they stand dumb or silent witnesses to the creed of a prehistoric age" [50].

Although Speight associates them with religious practice rather ancient trackways, his assertion that prehistoric standing stones in the West Riding (whatever their origin) were formerly known as Dumb Steeples is interesting. The term is not referenced anywhere else, but Speight is typically a reliable source and was writing at a time when old folk names may still have endured in the region.

Whether Speight is correct or not, it seems certain that the Dumb Steeple seen today did replace an earlier structure, which could have been some sort of wayside cross or boundary marker. Such landmarks are often found in clusters, and when you consider the existence of the Anglo-Saxon Walton Cross at Hartshead and a destroyed cross at Clifton (still evidenced by the existence of a 14th Century building recorded as Crosse Farm), it further supports the idea that Robin Hood's grave may once have been the site of a similar monument. Possibly Kirklees once lay at the convergence of several ancient trackways, or perhaps the whole area was considered sacred long before the Priory arrived, and this represented a reason for its foundation there.

To sum up: at one time, there was a stone monolith on the ridge of Castle Hill at Kirklees. It exact origins and function are difficult to delineate, but it may have been a prehistoric standing stone or an Anglo-Saxon wayside cross. By the medieval period, the local folk had long forgotten what purpose it served, and it became known as the burial site of a giant, the location having perhaps been selected when the stone was thrown there from a nearby hilltop. Numerous other supernatural properties were also attributed to the stone, including automatic return, retribution if it was moved, and healing properties.

When the ballads of Robin Hood were popularised in the late-medieval period, and the outlaw took on gigantic stature in the folk consciousness, his name was grafted onto the story of the monolith at Kirklees, which subsequently became known as Robin Hood's Grave. When the writer of *A Gest of Robyn Hode* – who was almost certainly personally familiar with the topography of the West Riding – came to write his epic ballad in the 15th Century, he wove this local legend into a narrative that was already stitched together from a patchwork of different sources. The dates certainly fit. The first place name associated with the outlaw, Robin Hood's Stone in Barnsdale, was recorded in 1422 [51]. The *Gest* was probably written slightly later than this [52].

With the location of Robin's grave 'fixed' by its inclusion in the ballads, the site became more credible to early antiquarians, who began to record it in their works, starting with John Leland in the 1530s. At some point, the original stone monolith was replaced by an ordinary grave slab to lend authenticity, or perhaps the monolith became the grave slab itself. If it was already a cross of some description, then this is not impossible. It is likely this occurred in the period following the dissolution of the Priory, when the land passed through a succession of owners [53], or when the Armytage family first purchased the estate. With the popularity of the Robin Hood legend in the 16th Century, no gentleman could fail to be aware of the cachet such a monument held.

Of course, this is mere speculation and it is best regarded as an interesting hypothesis, rather than any final word on the precise origins of the site known as Robin Hood's grave. Sadly, it is probably impossible to prove such supposition, unless medieval documents recording the existence of a standing stone at Kirklees prior to the Dissolution suddenly come to light. This contingency, however, now seems unlikely. There are also a number of potential objections to the theory that need to be examined.

Undoubtedly, such a hypothesis requires rejecting the idea that an actual historical figure on whom the Robin Hood legends were based is buried at Kirklees. Few serious historians admit such a possibility today, however. The orthodoxy now seems to be that he was a composite figure synthesised from a variety of different medieval outlaws, including the likes of Fulk Fitz-Warine and Eustace the Monk, and then further embellished by balladeers and chroniclers. Nonetheless, it is still possible that the grave represents that of Robert Hood of Wakefield, whether he was an outlaw or not, especially if the connection with Thomas Aleyn is considered [54].

But if this is the case, it begs the question of why the grave was located so far from the precincts of the Priory. It was definitely not on hallowed ground. One possibility is that it was a mass burial site for victims of the Black Death, which struck England in 1348, a date which would certainly be consistent with the possible lifespan of Robert Hood of Wakefield. Meanwhile, in her study of medieval nunneries, Eileen Power recorded an outbreak of the plague at Kirklees, which also claimed the life of the Prioress at the time [55]. Yet despite the widespread breakdown of the conventions of death and burial in this period, religious institutions still endeavoured to inter the deceased in consecrated ground.

There is also the question of Richard Grafton's description of the grave, with its mass of incidental detail, recorded in his *Chronicle* of 1569. However, the reliability of Grafton's account has never been settled. He was suspected of uncritically plagiarising material, and certainly never visited Kirklees himself, instead citing an 'ancient pamphlet' which has mysteriously not survived. Johnston's sketch of 1669 supports Grafton's account, but by this time the Armytages would have had ample time to fabricate a grave slab based on Grafton's report. Equally, William Stukeley may have embellished Johnston's sketch to better match Grafton's words.

Ultimately, the possibility that Robin Hood's grave may have been the site of an earlier standing stone, is as difficult to disprove as it is to prove. We can only resort to the balance of probabilities, and in that regard, it seems to be a respectable hypothesis, albeit one of several. But, even if the theory is rejected, it still illustrates a number of interesting parallels and correspondences between the grave and legends attached to a variety of prehistoric menhirs, Anglo-Saxon crosses, and other anomalous stone monuments. Interesting parallels and correspondences seem to abound in relation to Kirklees.

The discussion also demonstrates how easily the name of Robin Hood was attached to sites in the Calder Valley, a process that was still going on until quite recently. On the slopes of Luddenden Dean, across the valley from Robin Hood's Penny Stone on Midgley Moor, and a short distance from where Robin Hood's Penny Stone once stood at Wainstalls, is an earthfast rock which is traditionally painted white every May Day morning by persons unknown. The custom was first recorded in the 1890s, and has been observed most years ever since [56].

Whilst it seems unlikely that this practice is any older than the 19th Century, it has become associated with a variety of legends, including one concerning Robin Hood. This tale claims that the outlaw once took refuge at the *Cat i'th'Well* pub, a short distance down the hillside from the White Rock. Needing to conceal his loot from his pursuers, he buried it beneath the stone, which the landlord of the inn then painted every May Day as a signal that the treasure was still safe [57].

Thus, even in the 20th Century, the tradition of Robin Hood in Calderdale was still strong enough for his name to become attached to sites of topographic significance. It is perhaps curious that local legend also claims Saltonstall, where the *Cat i'the'Well* pub and its namesake, St. Catherine's Well, are situated, to have been where a number of nuns settled following the dissolution of Kirklees Priory. Indeed, one of the nuns at the time of the Dissolution went by the name of Isabel Saltonstall [58]. However, this is just another one of those interesting parallels and correspondences, which it is seemingly impossible to escape.

CHAPTER TEN

There's Something Happening Here

There are now two issues to consider. Firstly, why has the site of an obscure medieval nunnery in an overlooked corner of the South Pennines become so strongly associated with the death and burial of the legendary outlaw, Robin Hood? Secondly, why has this place emerged as such a focus for paranormal and occult belief in the late 20th Century? Of course, some would argue that the reasons are quite simple: a historical figure known as Robin Hood was actually buried at Kirklees, and that the area has been haunted by the unquiet spirits of his murderers ever since. However, given that the balance of probabilities is rather weighted against such an explanation, it behoves us to consider other possibilities for the strength of these traditions.

And the tradition placing Robin's death and burial at Kirklees is very strong indeed. As the first chapter noted, whilst there are manifold locations across England purporting to display the grave of other legendary heroes such as King Arthur, this is not the case with Robin Hood. Indeed, only one other site bears the name "Robin Hood's Grave", a prehistoric burial cairn in Cumbria with no attached legend. It bears emphasising that Kirklees is the only place to have been consistently associated with the outlaw's end, in terms of both documentary sources and material antiquities.

There appears to be three possible options concerning the origins of the monument known as Robin Hood's grave at Kirklees and tales attached to it. The first, as discussed, proposes that it is indeed the burial site of the 'real' Robin Hood. The second is that the grave belongs to a 14th Century yeoman who just happened to be called Robert Hood and who died at Kirklees Priory, only ten miles from his home in Wakefield. Finally, the third holds that it was originall a prehistoric or early Christian monolith which, like so many other sites of this nature in the region, found itself associated with Robin's name in the medieval period.

Whilst the first option would undoubtedly be the simplest and most parsimonious, it is also the east historically credible. In the absence of authoritative documentary or archaeological evidence, t would be unwise to dismiss the possibility entirely, but it is nonetheless the least favoured hypothesis amongst reputable scholars of the legend. The likelihood is that even if Robin Hood wasn't a purely literary invention, then he was synthesised from the narratives of a number of historical medieval outlaws to create a more durable and heroic archetype.

The latter two options both present a similar problem. If the grave is that of Robert Hood of Wakefield, how did this become transmuted into the grave of the outlaw Robin Hood? Robert Hood was apparently a popular name in the medieval period and presumably, it would have been visible on a number of gravestones across the country. Similarly, if it was a standing stone of some description, how did it become known as the 'definitive' Robin Hood's grave, when other sites such as the prehistoric burial cairn in Cumbria did not? In other words, how did monuments, which were only accidentally connected to the legendary outlaw, generate such a strength of tradition?

Certainly, one of the primary factors must be the inclusion of Kirklees in *A Gest of Robyn Hode*. The survival rate of early copies of this epic ballad suggests that in the 15th and 16th Centuries at least, it was one of the most popular retellings of the legend. However, this conclusion then raises the fundamental question of which came first, the grave or *Gest*? Did the author of the ballad simply report an existing tradition connected to Kirklees, or was the monument in some way manufactured to capitalise on the fame provided by the *Gest*?

The most likely scenario seems to be that, whatever its true origins, the monument at Kirklees preceded the *Gest*. Whilst the earliest surviving copy of the ballad dates from the late 15th Century, and the first documentary reference to the grave does not appear until the 1530s, this still means there was definitely a material site known as Robin Hood's grave at Kirklees in existence prior to the dissolution of the priory [1]. It seems unlikely that Cistercian nuns would have been responsible for faking the burial site of an outlaw famous for his antipathy towards organised religion.

Conversely, evidence throughout the ballad suggests that the author of the *Gest* was personally familiar with the topography of the West Riding of Yorkshire [2]. As such, it is reasonable to suppose he was aware of the reputation of the site at Kirklees, and thus included it in his narrative. Subsequent antiquarian mentions of the monument by John Leland, Richard Grafton and William Camden over the next hundred years only helped to cement the idea of Kirklees as the location of Robin Hood's grave in the antiquarian consciousness.

However, in examining why Kirklees became known as the site of Robin's grave to the exclusion of almost anywhere else, it is also necessary to consider the role of the Armytage family and the extent to which they promoted the connection to serve their own interests [3]. Towards the end of the 16th Century, when the outlaw was increasingly regarded as an unjustly disenfranchised noble rather than a mere yeoman, an association with this national hero would undoubtedly have been a valuable asset for a merchant family seeking to establish a position amongst the landed gentry [4].

The relationship seems to have been cultivated accordingly, and it was evidently regarded as a source of pride throughout the extended family. As David Hepworth observes, Robin Hood place names appear in the landholdings of branches of the Armytage family at both Armitage Bridge near Huddersfield and Outwood near Wakefield during the 17th Century [5]. Such reinforcement was surely helpful in establishing the Armytages as custodians of the Robin Hood 'brand' in the regional consciousness.

Meanwhile, suspicions have been raised that the Armytages may even have embellished the legend. In 1618, the antiquarian Roger Dodsworth visited John Armytage III at Kirklees to copy the estate muniments and recorded a local tradition, which held that Robin Hood "came to Clifton upon Calder and came acquainted with Little John" [6]. Around one hundred and thirty years later, Reverend Joseph Ismay noted, "Little John was an ancestor of ye Naylors of Clifton". As Dodsworth's manuscript was not published until Joseph Hunter quoted it in 1852, the tale must have been sufficiently well-known to endure in the folk memory independently for over a century [7].

Hepworth notes that at the time Dodsworth visited Kirklees, John III was rapidly buying up land in the village of Clifton. Hence, he wonders:

> "Was the Little John story developed by the Armytage family for their children (and they were, after all, a family of Johns), adding colour to the grave on their estate? Even before the advent of early tourism, the popularity of the Robin Hood ballads must have added a degree of pride in the grave, for the children if not the parents" [8].

Such speculation does not seem improbable. By the late-17th Century, the Armytage family were further showing off their Robin Hood connections with wooden statues of the hero and his merry men on display at Kirklees Hall, plus a number of supposed relics, including his bow, kept in the library [9]. It also seems likely that the identification of the Gatehouse as the building from which Robin fired his final arrow was the responsibility of the Armytage family. There is certainly no textual support for this aspect of the legend beyond what is recorded in topographical works by visitors to Kirklees in the 19th Century.

David Hepworth also acknowledges the extent to which Robin Hood's grave would have lent Kirklees Park, and the Armytage family, considerable cache during the fashion for landscape gardens amongst the gentry in the 18th Century. As he astutely points out:

> "Designers such as Capability Brown and Repton included classical follies and statuary into newly reworked estates: Kirklees apparently did not need such embellishments because of the presence of the grave of the nation's legendary hero" [10].

Sepulchral monuments were an especially popular aesthetic addition to such landscaped parklands, having an authentic touch of the Arcadian about them following Nicolas Poussin's famous painting of 1638, *Les Bergers d'Arcadie* [11]. The famed architect Nicholas Hawksmoor constructed Castle Howard's famous mausoleum in the 1730s, whilst similar shrines were added to the renowned estates of Stowe and West Wycombe. We know that the enclosure of Robin's grave by the Armytage family occurred during the 1750s and 1760s, perhaps inspired by this trend, as much as by a desire to protect it from souvenir hunters.

However, the enclosure of the grave has led many commentators (some of whom really should know better) to write of the monument as nothing more significant than a gentrified folly. One of the current standard popular reference works for folklore baldly states:

> "There is a tomb in Kirklees Park (Yorkshire) alleged to be his (Robin Hood's); 16th and 17th Century antiquarians mention an inscribed gravestone there, but their accounts are inconsistent with one another and with the existing monument. There is no reason to suppose it is authentic" [12].

Although there is a degree of truth in the charge of inconsistency between antiquarian reports, writers who deploy the current 18th Century enclosure and epitaph as proof against the grave's 'authenticity' (whatever that might mean in this context) invariably overlook one thing. That is the fact that the stone on the floor of the enclosure is almost certainly the original gravestone, and of a much older provenance than its surroundings. Whilst the grave is now contained within an 18th Century folly, it is not 18th Century itself.

Often, the accusation that the grave is somehow 'inauthentic' is not merely a suggestion that Robin Hood is not buried at the site, it also carries with it an insinuation that the monument is not the product of popular belief, but an artificial construction to advance the interests of the Armytage family. Folklorists call such a phenomenon 'folklorismus' or 'fakelore', representing the distinction between "folk practices wholly belonging to the innermost folk life of the people or something adopted or imposed from some understood or ulterior motive" [13]. It is a serious charge, for as one modern folklorist puts it, "Fakelore is the antithesis of folklore; whereas folklore exercises a critical function in nation states, fakelore contributes to social coordination and ideological and cultural hegemony" [14].

A degree of this can certainly be seen in Robin Hood's transmutation from yeoman outlaw fighting against the corruption of the medieval Church, to the wrongly disinherited Earl of Huntington, fighting to regain what is rightfully his. Whereas in the medieval period, Robin functioned as a symbol of rebellion against hegemonic institutions, the establishment recognised the threat such a symbol posed, and so co-opted the outlaw to serve and reinforce their own social orthodoxy. During the 16th Century, Robin Hood became a national hero in the sense that he now embodied dominant national interests rather than undermine them.

By promoting their association with the burial site of this newly-respectable champion of English values, the Armytage family undoubtedly strengthened their own position amongst the landed gentry and throughout the local population. However, whilst they may have been responsible for maintaining both the physical condition and its place in the national consciousness, they cannot be accused of having created the monument, and of introducing it into the national consciousness in the first place. The latter feat was almost certainly the work of the author of the *Gest,* or perhaps the composer of an even earlier ballad, now lost. But, as these individuals remain anonymous we cannot speculate what their motives might have been.

Perhaps without these nameless writers, and the Armytage family's perpetuation of the myth between the 17th and early 20th Centuries, then the grave at Kirklees would not have become nearly as well-known as it did. It may have remained one of the many Robin Hood toponyms scattered throughout the country, its legend taken no more seriously than those attached to the numerous Robin Hood's Stones, Robin Hood's Wells or Robin Hood's Butts. In that sense, the fame of the grave is perhaps artificial but it would still be wrong to dismiss it as manufactured fakelore, created purely to serve the agendas of individuals.

Moreover, it is increasingly considered naïve to believe that any particular constituent of the vast corpus of beliefs which has been dubbed 'folklore', and collected only in comparatively recent times, is an entirely native or spontaneous product of the folk consciousness. There have always been biases of selection and preservation [15]. Certain legends, which are now so familiar that we scarcely ever question their origins or mode of transmission, have always been promoted for particular ends and it is precisely this promotion that has ensured their survival into the modern period.

In that respect, not only was the patronage of the Armytage family relevant in so firmly establishing Kirklees as the site of Robin Hood's grave, it also gathered a great deal of momentum from its mention in seminal antiquarian texts such as Grafton's *Chronicle* and Camden's *Britannia*. Scholarly interest in folk traditions often feeds back into the traditions themselves, and reference to Kirklees as the site of the outlaw's burial in these tomes no doubt reinforced the notion amongst the wider populace [16]. Similarly, although Joseph Hunter's Robert Hood of Wakefield hypothesis has long since been discredited in the eyes of academic writers on Robin Hood, it still endures in the public psyche, especially (and unsurprisingly) in Yorkshire [17].

Whatever the Armytages' role in cementing the idea of Kirklees as the location of Robin Hood's grave, there were clearly thriving local folk traditions connected to the site itself, which arose independently of any 'official' narrative. As we have seen, the tale given by Thomas Gent is typical of the migratory legends, which attach themselves to anomalous stones throughout Britain. Equally, the custom of taking a chipping from the gravestone to cure toothache is a characteristic 'folk' practice, unapproved by the powers that be. Such traditions are likely to have originated in the local community, and were primarily sustained through oral transmission alone. There may have been many other popular beliefs connected to the grave, which were simply never recorded by antiquarians, so are now wholly forgotten.

However, the provenance of much of the modern lore associated with the grave and surrounding area is much more dubious and does perhaps deserve the term 'fakelore'. The notion of vampiric activity, especially, did not originate in any sincerely held local tradition; it was manufactured by a select number of individuals then perpetuated through media manipulation, and whilst it may have been generated unconsciously, it undoubtedly served certain ideological aims. But, although this strategy largely backfired, leading the progenitors of the Kirklees Vampire to quietly abandon their creation, it lives on in the annals of popular mystery books, and even amongst the local population, illustrating how easily fakelore can feed back into folklore.

As noted in Chapter 7, the Kirklees Vampire initially arose purely as a hypothesis. Members of the Yorkshire Robin Hood Society noted similarities between the method by which the outlaw was murdered by the faithless Prioress, and before long confirmation bias led them to interpret a wide array of unconnected events and phenomena in vampiric terms, including everything from Sir Samuel Armytage's aborted excavation of the grave, to dead animals found in its vicinity.

Vampires, however, have never been a native ingredient of British folklore. Although the 12th Century chronicler William of Newburgh includes an account of a revenant with vaguely vampiric characteristics in *Historia rerum Anglicarum*, the image with which we are now familiar, and which was invoked in the Kirklees flap, is the product of 17th and 18th Century Eastern European folklore, further embellished by the literary imagination. It is instructive that very few accounts of 'vampirism' have emerged in Britain besides those associated with Highgate and Kirklees, in which the very same individual played a central role.

Indeed, similarities to the Highgate case, beyond the involvement of certain people, are noticeable in several respects. First amongst them is the condition of the site. Like Highgate Cemetery, the graves at Kirklees were in a ruinous and overgrown state, the sanctity of these monuments sadly disregarded by their proper guardians. Equally, both were in secluded locations (in relation to their surroundings) which positively encouraged clandestine nocturnal activity. Séan Manchester himself draws the parallel explicitly in his description of Kirklees in *The Vampire Hunter's Handbook*, "Anyone familiar with events at Highgate might get *déjà vu*" [18].

The Highgate hysteria drew a great deal of public attention to the cemetery, and an argument can be made that whilst it took some considerable time, this adverse publicity was causally responsible for its subsequent restoration. Doubtless, the Yorkshire Robin Hood Society hoped that some of the interest generated by rumours of vampiric activity at Robin Hood's grave would have a similar effect. However, the interests of their patron, Séan Manchester, were quite different. In the opinion of this author, he seems to have had scant regard for the site itself, later dismissing Robin Hood as a "cutthroat" and a "villain" [19]. For him - again in the opinion of this author - the affair was primarily an opportunity to indulge his interest in the undead, which (whether this was his intention or not) maintained his profile as Britain's foremost "vampirologist".

There are also correlations in the way the media story developed and the way in which the protagonists not only fashioned diverse phenomena into a coherent narrative, but attempted to retrospectively rewrite the sequence of events in order to fit that narrative. As we have seen the speculation began quite innocently enough, with the *Huddersfield Daily Examiner* article of 13th June 1988 titled, "Is there a curse of Kirklees", which noted a number of disparate historical tragedies connected to the area around the grave. These included Sir John Armytage's fatal riding accident in 1677, and the disastrous consequence of the Luddite assault of 1812.

The Kirklees 'curse' only ballooned into a full-blown vampire story in the press somewhat later when Séan Manchester became increasingly involved. Very quickly, a diverse assortment of events had been marshalled to support the theory, with the 1985 haunting at the *Three Nun* linked to it, along with Robert Reid's suggestive, but ultimately, vague passage from *Land of Lost Content: The Luddite Rebellion 1812*. Manchester would also cite dead animals seen in proximity to the grave (a perfectly natural phenomenon) and occult symbols drawn on nearby buildings as evidence of malefic activity [20], much as he did in the Highgate case [21]. However, none of these things are necessarily intrinsically connected, unless one is already looking for evidence of vampiric activity. They form interesting correspondences but little more.

It is equally notable that it could be argued that Manchester would later attempt to revise the date of his involvement with events to predate the period in which the story broke in the press. In *The Vampire Hunter's Handbook* he suggests that he was familiar with Roger Williams' experiences prior to 1987 [22], even though Williams did not relate the story until 1994 [23]. Manchester also claims that "finger-width holes" around the grave had been observed in the winter of 1987, even though they are not referred to in any documentary source until early 1989 [24]. This all echoes how it also could be argued that Manchester retrospectively predated his involvement with the Highgate case to 1967, through his involvement with Elizabeth Wojdyla and 'Lusia'.

The Kirklees Vampire narrative was further propagated by the media, rather than any oral transmission. The principal organs of circulation seem to have been the local press, in conjunction with national tabloids. The former are typically starved of genuine news and will leap at any story that comes their way, whilst the latter delight in reporting on the activities of what they perceive as the lunatic fringe, especially when such stories lend themselves to an excrescence of groan-inducing puns.

However, whilst much of the coverage was tongue-in-cheek in tone, it is worth observing that the Kirklees case came at a time when hysteria regarding black magic was going through one of its periodic upswings in Britain. The late 1980s and early 1990s were marked by a succession of Satanic child-abuse scares, which resulted in the authorities in Rochdale, Orkney and elsewhere taking numerous children into protective custody on the basis of scant evidence. These incidents are now regarded as little more than modern witch-hunts, and the social services departments in question were subsequently severely criticised for their handling of the affair in official reports. Yet at the time, many people took them quite seriously indeed, prompting a spate of prurient exposés of supposed Satanic activity in the media.

Bill Ellis has observed how the Highgate flap erupted following similar hysteria in the late 1960s, generated by a rise in cemetery vandalism, the emergence of neo-pagan religions and horror films such as *The Devil Rides Out* [25]. He notes, "However campy the idea of a 'King Vampire from Wallachia' might have been, many were quite willing to believe that occultists were using the grounds for weird rituals" [26]. Similarly, whilst claims about vampiric activity at Kirklees may not have been taken seriously by many people, as the idea was developed to suggest that black magic covens were using Robin Hood's grave for their own nefarious rites, it increasingly conformed to an extant media narrative, which was all too widely accepted at the time. It was a narrative on which Séan Manchester thrived.

Much of the 'evidence' produced by the media and fundamentalist religious groups to support assertions regarding Satanic activity over the decades has rarely been convincing. It is more often merely evidence of bored teenagers consciously acting out black magic narratives, which they have gleaned from the media [27]. This phenomenon has been recognised by folklorists as a manifestation of two closely related practices dubbed 'legend-tripping' and 'ostension'. These phenomena also seem to have been integral to the propagation of the supernatural lore at Kirklees.

Legend-tripping has become a well-studied aspect of adolescent tradition in the last couple of decades, especially in the United States. The typical legend-trip involves a nocturnal visit by a group of young people to some spooky local site, such as a cemetery or derelict house, often under the influence of alcohol or drugs [28]. The location in question tends to have some vague lore associated with it, usually that it was the scene of some terrible tragedy, as a result of which it is now haunted [29]. The precise story, however, may vary between generations or neighbourhoods and often has little basis in historical events [30]. Indeed, the legend itself is frequently of lesser importance than the performance of the trip itself [31].

Favoured sites for legend-trips tend to be in liminal locations, on the very borders of the neighbourhood and sometimes verging on open countryside, but still within relatively easy reach [32]. If access is supposedly prohibited, then the prospect of getting caught by the authorities adds an extra frisson to proceedings for the legend-trippers [33]. Equally, whilst at the site petty vandalism may also occur, sometimes as part of an invented ritual designed to invoke or protect against the supernatural forces supposed to lurk there [34].

The legend-trip is largely regarded as a beneficial aspect of the adolescent experience. It provides teenagers with a relatively undisruptive way of rebelling against societal norms and allow them the experience of confronting and overcoming their fears in a safe context [35]. The tr also seems to operate outside the normal conventions of belief, involving a willing suspension of scepticism by the participants, which temporarily re-enchants the mundane world around them [36]. Much has been made of the similarities between the legend-trip and other rites of passage, occurring as it does at liminal places and in liminal states of mind. Indeed, teenagers often perceive the legend-trip as an initiatory practice themselves [37].

Bill Ellis studied the Highgate case as a classic British example of the legend-tripping phenomenon that got out-of-hand. He cites a statement made by Mary Farrant during her ex-husband's 19 court case, in which she claims they had originally started visiting the cemetery at night "for laugh and a joke... (to) wander about, frighten ourselves to death and come out again" [38]. also concludes that, "most of the damage was caused by adolescent gangs expressing rebelli to adult norms or carrying out dares or hoaxes" [39]. Ellis' analysis provoked a predictably furio response from Séan Manchester [40], but it seems difficult to argue with, unless we accept t existence of uncharacteristically flagrant Satanic cults and 'predatory demonic wraiths'.

Similarly, however, if Séan Manchester truly discovered occult symbols etched on stonewo at Kirklees other than the well-known masons' marks (and no credible evidence has yet be produced in support of this claim), then it is just as likely to have been the remnants of legen tripping and related activities. A pentagram graffitied on a wall is not necessarily evidence

Satanic activity. It could just as easily have be drawn in joking imitation of such practices, or simply because the culprit enjoyed drawing unicursal stellated polygons.

There is certainly reason to believe that Robin Hood's grave enjoyed a reputation as a legend-tripping destination even before stories about the Kirklees Vampire began to circulate. We know Roger Williams visited the site illicitly at least twice in the 1960s and 1970s, whilst a 1974 article in the *Huddersfield Examiner* reported on evidence of vandalism at the monument [41]. Lady Armytage frequently cited persistent wilful damage observed over several decades as a reason for refusing wider access to the grave [42].

What Lady Armytage failed to appreciate is that it was precisely the grave's taboo reputation that made it an appropriate destination for pursuits such as legend-tripping. Located amongst dense vegetation in a small rural hinterland between several urban settlements, it already occupied the sort of liminal region that breeds legend-tripping, whilst an awareness of intruding on forbidden territory will only have magnified the rebellious aspect of such behaviour. Meanwhile, an overgrown and ruinous grave situated alone in the woods is the very definition of a spooky site, especially when it has a grisly legend already attached.

Perhaps inevitably, once word of the 'vampire' at Kirklees got out, the grave's potential for legend-tripping only increased further. Numerous anecdotal reports of illicit visits to the grave circulated amongst teenagers in Brighouse during the 1990s [43], whilst Barbara Green's published accounts of her expeditions frequently fulfil the criteria for a legend trip. Her 1994 late-night visit in the company of three young men who were under the influence of alcohol, cannabis and lighter fuel [44], during which she believes to have encountered the phantom of Red Roger, is particularly ripe for analysis in these terms.

Although legend-trips are more usually the province of adolescents, if we accept that part of their attraction derives from the sense of rebellion against authority, then it is possible to understand how Barbara Green's activities also fit the template. Whilst Green may have been a couple of decades past adolescence, having been repeatedly rejected by the Kirklees establishment, such unsanctioned visits to the grave were a perfect way to subvert Lady Armytage's unrecognised authority and provide a small sense of victory against the otherwise immovable forces ranked in opposition to the YRHS campaign.

It was largely through legend-tripping that the notion of paranormal activity at Robin Hood's grave was sustained. Had the grave not possessed the potential to generate such activity, the 'Kirklees Vampire' flap would, in all likelihood, have been forgotten, dismissed as nothing more than an outbreak of tabloid silliness. Yet in an age when oral tradition is compromised by shifting populations and the influence of the media, legend-tripping is increasingly one of the most common means by which such lore is preserved. As a performative and participatory mode of transmission, its appeals are obvious. Legend-tripping allows those who partake to feel as if they are actively involved in the legend, thus adding lustre to their quotidian lives.

Indeed, much of the supernatural reputation of Robin Hood's grave has been generated through performative acts, from Séan Manchester's vampire vigil to Barbara Green's legend-trips and David Farrant's blessing ceremony. In this respect, it has much in common with a phenomenon folklorists have dubbed 'ostension'. This term was originally borrowed from semiotics, where it refers to communication through symbolic gestures, such as supping an imaginary pint to inquire if somebody wants a drink from the bar [45]. Folklorists have used it to refer to incidences of real people acting according to the terms of a legend, thereby reinforcing and perpetuating the survival of that legend [46].

Several different varieties of ostension were defined by Linda Dégh and Andrew Vázsonyi in their influential paper introducing the concept. Pure ostension involves behaviour that corresponds to a famous folkloric narrative, in the unwitting belief that the narrative was authentic rather than legendary [47]. One commonly cited example is the warning often issued at Hallowe'en in the United States, cautioning trick-or-treaters to beware of contaminated confectionaries. Rumours of razorblades and poison concealed within Hallowe'en 'treats' originally emerged as little more than an urban legend, but that did not stop parents and authorities increasingly behaving as if the story was true. More worryingly, it led to a number of sociopathic individuals actually committing the crime, in the belief that they were copying actual behaviour [48].

Dégh and Vázsonyi also identified 'pseudo-ostension', whereby a legend is deliberately acted out, often involving a hoax [49]. Legend-tripping frequently involves this type of ostension and it is likely that most 'evidence' of Satanic activity heralded by the media in the last fifty years is a product of pseudo-ostension rather than genuine occultism. Meanwhile, 'proto-ostension' involves cases where an individual claims a legendary narrative as their own experience, and 'quasi-ostension' refers to cases where natural phenomenon are misinterpreted as evidence for the reality of a legend [50]. Frequently these various types of ostension are present as a unified complex of behaviour, and this is certainly the case at Kirklees.

Bill Ellis has already commented with regard to Highgate that, "Both Manchester and Farrant from the start seemed eager to carry legend-making into... ostension, literally acting out the terms of their narrative" [51] and their activities at Kirklees invite a similar interpretation. Manchester's report of his 1990 vigil at Robin Hood's grave, with his "armoury of crucifixes holy water, garlic, candles and all known vampire repellents" bears more relation to popular images of the vampire-hunter, largely derived from Bram Stoker's 'Abraham Van Helsing' than any officially sanctioned ritual of the Catholic Church [52].

Citing the proximity of dead animals and Sir John Armytage's riding accident in the vicinity of Robin Hood's grave as evidence of supernatural activity, meanwhile, is a perfect example of quasi-ostension. Much the same can be said for attempts to suggest that institutional indifference, and logistical difficulties, are evidence of a conspiracy to suppress knowledge of the grave. Independent film projects such as that undertaken by Red Monkey fail all the time due to the constraints of time and money.

There also seems to have been a desire on the part of YRHS members to participate in the Robin Hood narrative itself. From their inception, the YRHS exhibited a passion for re-enactment often attending public events in costume and performing dramatisations of the outlaw's death. The hostility shown towards them by institutions such as the Nottingham tourist industry and the Kirklees Estate increasingly turned their activities into a crusade against what they perceived as an unjust hegemony. Whilst in the early 1990s trespass was the only option available to those wishing to visit the grave of their hero, the YRHS were fully aware of the similarities between their own actions and those of the legendary outlaw [53]. To an extent, they even revelled in it.

The Kirklees Vampire narrative also permitted Robin Hood enthusiasts to insert themselves into his myth. By seeking to defend his resting place against the lingering vampiric influence of the Prioress even after death through blessing ceremonies and the like, they could imagine themselves as Robin's protectors. Barbara Green had always identified strongly with the female characters in the Robin Hood myth, evident from her first published work on the subject, *Marion's Christmas Rose,* retelling the story from the women's perspective. The creation of the Kirklees Vampire and the efforts to banish its influence, resulting in a literal confrontation with the ghosts of Red Roger and the Prioress, can be seen as a continuation of this identification.

Equally, by moving their fight against 'dark forces' at Kirklees into the spiritual realm, the YRHS could continue their battle to protect Robin's grave even after their efforts to preserve the physical monument had been thwarted. Whilst they could not gain proper access to the grave to save it from the material ravages of time, they were able to bless the nodes on the leys to guard the site against spiritual rot. This contingency may not have been nearly as satisfactory, but it still provided the feeling of having achieved something. Moreover, this achievement occurred on a level that disinterested council officials, and obstructive estate managers would never hope to understand.

Indeed, the Kirklees Vampire can be understood as an unconscious personification of the situation at Robin Hood's grave in the late 1980s and early 1990s. The vampire is a creature in which the human life force has been perverted, which attacks its enemies by sapping their vitality. It is the perfect metaphor for a once-hallowed site, which had been corrupted by neglect, and the wearying opposition presented to any effort to restore its sanctity. As Bill Ellis observes:

> "Contemporary legends often embody emergencies – a social problem that urgently needs attention. Legends embody social stresses and attempt to define ambiguous feelings of threat in vivid, dramatic form... One role of legend is to redefine reality in a way that restores the narrator's control over the situation" [54].

Arguably, the Kirklees Vampire restored the YRHS's feeling of control in a number of ways. Not only did it provide a tangible (and potentially conquerable) symbol of the forces stacked against them, the very creation of a supernatural narrative was a subversive act [55]. It established a new narrative for the site in opposition to the neutered orthodox narrative and sceptical claims, which had been repeatedly used to disenfranchise the YRHS. The vampire legend created new significance for the site and pushed the media focus onto areas with which the existing authorities were unprepared to deal. The balance of expertise shifted to the YRHS and their vampirologist patron, Séan Manchester.

As such, the Kirklees Vampire represented an attack on the authoritarian forces of class and academia, which had persistently refused to acknowledge the YRHS's investment in the future of Robin Hood's grave. Whilst we might dismiss the vampire story as artificial, in that it was largely manufactured by a small group of people through the media for defined purposes, it nonetheless fulfilled an authentic purpose of folklore: to present a challenge and alternative to dominant hegemonic narratives. This was precisely the function the Robin Hood myth had once fulfilled itself, before it was sanitised in the 16th and 17th Centuries.

But, if we analyse the Kirklees Vampire in these sociological terms, what are we to make of the validity of the accounts of supernatural encounters in the area? Even if the vampiric motif was fabricated, the media attention brought to light a number of independent reports of paranormal activity around Robin Hood's grave. Some, such as the experience of Sue Ellis and Judith Broadbent, involved seemingly credible witnesses. Others, such as the spectre seen by Roger Williams, predated the Kirklees Vampire flap by many years.

Perhaps in the case of the phenomena experienced at various times by Séan Manchester's companion, Barbara Green, and Mark Gibbons, the sceptic might agree with Dégh and Vázsonyi:

> "It is the narrator who experiences the supernatural due to a variety of possible reasons: personal, psychological or physiological conditions, or an excited imagination... The otherwise normal, but visionary and perhaps slightly neurotic person creates stories from unconsciously preserved memories. The teller is supported by co-authors – the legend-bearers of society help to form the stereotype the teller visualises as vividly as if it were there. Yet there is no one and nothing on the 'stage' where the imagined apparition is reported. For the visionary, the subjective authentic witness of the legend event, this makes no difference: the non-existent apparition will be seen in any case" [56].

Whilst such an explanation preserves the veracity of the experience for the subject, it admits no external aspect, reducing the encounters to the status of mere internal projections. Yet there is one thing the many apparitions sighted in the vicinity of Robin Hood's grave have in common and that is the area in which they were seen. The landscape of Kirklees has proved fertile territory for ghostly manifestations over many years, even amongst those who were not necessarily familiar with its haunted reputation. Perhaps it is not the idea of the place which generates these experiences, but something intrinsic to the site itself?

The correspondences between the figures observed at Kirklees by various witnesses, and the tradition of spectral ladies in English ghost lore, has already been remarked upon. Such apparitions are often associated with specific sites, and some commentators believe that the phenomenology of the experience has much in common with certain other paranormal encounters, including sightings of fairies and the Blessed Virgin Mary, which also tend to occur at particular locations [57]. It is possible that they all represent the same type of anomalous experience, which is subsequently interpreted according to the subject's own cultural background.

It may be significant that Kirklees Priory, like all Cistercian houses, was dedicated to the Blessed Virgin Mary [58]. Indeed, there seems to have been a strong Marian tradition in the area, with the Lady Well near St. Peter's Church at Hartshead also taking its name from the mother of Christ (her full title in the Catholic Church often being rendered as Our Lady, the Blessed Virgin Mary). Given the well's proximity to the Walton Cross, a 10th Century Anglo-Saxon preaching cross, its provenance may be of some considerable antiquity [59]. As some have argued that many holy wells originated in the pre-Christian period, it is possible the Lady Well was already associated with some female deity before it was re-dedicated to Mary.

When considering why a Cistercian nunnery was founded at Kirklees, historians have only considered the topographical features of the site. However, many religious houses throughout Christendom were sited according to spiritual considerations too, and perhaps Kirklees was no different. The foundation charter certainly suggests that a cenobitic community had already settled there before the land was expressly donated [60]. Although it would probably be impossible to prove, the area may have been considered holy before the official establishment of the Priory, maybe as the scene of religious experiences, which were associated with the Blessed Virgin Mary.

Such a hypothesis is pure speculation and should not be taken as anything more. However, wading further into the mire of idle fancy, it seems worth considering that if Kirklees was once intrinsically connected to the principal female figure of veneration in the Christian mythos, maybe the female apparitions seen in the area in more recent times are modern interpretations of the same experiential property. In other words, it is feasible that Kirklees has a lengthy tradition of sightings of a female tutelary spirit, which each witness has subsequently woven into their preferred narrative.

Thus, the paranormal phenomena at Kirklees should not be regarded as visions of the unquiet dead, but manifestations of the *genius loci* (spirit of place). It is significant that between the 18th and early 20th Centuries, when Kirklees Park was at its prime, descriptions of the place are positively rhapsodic, whilst the supernatural associations are invariably interpreted as benign. However, as the area has fallen into decline over the course of the last fifty years particularly, the apparitions have become increasingly perceived as hostile. As the site has been allowed to fall into a state of neglect, its *genius loci* has grown similarly corrupt.

The sceptic might dismiss this as nothing more than an imaginative, aesthetic response. According to this school of thought, witnesses to the supernatural phenomena at Kirklees have projected their own feelings about the place into a symbolic, but ultimately illusory experience. Yet this seems to ignore the extent to which perception is always a fundamentally imaginative process [61]. Our awareness of the world is a construct generated as much by internal maps as external inputs. The qualitative appearance of the colour red, for instance, has no reality beyond our own consciousness. All that exists independently of our minds is an object with a surface texture that reflects light at a certain wavelength; the redness of the red remains entirely in the eye of the beholder [62]. Nonetheless, we behave as if redness is an objective feature of the world.

It therefore seems parochial to deny a similar degree of quasi-objectivity to perceptual experiences produced by the features of a certain place. Manifestations of the *genius loci* may depend upon both the external environment and the subjective observer, but they should be regarded as emergent phenomena whose existence transcends their individual components. In other words, these experiences are more than just the sum of their parts and may be considered trans-personal, in that whilst they emerge from individual consciousnesses, they synergise with something beyond ourselves to attain their own reality [63].

Kirklees is clearly exactly the sort of region that produces these manifestations. Even on a purely symbolic or aesthetic level, it can be said to possess a powerful *genius loci* and as such, it may have been regarded a sacred place long before the Priory was founded. This atmosphere has engendered a complex symbiotic relationship, in which human history has both responded to, and further influenced the spirit of place. It has become an archetype of liminality, poised between town and country, the sacred and the profane, this world and the Other. As Robert Reid so rightly observed in that oft-quoted passage from *Land of Lost Content:* "There was more than an insularity about it which local people only reluctantly tried to penetrate" [64].

Perhaps appropriately, the best approach to the many mysteries surrounding Kirklees is itself liminal. Rather than insisting on an answer to the question of whether Robin Hood is 'really' buried there, or if the ghosts 'really' exist, we should instead embrace their inherent ambiguity. As a monument, the very ambiguity of Robin Hood's grave allows a multiplicity of interpretations to be projected onto it and it is richer to embrace all these interpretations than demand a definitive analysis where none is forthcoming. The Romantic poet John Keats described this approach as, "Negative capability – that is when a man is capable of being in uncertainties, Mysteries, doubts without any irritable reaching after fact and reason" [65].

Such an attitude might be dismissed by some as mere postmodern relativism. Surely it *matters* whether or not the historical Robin Hood is buried at Kirklees? To an extent, it does, and hopefully this book has demonstrated that the grave cannot be easily dismissed as little more than a gentrified folly, as many commentators have attempted to do. Yet it should also have shown that the site's historical value derives from so much more than that. It has become a focus for the hopes and fears of so many individuals that it has attained a significance greater than its origins alone.

To quote philosopher Gabriel Marcel:

> "A problem is something which I meet, which I find completely before me, but which I can therefore lay siege to and reduce. But a mystery is something in which I am myself involved, and it can therefore only be thought of as a sphere where the distinction between what is in me and what is before me loses its meaning and initial validity" [66].

Mystery defines Kirklees, and it is the mystery that absorbs and enraptures. It is the mystery that has led so many to devote themselves to it over the centuries, and - whatever becomes of the place - it is the mystery that will endure.

REFERENCES

(Here it should be noted that Bishop Manchester has asked us to include that he believes that some of the letters attributed to him are fakes and that some of the quotes attributed to him are false)

CHAPTER ONE

1. J.C. Holt, *Robin Hood,* Rev. Ed. (Thames & Hudson Ltd, 1989), p16
2. Nigel Cawthorne, *A Brief History of Robin Hood,* (Robinson Publishing, 2010), p58
3. Holt, p190
4. Holt, p188
5. Holt, p193
Stephen Knight and Thomas Ohlgren (1), "The Death of Robin Hood: An Introduction" in *Robin Hood and Other Outlaw Tales* (Medieval Institute Publications, 1997)
       Online at http://www.lib.rochester.edu/camelot/teams/dearhint.htm
7. Stephen Knight, *Robin Hood: A Mythic Biography* (Cornell University Press, 2010) p3
8. Cawthorn, p64-5
9. Knight, p18
10. Fran and Geoff Doel, *Robin Hood: Outlaw and Greenwood Myth* (NPI Media Group, 2000), p13
Stephen Knight and Thomas Ohlgren (2), "A Gest of Robyn Hode: An Introduction" in *Robin Hood and Other Outlaw Tales* (Medieval Institute Publications, 1997)
       Online at http://www.lib.rochester.edu/camelot/teams/gestint.htm
12. Loc. cit.
13. Holt, p15
14. Loc. cit.
15. Holt, p200
16. Loc. cit.
17. Knight and Ohlgren (2), Op. cit.
18. Doel, p17
19. Knight and Ohlgren (2), Op. cit.

20. Doel, p18

21. Holt, p74-5

22. Knight and Ohlgren (2), Op. cit.

23. Holt, p17

24. Ibid, p200

25. David Hepworth, "A Grave Tale" in Helen Phillips, Ed., *Robin Hood: Medieval and Post-Medieval* (Four Courts Press, 2005), p93

26. Quoted in Stephen Knight and Thomas Ohlgren, *Robin Hood and Other Outlaw Tales* (Medieval Institute Publications, 1997) Online at http://www.lib.rochester.edu/camelot/teams/large.htm

27. E.J. Devereux, "Richard Grafton's Historical Publications" in *The Sixteenth Century Journal* Vol. 21 No. 1 (1990)

28. Cawthorne, p42-3

29. Holt, p41

30. Cawthorne, p42-3

31. Quoted in Barbara Green, *The Outlaw Robin Hood: His Yorkshire Legend* (Kirklees Cultural Services, 1991) p38

32. Knight, p26

33. Holt, p162

34. Ibid, p176

35. Doel, p72

36. Holt, p184

37. Ibid, 162-3

38. Hugh Chisholm, Ed., "Martin Parker" in *Encylopedia Britannica* Eleventh Edition, Vol. 20 (Cambridge University Press, 1911)
Stephen Knight and Thomas Ohlgren (3), "A True Tale of Robin Hood: An Introduction" in *Robin Hood and Other Outlaw Tales* (Medieval Institute Publications, 1997)
        Online at http://www.lib.rochester.edu/camelot/teams/trueint.htm

40. Loc. cit.

41. Loc. cit.

42. Hepworth, p97

43. Cawthorne, p62

44. Thomas Percy, *Reliques of Ancient English Poetry* (1765), p7

45. Doel, p24

46. R.B. Dobson and John Taylor, *The Rymes of Robin Hood: An Introduction to the English Outlaw,* Rev. Ed. (Sutton Publishing, 1997), p134

47. Knight and Ohlgren (1), Op. cit.

48. Loc. cit.

49. Loc. cit.

50. Loc. cit.

51. Loc. cit

52. R.H. Hilton, "The Origins of Robin Hood" in *Past and Present* No. 14 (1958), p36

53. Holt, p28

54. Dobson and Taylor, p134

55. Knight and Ohlgren (1), Op. cit.

56. Loc. cit.

57. Dobson and Taylor, p134

58. Knight and Ohlgren (1), Op. cit.

59. Green, p37

60. A.H. Smith, *The Place Names of the West Riding of Yorkshire* Vol. 3 (Cambridge University Press, 1961), p3-4

61. Holt, p74

62. Knight, p29
Doel, p24

CHAPTER TWO

1. David Hepworth, "A Grave Tale" in Helen Phillips, Ed., *Robin Hood: Medieval and Post-Medieval* (Four Courts Press, 2005), p96

2. Kerry Sykes, *An Archaeological Survey of Kirklees Park* (Publisher and date unknown). p7

3. Ibid, p5

4. Loc. cit.

5. Ibid, p6-7

6. Rev. John Watson, *The History and Antiquities of the Parish of Halifax* (Lowdnes, 1775), p39

7. Loc. cit.

8. Sykes, p5

9. Ibid, p5, 7

10. Ibid, p9

11. Ibid, p9, 10

12. Sykes, p11

13. S.J. Chadwick, "Kirklees Priory" in *Yorkshire Archaeological Journal* 16 (1902), p319

14. Chas P. Hobkirk, *Huddersfield: Its History and Natural History* (Ward and Lock, 1859), p73

15. Chadwick, p319

16. Ibid, p320, 323

17. James Parker, *Illustrated Rambles from Hipperholme to Tong* (Percy Lund, Humphries

and Co. 1904), p517

18. Chadwick, p319

19. Ibid, p335

20. Loc. cit.

21. Sir George Armytage, "Kirklees Priory" in *Yorkshire Archaeological Journal* 20 (1906), p25

22. Ibid, p27

23. H.N. & Marion Pobjoy, *The Story of the Ancient Parish of Hartshead-cum-Clifton* (Ridings Publishing Co. 1972), p39

24. Ibid, p40

25. Chadwick, p328

26. Pobjoy, p39

27. Ibid, p40

28. Hobkirk, p74

29. Pobjoy, p36

30. Eileen Power, *Medieval English Nunneries* (Cambridge University Press, 1922), p597

31. Chadwick, p353

32. Pobjoy, p42

33. Hobkirk, p74

34. J.W. Walker, "Robin Hood Identified" in *Yorkshire Archaeological Journal* 36 (1944), p38

35. Loc. cit.

36. Loc. cit.

37. S.J. Chadwick, "Kirklees Priory" in *Yorkshire Archaeological Journal* 17 (1903), p422

38. Pobjoy, p38; Sykes, p19

39. Joseph Hunter, *The great hero of the ancient minstrelsy of England: Robin Hood* (John Russell Smith, 1852), p53

40. Pobjoy, p53

41. Hobkirk, p75

42. Chadwick (1906), p328-9

43. Ibid, p334

44. Hopkirk, p75

45. Chadwick, p322

46. Pobjoy, p45

47. Chadwick, p322

48. Ibid, p348-9

49. Ibird, p350

50. Sykes, p15

51. Loc. cit.

52. Armyatge, p27

53. Sykes, p15

54. Sykes, p20

55. Loc. cit.

56. Loc. cit.

57. Armytage, p26

58. David Nortcliffe, "The Restyling of Kirklees Hall 1753-90" in *Transactions of the Halifax Antiquarian Society* (1982), p28

59. *Brighouse Echo*, 14th June 1991

60. Hepworth, p107

61. Ibid, p107-8

62. Joseph Hunter, *The rise of old dissent exemplified in the life of Oliver Heywood 1630-1702* (1842), p282

63. Hepworth, p108

64. Richard Griffith, "Kirk-Leas: A descriptive poem" (T. Burton, 1802)

65. Nortcliffe, p28

66. Ibid, p29

67. Ibid, p30

68. Ibid, p32

69. Loc. cit.

70. Robert Reid, *Land of Lost Content: The Luddite Rebellion of 1812,* (William Heinemann Ltd. 1986), p105

71. *The Times,* 8th August 1974

72. David Nortcliffe, "The Development of North Brighouse 1790-1910" in John Billingsley, Ed., *Aspects of Calderdale* (Wharncliffe Books, 2002) p22-3

73. *Brighouse Echo,* 10th April 1987

74. Loc. cit.

75. *Halifax Evening Courier,* 24th November 1988

76. *Brighouse Echo,* 24th March 1989

77. Ibid, 6th May 1994

78. Ibid, 13th June 1997

79. Ibid, 4th February 2000

Huddersfield Daily Examiner, 23rd October 2010

CHAPTER THREE

1. Barbara Green, *Secrets of the Grave,* (Palmyra Press, 2001), p21

2. J.C. Holt, *Robin Hood,* Rev. Ed. (Thames & Hudson Ltd, 1989), p42

3. Nigel Cawthorne, *A Brief History of Robin Hood,* (Robinson Publishing, 2010), p44

4.   Holt, p41

5.   J. Horsfall Turner, Ed. *Yorkshire Notes & Queries* Vol. 1, (T. Harrison, 1888), p106

6.   David Hepworth, "A Grave Tale" in Helen Phillips, Ed., *Robin Hood: Medieval and Post-Medieval* (Four Courts Press, 2005), p94

7.   Ibid, p95

8.   Bob Trubshaw, *Sacred Places: Prehistory and the PopularImagination,* (Heart of Albion Press, 2005), p90

9.   Hepworth, p94-5

10. D.R. Woolf, "The Common Voice: History, Folklore and Oral Tradition in Early Modern England" in *The Past and Present Society* No. 120 (1988), p29-30

11. W.H. Herendeen, "William Camden: Historian, Herald and Antiquary" in *Studies In Philology* Vol. 85. No. 2 (1988), p202

12. Hepworth, p94

13. Richard Grafton, *Chronicle At Large* Volume 1 (1569), p84-5

14. John Paul Davis, *Robin Hood: The Unknown Templar* (Peter Owen Publishers, 2009), p181

15. Stephen Knight and Thomas Ohlgren, *Robin Hood and Other Outlaw Tales* (Medieval Institute Publications, 1997) Online at http://www.lib.rochester.edu/camelot/teams/large.htm

16. E.J. Devereux, "Richard Grafton's Historical Publications" in *The Sixteenth Century Journal* Vol. 21 No. 1 (1990), p34, 38

17. W.B. Crump, "The Site of Robin Hood's Grave" in *Yorkshire Archaeological Journal* Volume 37 (1950), p105

18. Crump, p106

William Camden, *Britannia,* Trans. Philemon Holland (1610)
        Online at http://www.philological.bham.ac.uk/cambrit/yorkseng.html#yorks1

20. George Laurence Gomme, Ed., *The Gentleman's Magazine Library: English Traditional Lore* (Elliot Stock, 1885), p87

21. Richard Gough, Ed., *William Camden's Britannia, Englarged by the Latest Discoveries by Richard Gough* Volume 3 (John Nichols, 1789), p38

22. J.W. Walker, "Robin Hood Identified" in *Yorkshire Archaeological Journal* 36 (1944), p41

23. See for example Davis, p181; Barbara Green, *The Outlaw Robin Hood: His Yorkshire Legend* (Kirklees Cultural Services, 1991) p42; Jim Lees, *The Quest for Robin Hood* (Temple Nostalgia Press, 1987), p147; Richard Rutherford-Moore, *Robin Hood: On the Outlaw Trail Again* (Capell Bann Publishing, 2004), p107

24. Herendeen, p200

25. Quoted in Joseph Ritson, *Robin Hood: A Collection of All the Ancient Poems, Songs, and Ballads, Now Extant Relative to That Celebrated English Outlaw: To Which are Prefixed Historical Anecdotes of His Life* Volume 1, Rev. Ed. (1832), piii

26. H.N. & Marion Pobjoy, *The Story of the Ancient Parish of Hartshead-cum-Clifton* (Ridings Publishing Co. 1972), p39

27. S.J. Chadwick, "Kirklees Priory" in *Yorkshire Archaeological Journal* 16 (1902), p348-9

28. Hepworth, p102

29. Ibid, p101-2

30. Ibid, p97

31. West Yorkshire Archive Service, Calderdale, KMB 887/2

32. Holt, p43

33. Thomas Hearne, *Reliquiae Hearnianae: The Remains of Thomas Hearne,* Ed. Philip Bliss (John Russell Smith, 1869) p207

34. Hepworth, p103-4

35. Knight & Ohlgren, op. cit.

36. Hepworth, p102

37. Joseph Hunter, *The rise of old dissent exemplified in the life of Oliver Heywood 1630-1702* (1842), p282

38. Thomas Hearne, *Remarks and Collections of Thomas Hearne* Vol. 3, Ed. C.E. Doble (Clarendon Press, 1889), p449

39. Richard Gough, *Sepulchral Monuments of Great Britain* Volume 1 (J. Nichols, 1796), pcviii

40. Charles A. Federer, "Robin Hood: Myth or Mystery" in *Bradford Antiquary* First Series, Vol. 3 (1897), p92

41. Green (2001), p21

42. Ralph Thoresby, *Ducatus Leodiensis,* (Maurice Atkins, 1715), p576

43. Hepworth, p97

44. Ritson, pxlvii

45. Hepworth, p100

46. Thomas Gent, *The Ancient and Modern History of the Famous City of York* (Thomas Hammond, 1730), p234

47. Hepworth, p107

48. Davis p187; Rutherford-Moore p105-6

49. J. Horsfall-Turner, *The History of Brighouse, Rastrick and Hipperholme* (Thomas Harrison and Sons, 1893), p204

50. Walker, p42

51. Holt, p42

52. Joseph Ismay, notebook entry, 14th April 1752, as quoted in Hepworth, p101

53. Hepworth, p100

54. Hepworth p101-2

55. Loc. cit.

56. Davis, p188

57. John Watson, note dated 1758, as quoted in Hepworth, p98

58. WYAS, KMB 868

59. WYAS, KMA 732/28

60. WYAS, KMA 732/40

61. Richard Gough, as quoted in Rosemary Sweet, "Antiquaries and Antiquities in Eight-eenth-Century England" in *Eighteenth Century Studies* Vol. 34 No. 2 (2001), p189

62. Hepworth, p104

63. Maurice Keen, *The Outlaws of Medieval Legend* Rev. Ed. (Routledge, 1987), p181

64. Charles Alfred Stothard, *The Monumental Effigies of Great Britain* (J. M'Creery, 1817), p5

65. Thomas Percy, *Reliques of Ancient English Poetry* (1765), p116

66. Gough (1796), pcviii

67. Loc. cit.

68. Thomas Dunham Whitaker, *Loidis and Elmete* (T. Davison, 1816), p307-9

69. Keen, p181-2

70. Green (1991), p42

71. *Brighouse Echo,* 27th December 2002

72. Horsfall Turner, p204

73. Rutherford-Moore, p205

74. Ibid, p211

75. Ibid, p127
Sacheverell Sitwell, as quoted in Robert Aickman, *Cold Hand In Mine* (Robinson Publishing, 1988), p9

CHAPTER FOUR

1. Stephen Knight, *Robin Hood: A Mythic Biography* (Cornell University Press, 2010) pxii

2. William Simeone, "The Historic Robin Hood" in *The Journal of American Folklore* Vol. 62, No. 262 (1953), p303

3. J.W. Walker, "Robin Hood Identified" in *Yorkshire Archaeological Journal* 36 (1944), p7

4. Fran and Geoff Doel, *Robin Hood: Outlaw and Greenwood Myth* (NPI Media Group, 2000), p58

5. J.C. Holt, *Robin Hood,* Rev. Ed. (Thames & Hudson Ltd, 1989), p49

6. Ibid, 45

7. Ibid, p74-5

8. Ibid, p83

9. Brian Lewis, *Robin Hood: A Yorkshireman* (Briton Press, 1994), p12

10. Walker, p22

11. Holt, p176-8

12. Walker, p22

13. Holt, p84-6

14. Ibid, p179
15. Ibid, p199
16. Joseph Hunter, *The great hero of the ancient minstrelsy of England: Robin Hood* (John Russell Smith, 1852), p12
17. Philip Ahier, *Legends and Traditions of Huddersfield and Its District* Vol. 2 (The Advertiser Press, 1943), p52
18. Ibid, p65
19. Hunter, p35
20. Ibid, p37
21. Loc. cit.
22. Ibid, p43-4
23. Walker, p33
24. Hunter, p46
25. Ibid, p46-7
26. Ibid, p50
27. Barbara Green, *The Outlaw Robin Hood: His Yorkshire Legend* (Kirklees Cultural Services, 1991), p14
28. Hunter, p55
29. Ibid, p55-6
30. Ibid, p61-2
31. Ibid, p56
32. Holt, p160
33. Hunter, p53
34. Ibid, p59
35. Pobjoy, p53
36. Walker, p18
37. Loc. cit.
38. Ibid, p18-19
39. Ibid, p20
40. Ibid, p21
41. Loc. cit.
42. Ibid, p42
43. Percy Valentine Harris, *The Truth About Robin Hood,* Rev. Ed. (Linneys of Mansfield, 1973), p79
44. Loc. cit.
45. Simeone, p308
46. Holt, p197
47. Ibid, p46

48. Ibid, p47
49. Ibid, p49
50. Ibid, p50
51. Ibid, p47
52. Loc. cit.
53. Ibid, p48
54. Loc. cit.
55. Ibid, p52
56. Ibid, p188
57. Ibid, p190
58. Holt, p106
59. Richard Grafton, *Chronicle At Large* Volume 1 (1569), p84-5
60. David Hepworth, "A Grave Tale" in Helen Phillips, Ed., *Robin Hood: Medieval and Post-Medieval* (Four Courts Press, 2005), p111
61. Loc. cit.
62. Ibid, p112
63. Ibid, p97
64. John Paul Davis, "Robin Hood and the Templars of Doom" in *Fortean Times* No. 259 (2009), p38
65. Ibid, p39
66. Ibid, p38
67. Loc. cit.
68. Hepworth, p102
69. Hunter, p7
70. Sir Sidney Lee, Ed., *Dictionary of National Biography* Vol. 27 (MacMillan and Co., 1891), p258-9
71. Barbara Lowe, "Robin Hood In the Light of History" in *Journal of the English Folk Dance and Song Society* Vol. 7, No. 4 (1955), p228
72. William Simeone, "The Mythical Robin Hood" in *Western Folklore* Vol. 17, No. 1 (1958), p22
73. Thomas Wright, *Essays Concerned With the Literature, Popular Superstitions and History of England During the Middle Ages* (John Russell Smith, 1846), p207
74. Ibid, p208-9
75. Lewis Spence, "The Supernatural Character of Robin Hood" in *Hibbert Journal* Vol. 40 (1947), p284
76. Bob Trubshaw, *Explore Folklore* (Heart of Albion Press, 2002), Chapter 4
77. Harris, p52
78. Ibid, p50-1
79. Ibid, p50

80. Holt, p106

81. Ibid, p176

82. Lord Raglan, *The Hero: A Study In Myth, Tradition and Drama* (Methuen, 1936), p54

83. Trubshaw (2002), p39

84. Raglan, p51-4

85. Ibid, p179-80

86. Ibid, p189

87. Margaret Murray, *The God of the Witches* (Faber, 1952), p15

88. Loc. cit.

89. Robert Graves, *The White Goddess,* Rev. Ed. (Faber & Faber, 1961), 396

90. Trubshaw (2002), p40

91. Lowe, p228-9

92. Ibid, p229

93. Ibid, p238

94. Murray, p15

95. Doel, p24

96. John Matthews, *Robin Hood: The Green Lord of the Wildwood* (Gothic Image Publications, 1993), p16

97. Lowe, p231

98. Bob Trubshaw, *Explore Mythology* (Heart of Albion Press, 2003), pxiv-v

99. Ibid, p25

100.Joseph Falaky Nagy, "The Paradoxes of Robin Hood" in *Folklore* Vol. 91, No. 2 (1980), p198-9

101.Ibid, p203

102.Ibid, p202

103.Ibid, p206-7

Trubshaw (2003), pxv

CHAPTER FIVE

1.   Michael Kerrigan, *Who Lies Where: A Guide to Famous Graves* (Fourth Estate, 1998), p8

2.   David Hepworth, "A Grave Tale" in Helen Phillips, Ed., *Robin Hood: Medieval and Post-Medieval* (Four Courts Press, 2005), p107

3.   David Nortcliffe, "The Restyling of Kirklees Hall 1753-90" in *Transactions of the Halifax Antiquarian Society* (1982), p36

4.   W.B. Crump, "The Site of Robin Hood's Grave" in *Yorkshire Archaeological Journal* Volume 37 (1950), p105-6

5.   Richard Griffith, "Kirk-Leas: A descriptive poem" (T. Burton, 1802)

5.   Hepworth, p101

7. Richard Rutherford-Moore, *Robin Hood: On the Outlaw Trail Again* (Capell Bann Publishing, 2004), p105-7

8. Griffith, op. cit.

9. Jim Lees, *The Quest for Robin Hood* (Temple Nostalgia Press, 1987), p111

10. *Brighouse Echo,* 12th September 1952

11. Federations of Women's Institutes, *The South and West Yorkshire Village Book* (Countryside Books, 1991), p104

12. Edward Chitham, *The Brontës' Irish Background* (Palgrave MacMillan, 1986), p105-6

13. Elizabeth Gaskell, *The Life of Charlotte Brontë* (Smith, Elder and Co., 1857), p101

14. Loc. cit.

15. Charlotte Brontë, *Shirley,* (Smith, Elder and Co., 1849), p158

16. Gaskell, op. cit.

17. Unknown, *The Life & Ballads of Robin Hood* (Milner & Sowerby, 1855)

18. Stephen Knight, *Robin Hood: A Mythic Biography* (Cornell University Press, 2010), p101

19. Ibid, p107

20. Ibid, p141

21. Griffiths, op. cit.

22. January Searle, *Essays, Poems, Allegories and Fables with an Elucidation and Analysis of the Bhagvat Geeta* (John Chapman, 1851), p51-4

23. Hepworth, p108

24. *Brighouse Echo,* 26th February 1999

25. Ibid, 26th August 1988

26. http://freepages.history.rootsweb.ancestry.com/~calderdalecompanion/m408_r.html

27. *Brighouse Echo,* 23rd August 1996

28. Barbara Green, *Secrets of the Grave* (Palmyra Press, 2001) p31

29. Green (2001), p76

30. Loc. cit.

31. *Brighouse Echo,* 13th June 1986

32. Green (2001), p26

33. Loc. cit.

34. *Daily Star,* 13th June 1986

35. Green (2001), p26

36. *Brighouse Echo,* 13th June 1986

37. YRHS foundation

38. Green (2001), p26

39. Barbara Green, email to author, 20th January 2011

40. Green (2001), p27

41. Bishop Séan Manchester, email to author, 19th March 2011

42. *Evening Courier,* 13th June 1986
43. Green (2001), p32
44. *Brighouse Echo,* 13th June 1986
45. Green (2001), p29
46. Loc. cit.
47. National Trust, *Out Of Town,* November 1986
48. Green (2001), p27
49. *Nottingham Evening Post,* 14th July 1987
50. Green (2001), p31
51. *Brighouse Echo,* 18th April 1987
52. *Huddersfield Daily Examiner*, 9th June 1987
53. *Brighouse Echo,* 10th April 1987
54. *Brighouse Echo,* 21st August 1987
55. Green (2001), p27
56. *Brighouse Echo,* 29th January 1988
57. Green (2001), p27
58. Ibid, p28
59. David Nortcliffe, *A Historical Note* (Trusthouse Forte, 1988)
60. Jane Branton, letter to Barbara Green, 23rd February 1988
61. Green (2001), p32
62. *Brighouse Echo,* 5th August 1988
63. D.J. Wyles, letter to Barbara Green, 5th January 1989
64. Barbara Green, Annual General Meeting Report (Yorkshire Robin Hood Society, 1989)
65. *Spenborough Guardian,* 4th May 1990
66. Green (2001), p33
67. Ann Taylor MP, letter to Barbara Green, 30th July 1990
68. *Spenborough Guardian,* op. cit.
69. Barbara Green, *The Conquest of Kirklees* (Yorkshire Robin Hood Society, 1990)
70. *Huddersfield Daily Examiner,* 13th January 1988
71. *Brighouse Echo,* 10th April 1987
72. *Spenborough Guardian,* 16th May 1990
73. Green (2001), p87
74. *Huddersfield Daily Examiner,* 1st August 1991
75. *Evening Courier,* 1st August 1991
76. Green (2001), p88
77. *Brighouse Echo,* 19th July 1996
78. *Bradford and Pennine News,* 18th April 1996

79. Green (2001), p109

80. Ibid, p98-104

81. Ibid, p99

82. Ibid, p101

83. Ibid, p78

84. *Brighouse Echo,* 13th June 1997

85. Green (2001), p111-2

86. *Nottingham Evening Post,* 23rd March 2002

87. *Brighouse Echo,* 14th March 1997

88. Green (2001), p27

89. *Brighouse Echo,* 2nd July 2000

90. *Brighouse Echo,* 6th July 2007

91. *Evening Courier,* 6th February 2004

92. *Brighouse Echo,* 12th October 2001

93. http://www.calderdaleheritagewalks.org.uk/atrium.html

94. *Evening Courier,* 9th October 2006

95. http://robinhoodconspiracy.blogspot.com/2007/11/summary-of-yrhs-history-so-far.html

96. http://www.redmonkeyfilms.co.uk/Red%20Monkey%20Films%20Web%20Site%20%28latest%29/robin%20hood.htm

97. Barbara Green, email to author, 3rd November 2010

98. Paul Weatherhead, *Weird Calderdale,* Rev. Ed. (Tom Bell Publishing, 2005), p47

99. Catherine Fearnley, email to author, 19th October 2010

100. *Brighouse Echo,* 13th May 2005

101. www.robinhoodforum.ltd.uk/newforum/showthread.asp?page=6&order=id&id=1908 Accessed 23rd June2005

102. *Evening Courier,* 2nd November 2007

103. Barbara Green, "Robin Hood: Conspiracy and Cover-up of Yorkshire's Buried Treasure" in Joan D'Arc and Al Hidell, *Paranoia: The Conspiracy Reader,* Vol. 1 (Paranoia Publishing, 2010), p64-72

104. Email to author, 30th January 2011

105. http://www.thesupernaturalworld.com/forum/index.php?showtopic=25743&view=findpost&p=472403

106. Brian L. Keeley, "Of Conspiracy Theories" in *The Journal of Philosophy,* Vol. 96, No. 3 (1999), p111

107. Ted Goertzel, "Belief In Conspiracy Theories" in *Political Psychology,* Vol. 15, No. 4 (1994), p740

108. *Spenborough Guardian,* 16th May 1997

109. *Brighouse Echo,* 13th June 1997

110. www.robinhoodforum.ltd.uk/newforum/showthread.asp?page=6&order=id&id=1908

Accessed 23rd June2005

111.Loc. cit.

112.Loc. cit.

113.www.robinhoodforum.ltd.uk/newforum/showthread.asp?page=4&order=id&id=31 Accessed 20th March 2002

www.robinhoodforum.ltd.uk/newforum/showthread.asp?page=6&order=id&id=1908 Accessed 23rd June2005

CHAPTER SIX

1. Barbara Green, *Secrets of the Grave,* (Palmyra Press, 2001), p42; Bishop Séan Manchester, e-mail to author, 19th March 2010

2. http://www.highgate-cemetery.org/index.php/history

3. Bill Ellis, "The Highgate Cemetery Vampire Hunt: The Anglo-American Connection In Cult Lore" in *Folklore* Vol. 104, No 1/2 (1993), p19

4. Ibid, p17-8

5. Ibid p20

6. Ibid, p18

7. Ronald Hutton, *Triumph of the Moon: A History of Modern Pagan Witchcraft* (Oxford Paperbacks, 1995)

8. Ellis, p18

9. *Hampstead and Highgate Express,* 6th February 1970

10. Ellis, p21

11. Ellis, p22

12. Loc. cit.

13. http://friendsofbishopseanmanchester.blogspot.com/2010/10/tony-hill.html

14. *Hampstead and Highgate Express,* 27th February 1970

15. Séan Manchester, *The Vampire Hunter's Handbook,* (Gothic Press, 1997) p72

16. *Hampstead and Highgate Express,* 6th March 1970

17. Séan Manchester, *The Highgate Vampire* (British Occult Society, 1985), p124

18. Manchester (1997), p29; p33

19. http://www.holygrail-church.fsnet.co.uk/24Hours.htm

20. http://friendsofbishopseanmanchester.blogspot.com/2011/02/vrs-founded.html

21. http://www.davidfarrant.org/about/bpos.html

22. http://dawwih.blogspot.com/2009/02/davids-response-to-my-queries.html

23. *Camden New Journal,* 29th January 2009

24. Ellis, p24

25. *Hampstead and Highgate Express,* 20th March 1970

26. Ellis, p25

27. Manchester (1985), p50-1

28. *Evening News,* 14th March 1970

29. *Hampstead and Highgate Express,* 20th March 1970

30. Ellis, p24

31. *Hampstead and Highgate Express,* 7th August 1970

32. Ellis, p26

33. Loc. cit.

34. *The Sun,* 19th August 1971

35. Ellis, p27

36. Manchester (1985), p54

37. *Hornsey Journal,* 6th November 1971

38. "The Right Rev. Dr. Séan Manchester OSG" in *Folklore* Vol. 10 (1996), p108

39. Ellis, p26

40. *Evening News,* 16th October 1971

41. Ellis, p27

42. Ibid, p29

43. *Hampstead and Highgate Express,* 15th October 1971

44. Rob Milne, *Return of the Vampire Hunter* (British Psychic and Occult Society, 2003), p22-6

45. Ellis, p30

46. *Hornsey Journal,* 8th October 1971

47. *The Sun*, 23rd November 1972

48. Ellis, p30-1

49. http://www.holygrail-church.fsnet.co.uk/Ecclesia%20Apostolica%20Sancti%20Graal.htm

50. *Hampstead and Highgate Express,* 5th May 1973

51. *Hornsey Journal*, 31st August 1973

52. Ellis, p31

53. Loc. cit

54. http://www.davidfarrant.org/faq.html

55. Ellis, p32

56. Loc. cit.

57. Loc. cit.

58. *Hornsey Journal,* 7th December 1973

59. http://plan9.150m.com/burning.htm

60. Ellis, p32

61. Manchester (1985), p91-114

62. Ellis, p32

63. Loc. cit.

64. Ibid, p33

65. Loc. cit.

66. *Hornsey Journal,* 28th June 1974

67. Ellis, p33

68. *Finchley Press,* 22nd February 1980

69. http://highgatevampire.blogspot.com/2009/08/prison-correspondence-from-lone-vampire.html

70. Manchester (1985), p22

71. Ibid, p46

72. http://dawwih.blogspot.com/2010/12/wojdyla-testimony-pt-2.html

73. Ramsey Campbell, "The Strange Case of Séan Manchester" in *Ramsey Campbell Probably* (PS Publishing, 2002), p147-8

74. http://plan9.150m.com/lusialives.htm

75. *Borehamwood Post,* 29th September 1977

76. *Sunday People,* 9th October 1977

77. http://www.holygrail-church.fsnet.co.uk/TheThorneConspiracy.htm

78. http://plan9.150m.com/MY%20DEATH%20-%20PART%201.htm

79. Loc. cit.

80. *Hornsey Journal,* 1st September 1978

81. http://plan9.150m.com/my%20death%20-%20part%202.htm

82. *Hornsey Journal,* 30th June 1978

83. http://plan9.150m.com/wwpod.htm

84. Loc. cit.

85. *City Limits,* July 6-12 1984

86. *Hampstead and Highgate Express,* 15th June 1984

87. http://plan9.150m.com/from%20satan%20to%20christ%20pt%20ii.htm

88. Manchester (1985), p62

89. http://www.gothicpress.freeserve.co.uk/Highgate%20Vampire%20Society.htm

90. http://www.davidfarrant.org/faq.html

91. Loc. cit.

92. Ellis, p30

93. http://www.gothicpress.freeserve.co.uk/The%20Right%20Reverend%20Sean%20Manchester.htm

94. Loc. cit.

95. http://www.holygrail-church.fsnet.co.uk/FarrantFacts.htm

96. Manchester (1985), p18

97. http://friendsofbishopseanmanchester.blogspot.com/2010/10/summoning-vampire.html

98. *Ofcom Broadcast Bulletin* Issue 58 (2006), p44

99. http://is-is.facebook.com/topic.php?uid=2208499322&topic=9515&post=41535
http://www.gothicpress.freeserve.co.uk/The%20Right%20Reverend%20Sean%20Manchester.htm

CHAPTER SEVEN

1. Thomas Gent, *The Ancient and Modern History of the Famous City of York* (Thomas Hammond, 1730), p234

2. Richard Griffith, "Kirk-Leas: A descriptive poem" (T. Burton, 1802)

3. Charlotte Brontë, *Shirley,* (Smith, Elder and Co., 1849), p158

4. Ibid, p385-6

5. Robert Reid, *Land of Lost Content: The Luddite Rebellion of 1812,* (William Heinemann Ltd. 1986), p10

6. Séan Manchester, *The Vampire Hunter's Handbook,* (Gothic Press, 1997) p31; Paul Weatherhead, *Weird Calderdale,* Rev. Ed. (Tom Bell Publishing, 2005), p42

7. Barbara Green, *The Outlaw Robin Hood: His Yorkshire Legend* (Kirklees Cultural Services, 1991), p40; Barbara Green, *Secrets of the Grave* (Palmyra Press, 2001), p20

8. Séan Manchester, email to author, 19th March 2011

9. *Brighouse Echo,* 27th December 2002

10. Green (2001), p38

11. Ibid, p39

12. Loc. cit.

13. Séan Manchester, email to author, 19th March 2011

14. Green (2001), p40

15. Séan Manchester, letter to Barbara Green, 22nd December 1987

16. Anonymous, "Lady Armytage, Robin Hood and Vampires" in *Spen Valley Spark* (July 1990)

17. Green (2001), p46

18. *Huddersfield Daily Examiner,* 13th June 1988

19. Green (2001), p40

20. Richard Firth Green, "The Hermit and the Outlaw: New Evidence for Robin Hood's Death?" in Helen Phillips, Ed., *Robin Hood: Medieval and Post-Medieval* (Four Courts Press, 2005)

21. Green (2001), p42

22. Ibid, p45

23. Manchester (1997), p36

24. Ibid, p31

25. Ruthwen Glenarvon, letter to Lady Margarete Armytage, 29th November 1988

26. Lady Margarete Armytage, letter to Ruthwen Glenarvon, 15th December 1988

27. Séan Manchester, letter to Barbara Green , 28th December 1988

28. Séan Manchester, email to author, 20th March 2011

29. http://vampireresearchsociety.blogspot.com/2009/02/kirklees-mystery-west-yorkshire.html

30. http://is-is.facebook.com/topic.php?uid=2208499322&topic=9515&post=41535

31. Green, p42

32. *Daily Star,* 5th January 1989

33. Green, p42

34. *Brighouse Echo,* 6th January 1989

35. *Daily Star,* 5th January 1989

36. *Yorkshire Post,* 5th January 1989

37. *Brighouse Echo,* 6th January 1989

38. Séan Manchester, letter to newspaper editors, 2nd February 1989

39. Séan Manchester, email to author, 19th March 2011

40. Séan Manchester, letter to Barbara Green, January 1989

41. *Yorkshire Post,* 5th February 1989

42. Séan Manchester, letter to Barbara Green, 17th February 1989

43. Green (2001), p45

44. Rev. John Flack, letter to Barbara Green, 6th February 1989

45. *Evening Courier,* 27th February 1989

46. *Yorkshire Post,* 27th February 1989

47. Barbara Green, letter to Lady Margarete Armytage, 25th February 1989

48. Green (2001), p45-6

49. *Yorkshire Post,* 3rd March 1989

50. *Evening Courier,* 3rd March 1989

51. Father Matthew Dwyer, letter to Barbara Green, 30th May 1989

52. Green (2001), p82

53. Bishop Anselm Genders, letter to Barbara Green, 2nd June 1990

54. Green (2001), p83

55. Manchester (1997), p32

56. Green (2001), p84

57. Barbara Green, email to author, 13th February 2011

58. Green (2001), p83

59. Ibid, p84

60. Séan Manchester, letter to Barbara Green, 7th September 1989

61. Green (2001), p83

62. Ibid, p84

63. Séan Manchester, "The Kirklees Vampire" in *The Unexplained* (Orbis Publishing, 1992)

64. Manchester (1997), p33
65. Ibid, p33-4
66. Ibid, p34
67. Manchester (1992),
68. Manchester (1997), p34
69. Loc. cit.
70. Ibid, p29
71. Loc. cit.
72. Barbara Green, *The Conquest of Kirklees* (Yorkshire Robin Hood Society, 1990)
73. Green (2001), p91
74. Séan Manchester, email to author, 19th March 2011
75. Manchester (1992)
76. Séan Manchester, letter to Barbara Green, 29th November 1989
77. Loc. cit.
78. Séan Manchester, email to author, 19th March 2011
79. Séan Manchester, letter to Barbara Green, 10th July 1990
80. Séan Manchester, letter to Barbara Green, 28th May 1992
81. Weatherhead, p47
82. Séan Manchester, letter to Barbara Green, 10th July 1990
83. Manchester (1997), p32
84. Green (2001), p91
85. Ibid, p91-2
86. Manchester (1997), p29
87. http://www.gothicpress.freeserve.co.uk/The%20Kirklees%20Vampire.htm
88. Jane C. Beck, "The White Lady of Great Britain and Ireland" in *Folklore* Vol. 81, No. 4 (1970), p292-306
89. Green (2001), p94
90. Loc. cit
91. Ibid, p95
92. Barbara Green, email to author, 19th February 2011
93. Quoted in Weatherhead, p44
94. Barbara Green, email to author, 19th February 2011
95. *Daily Mirror,* 23rd March 2007
96. Green (2001), p95
97. *Spenborough Guardian,* 29th December 1995
98. Judith Broadbent, letter to Barbara Green, 24th April 1997
99. Judith Broadbent, letter to Barbara Green, 30th April 1997
100. Quoted in Barbara Green (2001), p106

101.Weatherhead, p43

102.Green (2001), p98

103.Manchester (1997), p36

104.*Evening Courier,* 18th March 1997

105.*Brighouse Echo,* 14th March 1997

106.*Telegraph and Argus,* 20th March 1997

107.*Evening Courier,* 18th March 1997

108.Green (2001), p13

109.Quoted in Green (2001), p14

110.Green (2001), p98

111.*Telegraph and Argus,* 20th March 1997

112.Quoted in Green (2001), p113

113.*Brighouse Echo,* 13th June 1997

114.*Brighouse Echo,* 25th July 1997

115.Green (2001), p105

116.*Brighouse Echo,* 5th February 1998

117.Green (2001), p112

118.*Brighouse Echo,* 5th February 1998

119.Green (2001), p114

120.Loc. cit.

121.Ibid, p113

122.David Farrant, email to author, 17th February 2011

123.Loc. cit.

124.Séan Manchester, letter to Bearders & Co. Solicitors, 1st June 1998

125.Green (2001), p116

126.Séan Manchester, email to author, 22nd March 2011

127.David Farrant, email to author, 17th February 2011

128.Loc. cit.

129.http://davidfarrant.org/TheHumanTouch/?p=86

130.http://ghosts-uk.net/modules/news/article.php?storyid=719

131.David Farrant, email to author, 17th February 2011

132.*Brighouse Echo,* 13th May 2005

133.http://friendsofbishopseanmanchester.blogspot.com/2010/10/barbara-green.html

134.David Farrant, email to author, 17th February 2011

135.Gareth J. Medway, email to author, 17th February 2011

136.*Huddersfield Daily Examiner,* 2nd May 2005

137.Gareth J. Medway, email to author, 17th February 2011

138.*Brighouse Echo,* 1st July 2005

139.http://dawwih.blogspot.com/2010/08/interview-with-catherine-fearnley.html

140.http://davidfarrant.org/TheHumanTouch/?p=85

141.Barbara Green, email to author, 11th December 2010

142.David Farrant, email to author, 17th February 2011

143.Barbara Green, email to author, 11th December 2010

144.David Farrant, email to author, 17th February 2011

145.Séan Manchester, email to author, 21st March 2011
http://vampireresearchsociety.blogspot.com/2009/02/kirklees-mystery-west-yorkshire.html

CHAPTER EIGHT

1.   Adam Stout, *What's Real and What Is Not: Reflections Upon Archaeology and Earth Mysteries in Great Britain* (Runetree Press, 2006), p78

2.   Richard Hayman, *Riddles In Stone: Myths, Archaeology and the Ancient Britons* Rev. Ed. (Hambledon Continuum, 2006) p212

3.   Alfred Watkins, *The Old Straight Track* Rev. Ed. (Abacus, 1994) pxx

4.   Ibid, pxxi

5.   Ibid, Chapter 21

6.   Ibid, Chapter 16

7.   Hayman, Chapter 22

8.   Stout, p18-19

9.   Hayman, p226

10. Eg. Thomas Wright, *Essays Concerned With the Literature, Popular Superstitions and History of England During the Middle Ages* (John Russell Smith, 1846), p208-9

11. Hayman, p223

12. Hayman, p223; 237

13. David Farrant, email to author, February 17th 2011

14. Barbara Green, *Secrets of the Grave* (Palmyra Press, 2001), p79

15. Robin Ellis, letter to Barbara Green, undated

16. Robin Ellis, letter to Barbara Green, undated

17. Robin Ellis, letter to Barbara Green, undated

18. Green, p79

19. H. Whitaker, "Early British Trackways" in *Transactions of the Halifax Antiquarian Society* (1929)

20. E.A. Hilary Haigh, Ed., *Huddersfield: A Most Handsome Town* (Kirklees Cultural Services, 1992), p10-12

21. Loc. cit.

22. Loc. cit.

23. Philip Ahier, *The Story of Castle Hill* (The Advertiser Press, 1946), p73

24. Hilary Haigh, p13

25. Hayman, p218

26. H.N. & Marion Pobjoy, *The Story of the Ancient Parish of Hartshead-cum-Clifton* Ridings Publishing Co. 1972), p7

27. http://www.kirkheatononlineparishclerk.com/mirfield/joseph-ismay.htm

28. Federations of Women's Institutes, *The South and West Yorkshire Village Book* Countryside Books, 1991), p104

29. A. Ronald Bielby, *Churches and Chapels of Kirklees* (Kirklees Metropolitan Council, 1978), p14-5

30. J.H. Ogden, "Visit to Kirklees Priory and Hartshead Church" in *Transactions of the Halifax Antiquarian Society* (1902)

31. Watkins, Chapter 21

32. Ronald Hutton, *The Pagan Religions of the Ancient British Isles: Their Nature and Legacy* (Blackwell Publishing, 1993), p271-2

33. Valerie Shepherd, *Holy Wells of West Yorkshire and the Dales,* Rev.Ed. (Lepus Press, 2004), p35

34. Federations of Women's Institutes, op. cit.

35. Philip Ahier, *Legends and Traditions of Huddersfield and Its District* Vol. 1 (The Adveriser Press, 1943), p150

36. Green, p33

37. David Farrant, op. cit.

38. Watkins, p220

39. *Brighouse Echo,* 6th October 1994

40. Loc. cit.

41. Green, p81

42. *Brighouse Echo,* op. cit.

43. *Evening Courier,* 15th June 1985

44. S.J. Chadwick, "Kirklees Priory" in *Yorkshire Archaeological Journal* 16 (1902), p

45. Pobjoy, p44

46. Green, p81

47. http://freepages.history.rootsweb.ancestry.com/~calderdalecompanion/p200_t.html#t107

48. J. Horsfall Turner, *History of Brighouse, Rastrick and Hipperholme* (Thomas Harrison nd Sons, 1893), p205

49. Ahier (1943), p276-281

50. Stephen Knight, *Robin Hood: A Mythic Biography* (Cornell University Press, 2010), p100

51. http://mirfield-2ndlook.info/Luddites/Luddites_2/luddites_2.html

52. http://mirfield-2ndlook.info/Luddites/Luddites_6/luddites_6.html

53. http://mirfield-2ndlook.info/Luddites/Luddites_5/luddites_5.html

54. Robert Reid, *Land of Lost Content: The Luddite Rebellion of 1812,* (William Heinemann Ltd. 1986), p105

55. http://mirfield-2ndlook.info/Luddites/Luddites_7/luddites_7.html

56. Reid, p108-9

57. Ibid, p109

58. Ibid, p110

59. Ibid, p111-3

60. Ibid, p117

61. http://mirfield-2ndlook.info/Luddites/Luddites_8/luddites_8.html

62. Loc. cit.

63. http://mirfield-2ndlook.info/Luddites/Luddites_9/luddites_9.html

64. http://mirfield-2ndlook.info/Luddites/Luddites_10/luddites_10.html

65. *Huddersfield Daily Examiner,* 13th June 1988

66. *Evening Courier,* op. cit.

67. Green, p81

68. *Evening Courier,* op. cit.

69. Loc. cit.

70. Kenneth Goor, *Haunted Leeds* (Tempus Publishing, 2006), p75-6; Stephen Wade, *Hauntings In Yorkshire* (Halsgrove, 2008), p28

71. Goor, p75

72. Michelle Hynes, letter to Barbara Green, undated

73. Green, p81

74. Goor, p75

75. http://theblueboarinnrobinhooddiscussions.yuku.com/topic/522/t/Sir-Samuel-Armytage.html Accessed 30th June 2005

76. Green, p80

77. Barbara Green, *The Plot Thickens!* (Yorkshire Robin Hood Society, 1991)

78. Quoted in Stout, p19

79. Quoted in Bob Trubshaw, *Sacred Places: Prehistory and the PopularImagination,* (Heart of Albion Press, 2005), p87

80. Ibid, p4

81. Ibid, pxiii
Merlin Coverley, *Psychogeography,* Rev. Ed. (Pocket Essentials, 2010), p16

CHAPTER NINE

1.   Thomas Gent, *The Ancient and Modern History of the Famous City of York* (Thomas Hammond, 1730), p234

2.   Richard Rutherford-Moore, *Robin Hood: On the Outlaw Trail Again* (Capell Bann Pub-

lishing, 2004), p105-6

3. Lewis Spence, "The Supernatural Character of Robin Hood" in *Hibbert Journal* Vol. 40 (1947), p285-6

4. Ibid, p286

5. J.C. Holt, *Robin Hood,* Rev. Ed. (Thames & Hudson Ltd, 1989), p106

6. Janet Bord, *Footprints In Stone* (Heart of Albion Press, 2004), p124

7. Leslie V. Grinsell, *Folklore of Prehistoric Sites in Britain* (David and Charles PLC, 1976), p60

8. Ibid, p64

9. Ibid, p65

10. Julian Cope, *The Modern Antiquarian: A Pre-Millennial Odyssey Through Megalithic Britain* (Harper Collins, 1998) p238-9

11. Dudley Costello, *Holidays With Hobgoblins* (John Camden Hotton, 1861), p220-2

12. *Notes and Queries,* 8th April 1876

13. J. Horsfall Turner, *History of Brighouse, Rastrick and Hipperholme* (Thomas Harrison and Sons, 1893), p204

14. Grinsell, p15

15. Ibid, p60

16. Rev. John Watson, *The History and Antiquities of the Parish of Halifax* (Lowdnes, 1775), p27

17. Bord, p129

18. Paul Bennett, *The Old Stones of Elmet* (Capall Bann, 2003), p167

19. Jessica Lofthouse, *North Country Folklore* (Robert Hale Ltd., 1976), p158

20. Waton, p27

21. Bennett, p171

22. John Crabtree, *A Concise History of the Parish and Vicarage of Halifax* (Hartley and Walker, 1836), p28

23. Raymond Varley, "A Stone-Axe Hammer, Robin Hood's Penny Stone and Stone Circle at Wainstalls, Warley near Halifax" in *Yorkshire Archaeological Journal* Vol. 69 (1997), p9

24. Bennett, p169

25. Loc. cit.

26. John Billingsley, *Folk Tales from Calderdale: Place Legends and Lore from the Calder Valley* Vol. 1 (Northern Earth, 2007), p83

27. Bennett, p169

28. Billingsley, p59

29. David Staveley, "Giants of the Sussex Hills" in *Northern Earth* No. 125 (2011), p11

30. David Haigh, "Fax Fallacies" in *Transactions of the Halifax Antiquarian Society* (1991), p129-30

31. Bennett, p85

32. W.B. Crump, "The Site of Robin Hood's Grave" in *Yorkshire Archaeological Journal* Volume 37 (1950), p105-6

33. Abraham Newell, "Long Causeway Crosses from Yorkshire to Lancashire" in *Transactions of the Halifax Antiquarian Society* (1911), 178

34. Ibid, p177

35. Loc. cit.

36. http://www.calderdale.gov.uk/environment/conservation/ancient-monuments/monuments-full.jsp?propno=HSK54ODWL2000

37. Newell, p177

38. Alfred Watkins, *The Old Straight Track* Rev. Ed. (Abacus, 1994) p23-4

39. Gerald Findler, *Legends of the Lake Counties* (Dalesman Publishing Company, 1967), p49

40. Newell, p181

41. John Walker and Michael Nevell, *Folklore of Tameside: Myths and Legends* (Tameside Metropolitan Borough Council, 1988), p31

42. Thomas Middleton, *Legends of Longdendale* (Fred Higham, 1906), p35-6

43. J. Horsfall Turner, Ed., *Yorkshire Notes and Queries* Vol. 1, (T. Harrison, 1888), p62

44. Philip Ahier, *Legends and Traditions of Huddersfield and Its District* Vol. 2 (The Advertiser Press, 1943), p283

45. Ibid, p288

46. Kerry Sykes, *An Archaeological Survey of Kirklees Park* (Publisher and date unknown). p5

47. F.R. Pearson, *Roman Yorkshire* (A. Brown and Sons, 1937), p38

48. Watkins, p27

49. David Shepherd, "Prehistoric Standing Stones In the South Pennines" in *Transactions of the Halifax Antiquarian Society* (2009), p22

50. Ahier, p50

51. Holt, p107

Stephen Knight and Thomas Ohlgren (2), "A Gest of Robyn Hode: An Introduction" in *Robin Hood and Other Outlaw Tales* (Medieval Institute Publications, 1997)
        Online at http://www.lib.rochester.edu/camelot/teams/gestint.htm

53. Hepworth, p106

54. Hepworth, p111-2

55. Eileen Power, *Medieval English Nunneries* (Cambridge University Press, 1922), p180

56. Billingsley, p80

57. Loc. cit.

Ibid, p81

CHAPTER TEN

1. David Hepworth, "A Grave Tale" in Helen Phillips, Ed., *Robin Hood: Medieval and Post*

Medieval (Four Courts Press, 2005), p94

2. Hepworth, p112
3. Hepworth, p106
4. Ibid, p107
5. Ibid, p109-10
6. Ibid, p96
7. Loc. cit.
8. Ibid, p107
9. Richard Griffith, "Kirk-Leas: A descriptive poem" (T. Burton, 1802)
10. Hepworth, p107
11. Christopher McIntosh, *Gardens of the Gods: Myth, Magic and Meaning* (I.B. Tauris, 2004), p105
12. Jacqueline Simpson and Steve Roud, *A Dictionary of English Folklore* (Oxford University Press, 2000), p299
13. Venetia J. Newell, "The Adaptation of Folklore and Tradition (Folklorismus) in *Folklore* Vol. 98, No. 2 (1987), p131
14. William S. Fox, "Folklore and Fakelore: Some Sociological Considerations" in *Journal of the Folklore Institute,* Vol. 17, No. 2/3 (1980), p252
15. Newell, p146
16. Hepworth, p95
17. *Yorkshire Post,* 6th February 2004
18. Séan Manchester, *The Vampire Hunter's Handbook,* (Gothic Press, 1997), p31
19. Séan Manchester, email to author, 19th March 2011
20. Manchester, p29
21. *Hampstead and Highgate Express,* 6th March 1970
22. Manchester, p29
23. Barbara Green, *Secrets of the Grave* (Palmyra Press, 2001), p91
24. Séan Manchester, letter to Barbara Green, 17th February 1989
25. Bill Ellis, "The Highgate Cemetery Vampire Hunt: The Anglo-American Connection In Cult Lore" in *Folklore* Vol. 104, No 1/2 (1993), p18
26. Ibid, p24
27. Bill Ellis, "Death By Folklore: Ostension, Contemporary Legend and Murder" in *Western Folklore* Vol. 48, No. 3 (1989), p208
28. Elizabeth Bird, "Playing With Fear: Interpreting the Adolescent Legend Trip" in *Western Folklore* Vol. 53, No. 3 (1994), p191
29. Donald H. Holly Jnr. and Casey E. Cordy, "What's In a Coin? Reading the Material Culture of Legend Tripping and Other Activities" in *Journal of American Folklore* Vol. 120 2007), p345
30. Ellis (2001), p191

31. Bird, p192
32. Bill Ellis, *Aliens, Ghosts and Cults: Legends We Live* (University of Mississippi Press, 2001), p188
33. Bird, p203
34. Holly and Cordy, p345
35. Bird, p199
36. Ellis (2001), p190
37. Ibid, p188
38. Ellis (1993), p20
39. Loc. cit.
40. "The Right Rev. Dr. Séan Manchester OSG" in *Folklore* Vol. 10 (1996), p108
41. *Huddersfield Daily Examiner,* 13th January 1988
42. *Spenborough Guardian,* 16th May 1997
43. Personal recollection by author
44. Green, p94
45. Linda Dégh and Andrew Vázsonyi, "Does the Word Dog Bite? Ostensive Action: A Means of Legend Telling" in *Journal of Folklore Research* Vol. 20, No. 1 (1983), p6-7
46. Ibid, p8
47. Ellis (2001), p162
48. Ibid, p9-15
49. Ibid, p19
50. Ibid, p20
51. Ellis (1993), p28
52. Loc. cit.
53. Green, p94
54. Ellis (2001), pxiv
55. Bob Trubshaw, *Sacred Places: Prehistory and the PopularImagination,* (Heart of Albion Press, 2005), p111
56. Dégh and Vázsonyi, p16
57. Patrick Harpur, *Daimonic Reality: A Field Guide to the Otherworld* (Arkana, 1995), p112-3
58. S.J. Chadwick, "Kirklees Priory" in *Yorkshire Archaeological Journal* 16 (1902), p319
59. Valerie Shepherd, *Holy Wells of West Yorkshire and the Dales,* Rev.Ed. (Lepus Press, 2004), p35
60. Sir George Armytage, "Kirklees Priory" in *Yorkshire Archaeological Journal* 20 (1906), p26
61. Harpur, p92
62. Colin McGinn, *The Subjective View: Secondary Qualities and Indexical Thoughts* (Oxford University Press, 1983)

63. Harpur, p35

64. Robert Reid, *Land of Lost Content: The Luddite Rebellion of 1812,* (William Heinemann Ltd. 1986), p10

65. Quoted in Duncan Wu, Ed., *Romanticism: An Anthology Rev. Ed.* (Blackwell, 2005), p1351

Gabriel Marcel, *Being and Having,* Trans. Katherine Farrer (Dacre Press, 1949), p117

ROBIN HOOD & CLORINDA

A mery geſte of

Robyn Hoode and othys lyfe, wyth
a newe playe for to be played
in Maye games very ple-
ſalinte and ſtill of paſtyme.

Lytel John

APPENDIX ONE

ROBIN HOOD'S DEATH

(PERCY FOLIO)

'I WILL neuer eate oor drinke,' Robin Hood said,
'Nor meate will doo me noe good,
Till I haue beene at merry Churchlees,
My vaines for to let blood.'

'That I reade not,' said Will Scarllett,
'Master, by the assente of me,
Without halfe a hundred of your best bowmen
You take to goe with yee.

'For there a good yeoman doth abide
Will be sure to quarrell with thee,
And if thou haue need of vs, master,
In faith we will not flee.'

'And thou be feard, thou William Scarlett,
Att home I read thee bee:'
'And you be wrothe, my deare master,
You shall neuer heare more of mee.'

'For there shall noe man with me goe,
Nor man with mee ryde,
And Litle Iohn shall be my man,
And beare my benbow by my side.'

'You'st beare your bowe, master, your selfe,
And shoote for a peny with mee:'
'To that I doe assent,' Robin Hood sayd,

'And soe, Iohn, lett it bee.'

They two bolde children shotten together,
All day theire selfe in ranke,
Vntill they came to blacke water,
And over it laid a planke.

Vpon it there kneeled an old woman,
Was banning Robin Hoode;
'Why dost thou bann Robin Hoode?' said Robin,

...BREAK...

'To giue to Robin Hoode;
Wee weepen for his deare body,
That this day must be lett bloode.'

'The dame prior is my aunts daughter,
And nie vnto my kinne;
I know shee wold me noe harme this day,
For all the world to winne.'

Forth then shotten these children two,
And they did neuer lin,
Vntill they came to merry Churchlees,
To merry Churchlee[s] with-in.

And when they came to merry Churchlees,
They knoced vpon a pin;
Vpp then rose dame prioresse,
And lett good Robin in.

Then Robin gaue to dame prioresse
Twenty pound in gold,
And bad her spend while that wold last,
And shee shold haue more when shee wold.

And downe then came dame prioresse,
Downe she came in that ilke,
With a pair off blood-irons in her hands,
Were wrapped all in silke.

'Sett a chaffing-dish to the fyer,' said dame prioresse,
'And stripp thou vp thy sleeue:'
I hold him but an vnwise man

That will noe warning leeve.

Shee laid the blood-irons to Robin Hoods vaine,
Alacke, the more pitye!
And pearct the vaine, and let out the bloode,
That full red was to see.

And first it bled, the thicke, thicke bloode,
And afterwards the thinne,
And well then wist good Robin Hoode
Treason there was within.

'What cheere my master?' said Litle Iohn;
'In faith, Iohn, litle goode;'

...BREAK...

'I haue upon a gowne of greene,
Is cut short by my knee,
And in my hand a bright browne brand
That will well bite of thee.'

But forth then of a shot-windowe
Good Robin Hood he could glide;
Red Roger, with a grounden glaue,
Thrust him through the milke-white side.

But Robin was light and nimble of foote,
And thought to abate his pride,
Ffor betwixt his head and his shoulders
He made a wound full wide.

Says, Ly there, ly there, Red Roger,
The doggs they must thee eate;
'For I may haue my houzle,' he said,
'For I may both goe and speake.

'Now giue me mood,' Robin said to Litle Iohn,
Giue me mood with thy hand;
I trust to God in heauen soe hye
My houzle will me bestand.'

Now giue me leaue, giue me leaue, master,' he said,
For Christs loue giue leaue to me,
To set a fier within this hall,

And to burne vp all Churchlee.'

'That I reade not,' said Robin Hoode then,
'Litle Iohn, for it may not be;
If I shold doe any widow hurt, at my latter end,
God,' he said, 'wold blame me;

'But take me vpon thy backe, Litle Iohn,
And beare me to yonder streete,
And there make me a full fayre graue,
Of grauell and of greete.

'And sett my bright sword at my head,
Mine arrowes at my feete,
And lay my vew-bow by my side,
My met-yard wi...

...BREAK...

APPENDIX TWO

A GEST OF ROBYN HODE
(EIGHTH FYTTE)

'Haste thou ony gren cloth,' sayd our kynge,
'That thou wylte sell nowe to me?'
'Ye, for God,' sayd Robyn,
'Thyrty yerd s and thre.'

'Robyn,' sayd our kynge,
'Now pray I the,
Sell me some of that cloth,
To me and my meyn .'

'Yes, for God,' then sayd Robyn,
'Or elles I were a fole;
Another day ye wyll me clothe,
I trowe, ayenst the Yole.'

The kynge kest of his col then,
A grene garment he dyde on,
And euery knyght also, i-wys,
Another had full sone.

Whan they were clothed in Lyncolne grene,
They keste away theyr graye;
'Now we shall to Notyngham,'
All thus our kynge gan say.

They bente theyr bowes, and forth they went,
Shotynge all in-fere,
Towarde the towne of Notyngham,

Outlawes as they were.
Our kynge and Robyn rode togyder,
For soth as I you say,
And they shote plucke-buffet,
As they went by the way.

And many a buffet our kynge wan
Of Robyn Hode that day,
And nothynge spared good Robyn
Our kynge in his pay.

'So God me help ,' sayd our kynge,
'Thy game is nought to lere;
I sholde not get a shote of the,
Though I shote all this yere.'

All the people of Notyngham
They stode and behelde;
They sawe nothynge but mantels of grene
That couered all the felde.

Than euery man to other gan say,
I drede our kynge be slone;
Com Robyn Hode to the towne, i-wys
On lyue he lefte neuer one.'

Full hastily they began to fle,
Both yemen and knaues,
And olde wyues that myght euyll goo,
They hypped on theyr staues.

The kynge l[o]ughe full fast,
And commaunded them agayne;
When they se our comly kynge,
I-wys they were full fayne.

They ete and dranke, and made them glad,
And sange with not s hye;
Than bespake our comly kynge
To Syr Rycharde at the Lee.

He gaue hym there his londe agayne,
A good man he bad hym be;
Robyn thanked our comly kynge,
And set hym on his kne.

Had robyn dwelled in the kyng s courte
But twelue monethes and thre,
That [he had] spent an hondred pounde,
And all his mennes fe.

In euery place where Robyn came
Euer more he layde downe,
Both for knyght s and for squyres,
To gete hym grete renowne.

By than the yere was all agone
He had no man but twayne,
Lytell Johan and good Scathlocke,
With hym all for to gone.

Robyn sawe yonge men shote
Full fayre vpon a day;
'Alas!' than sayd good Robyn,
'My welthe is went away.

'Somtyme I was an archere good,
A styffe and eke a stronge;
I was compted the best archere
That was in mery Englonde.

'Alas!' then sayd good Robyn,
'Alas and well a woo!
Yf I dwele lenger with the kynge,
Sorowe wyll me sloo.'

Forth than went Robyn Hode
Tyll he came to our kynge:
'My lorde the kynge of Englonde,
Graunte me myn askynge.

'I made a chapell in Bernysdale,
That semely is to se,
It is of Mary Magdaleyne,
And thereto wolde I be.

I myght neuer in this seuen nyght
No tyme to slepe ne wynke,
Nother all these seuen dayes
Nother ete ne drynke.

'Me longeth sore to Bernysdale,
 I may not be therfro;
 Barefote and wolwarde I haue hyght
 Thyder for to go.'

'Yf it be so,' than sayd our kynge,
 'It may no better be,
 Seuen nyght I gyue the leue,
 No lengre, to dwell fro me.'

'Gramercy, lorde,' then sayd Robyn,
 And set hym on his kne;
 He toke his leu full courteysly.
 To gren wode then went he.

Whan he came to gren wode,
 In a mery mornynge,
 There he herde the not s small
 Of byrd s mery syngynge.

'It is ferre gone,' sayd Robyn,
 'That I was last here;
 Me lyste a lytell for to shote
 At the donn dere.'

Robyn slewe a full grete harte;
 His horne than gan he blow,
 That all the outlawes of that forest
 That horne coud they knowe,

And gadred them togyder,
 In a lytell throwe.
 Seuen score of wyght yonge men
 Came redy on a rowe,

And fayre dyde of theyr hodes,
 And set them on theyr kne:
 'Welcome,' they sayd, 'our [der] mayster,
 Under this gren -wode tre.

Robyn dwelled in gren wode
 Twenty yere and two;
 For all drede of Edwarde our kynge,
 Agayne wolde he not goo.

Yet he was begyled, i-wys,
Through a wycked woman,
The pryoresse of Kyrk sly,
That nye was of hys kynne:

For the loue of a knyght,
Syr Roger of Donkesly,
That was her own speciall;
Full euyll mot they the!

They toke togyder theyr counsell
Robyn Hode for to sle,
And how they myght best do that dede,
His banis for to be.

Than bespake good Robyn,
In place where as he stode,
'To morow I muste to Kyrke[s]ly,
Craftely to be leten blode.'

Syr Roger of Donkestere,
By the pryoresse he lay,
And there they betrayed good Robyn Hode,
Through theyr fals playe.

Cryst haue mercy on his soule,
That dyed on the rode!
For he was a good outlawe,
And dyde pore men moch god.

APPENDIX THREE

ROBIN'S HOOD'S DEATH

(GARLAND)

WHEN Robin Hood and Little John
Down a down a down a down
Went oer yon bank of broom,
Said Robin Hood bold to Little John,
We have shot for many a pound.
Hey, etc.

But I am not able to shoot one shot more,
My broad arrows will not flee;
But I have a cousin lives down below,
Please God, she will bleed me.

Now Robin he is to fair Kirkly gone,
As fast as he can win;
But before he came there, as we do hear,
He was taken very ill.

And when he came to fair Kirkly-hall,
He knockd all at the ring,
But none was so ready as his cousin herself
For to let bold Robin in.

Will you please to sit down, cousin Robin,' she said,
And drink some beer with me?'
No, I will neither eat nor drink,
Till I am blooded by thee.'

'Well, I have a room, cousin Robin,' she said,
'Which you did never see,
And if you please to walk therein,
You blooded by me shall be.'

She took him by the lily-white hand,
And led him to a private room,
And there she blooded bold Robin Hood,
While one drop of blood would run down.

She blooded him in a vein of the arm,
And locked him up in the room;
Then did he bleed all the live-long day,
Until the next day at noon.

He then bethought him of a casement there,
Thinking for to get down;
But was so weak he could not leap,
He could not get him down.

He then bethought him of his bugle-horn,
Which hung low down to his knee;
He set his horn unto his mouth,
And blew out weak blasts three.

Then Little John, when hearing him,
As he sat under a tree,
'I fear my master is now near dead,
He blows so wearily.'

Then Little John to fair Kirkly is gone,
As fast as he can dree;
But when he came to Kirkly-hall,
He broke locks two or three:

Until he came bold Robin to see,
Then he fell on his knee;
'A boon, a boon,' cries Little John,
'Master, I beg of thee.'

'What is that boon,' said Robin Hood,
'Little John, [thou] begs of me?'
'It is to burn fair Kirkly-hall,
And all their nonnery.'

'Now nay, now nay,' quoth Robin Hood,
'That boon I'll not grant thee;
I never hurt woman in all my life,
Nor men in woman's company.

'I never hurt fair maid in all my time,
Nor at mine end shall it be;
But give me my bent bow in my hand,
And a broad arrow I'll let flee;
And where this arrow is taken up,
There shall my grave digged be.

'Lay me a green sod under my head,
And another at my feet;
And lay my bent bow by my side,
Which was my music sweet;
And make my grave of gravel and green,
Which is most right and meet.

'Let me have length and breadth enough,
With a green sod under my head;
That they may say, when I am dead
Here lies bold Robin Hood.'

These words they readily granted him,
Which did bold Robin please:
And there they buried bold Robin Hood,
Within the fair Kirkleys.

SOME PLACES MENTIONED IN THE TEXT

SITE	GRID REFERENCE
(Site of) Alegar Well, Brighouse	SE 151 228
Castle Hill, Almondbury	SE 152 140
Castle Hill, Kirklees	SE 173 216
Haigh Cross, Lindley	SE 107 188
Highgate Cemetery, London	TQ 284 870
Kirklees Hall, Kirklees	SE 170 222
(Site of) Kirklees Priory	SE 175 221
Kirklees Priory Gatehouse	SE 174 221
Lady Well, Hartshead	SE 177 235
Mount Cross, Todmorden	SD 915 272
Robin Hood's Bed, Blackstone Edge	SD 973 162
Robin Hood's Grave, Kirklees	SE 174 215
Robin Hood's Penny Stone, Midgley Moor	SE 018 284
(Site of) Robin Hood's Penny Stone, Wainstalls	SE 046 287
Robin Hood's Picking Rods, Ludworth Moor	SK 006 909
Robin Hood's Well, Barnsdale Bar	SE 518 120
St. Peter's Church, Hartshead	SE 179 233
Stump Cross, Mereclough	SD 879 302
The Three Nuns, Cooper Bridge	SE 181 211
Walton Cross, Hartshead	SE 175 237
White Rock, Luddenden Dean	SE 040 284

INDEX

ANIMALS & MEN
ISSUES 16-20
THE JOURNAL OF THE CENTRE FOR FORTEAN ZOOLOGY

NEW HORIZONS

Edited by Jon Downes

BIG CATS
LOOSE IN BRITAIN

PREDATOR DEATHMATCH

NICK MOLLOY
WITH ILLUSTRATIONS BY ANTHONY WALLIS

THE WORLD'S WEIRDEST PUBLISHING COMPANY

...TER!
...E ZOO...M PHENOMENA

Edited by
Jonathan Downes and Richard Freeman

FOREWORD BY Dr. KARL SHUKER

A DAINTREE DIARY
Tales from Travels ... Daintree
tropical North ... nsland, A...

CARL PORTMAN

THE COLLECTED POEMS
Dr Karl P. N. Shuker

STRANGELYSTRANGE
...ly normal

an anthology of writings by
ANDY ROBERTS

HOW TO START A PUBLISHING EMPIRE

Unlike most mainstream publishers, we have a non-commercial remit, and our mission state
ment claims that "we publish books because they deserve to be published, not because w
think that we can make money out of them". Our motto is the Latin Tag *Pro bona caus*
facimus (we do it for good reason), a slogan taken from a children's book *The Case of the Si*
ver Egg by the late Desmond Skirrow.

WIKIPEDIA: "The first book published was in 1988. *Take this Brother may it Serv*
you Well was a guide to Beatles bootlegs by Jonathan Downes. It sold quite well, bu
was hampered by very poor production values, being photocopied, and held togethe
by a plastic clip binder. In 1988 A5 clip binders were hard to get hold of, so the pub
lishers took A4 binders and cut them in half with a hacksaw. It now reaches surpris
ingly high prices second hand.

The production quality improved slightly over the years, and after 1999 all the book
produced were ringbound with laminated colour covers. In 2004, however, the
signed an agreement with Lightning Source, and all books are now produced perfec
bound, with full colour covers."

Until 2010 all our books, the majority of which are/were on the subject of mystery animal
and allied disciplines, were published by `CFZ Press`, the publishing arm of the Centre fc
Fortean Zoology (CFZ), and we urged our readers and followers to draw a discreet veil ove
the books that we published that were completely off topic to the CFZ.

However, in 2010 we decided that enough was enough and launched a second imprin
`Fortean Words` which aims to cover a wide range of non animal-related esoteric subject
Other imprints will be launched as and when we feel like it, however the basic ethos of th
company remains the same: Our job is to publish books and magazines that we feel are wort
publishing, whether or not they are going to sell. Money is, after all - as my dear old Mam
once told me - a rather vulgar subject, and she would be rolling in her grave if she thought tha
her eldest son was somehow in `trade`.

Luckily, so far our tastes have turned out nc
to be that rarified after all, and we have sol
far more books than anyone ever thought tha
we would, so there is a moral in there some
where…

Jon Downes,
Woolsery, North Devon
July 2010

CFZ PRESS

Other Books in Print

Weird Waters – The Mystery Animals of Scandinavia: Lake and Sea Monsters by Lars Thomas

The Inhumanoids by Barton Nunnelly

Monstrum! A Wizard's Tale by Tony "Doc" Shiels

CFZ Yearbook 2011 edited by Jonathan Downes

Karl Shuker's Alien Zoo by Shuker, Dr Karl P.N

Tetrapod Zoology Book One by Naish, Dr Darren

The Mystery Animals of Ireland by Gary Cunningham and Ronan Coghlan

Monsters of Texas by Gerhard, Ken

The Great Yokai Encyclopaedia by Freeman, Richard

NEW HORIZONS: Animals & Men *issues 16-20 Collected Editions Vol. 4*
by Downes, Jonathan

A Daintree Diary -
Tales from Travels to the Daintree Rainforest in tropical north Queensland, Australia
by Portman, Carl

Strangely Strange but Oddly Normal by Roberts, Andy

Centre for Fortean Zoology Yearbook 2010 by Downes, Jonathan

Predator Deathmatch by Molloy, Nick

Star Steeds and other Dreams by Shuker, Karl

CHINA: A Yellow Peril? by Muirhead, Richard

Mystery Animals of the British Isles: The Western Isles by Vaudrey, Glen

Giant Snakes - Unravelling the coils of mystery by Newton, Michael

Mystery Animals of the British Isles: Kent by Arnold, Neil

Centre for Fortean Zoology Yearbook 2009 by Downes, Jonathan

CFZ EXPEDITION REPORT: Russia 2008 by Richard Freeman *et al*, Shuker, Karl (fwd)

Dinosaurs and other Prehistoric Animals on Stamps - A Worldwide catalogue
by Shuker, Karl P. N

Dr Shuker's Casebook by Shuker, Karl P.N

The Island of Paradise - chupacabra UFO crash retrievals,
and accelerated evolution on the island of Puerto Rico by Downes, Jonathan

The Mystery Animals of the British Isles: Northumberland and Tyneside by Hallowell, Michael J

Centre for Fortean Zoology Yearbook 1997 by Downes, Jonathan (Ed)

Centre for Fortean Zoology Yearbook 2002 by Downes, Jonathan (Ed)

Centre for Fortean Zoology Yearbook 2000/1 by Downes, Jonathan (Ed)

Centre for Fortean Zoology Yearbook 1998 by Downes, Jonathan (Ed)
Centre for Fortean Zoology Yearbook 2003 by Downes, Jonathan (Ed)
In the wake of Bernard Heuvelmans by Woodley, Michael A
CFZ EXPEDITION REPORT: Guyana 2007 by Richard Freeman *et al*, Shuker, Karl (fwd)
Centre for Fortean Zoology Yearbook 1999 by Downes, Jonathan (Ed)
Big Cats in Britain Yearbook 2008 by Fraser, Mark (Ed)
Centre for Fortean Zoology Yearbook 1996 by Downes, Jonathan (Ed)
THE CALL OF THE WILD - Animals & Men issues 11-15
Collected Editions Vol. 3 by Downes, Jonathan (ed)
Ethna's Journal by Downes, C N
Centre for Fortean Zoology Yearbook 2008 by Downes, J (Ed)
DARK DORSET -Calendar Custome by Newland, Robert J
Extraordinary Animals Revisited by Shuker, Karl
MAN-MONKEY - In Search of the British Bigfoot by Redfern, Nick
Dark Dorset Tales of Mystery, Wonder and Terror by Newland, Robert J and Mark North
Big Cats Loose in Britain by Matthews, Marcus
MONSTER! - The A-Z of Zooform Phenomena by Arnold, Neil
The Centre for Fortean Zoology 2004 Yearbook by Downes, Jonathan (Ed)
The Centre for Fortean Zoology 2007 Yearbook by Downes, Jonathan (Ed)
CAT FLAPS! Northern Mystery Cats by Roberts, Andy
Big Cats in Britain Yearbook 2007 by Fraser, Mark (Ed)
BIG BIRD! - Modern sightings of Flying Monsters by Gerhard, Ken
THE NUMBER OF THE BEAST - Animals & Men issues 6-10
Collected Editions Vol. 1 by Downes, Jonathan (Ed)
IN THE BEGINNING - Animals & Men issues 1-5 Collected Editions Vol. 1 by Downes, Jonathan
STRENGTH THROUGH KOI - They saved Hitler's Koi and other stories by Downes, Jonathan
The Smaller Mystery Carnivores of the Westcountry by Downes, Jonathan
CFZ EXPEDITION REPORT: Gambia 2006 by Richard Freeman *et al*, Shuker, Karl (fwd)
The Owlman and Others by Jonathan Downes
The Blackdown Mystery by Downes, Jonathan
Big Cats in Britain Yearbook 2006 by Fraser, Mark (Ed)
Fragrant Harbours - Distant Rivers by Downes, John T
Only Fools and Goatsuckers by Downes, Jonathan
Monster of the Mere by Jonathan Downes
Dragons:More than a Myth by Freeman, Richard Alan
Granfer's Bible Stories by Downes, John Tweddell
Monster Hunter by Downes, Jonathan

Fortean Words

T he Centre for Fortean Zoology has for several years led the field in Fortean publishing. CFZ Press is the only publishing company specialising in books on monsters and mystery animals. CFZ Press has published more books on this subject than any other company in history and has attracted such well known authors as Andy Roberts, Nick Redfern, Michael Newton, Dr Karl Shuker, Neil Arnold, Dr Darren Naish, Jon Downes, Ken Gerhard and Richard Freeman.

Now CFZ Press are launching a new imprint. Fortean Words is a new line of books dealing with Fortean subjects other than cryptozoology, which is - after all - the subject the CFZ are best known for. Fortean Words is being launched with a spectacular multi-volume series called *Haunted Skies* which covers British UFO sightings between 1940 and 2010. Former policeman John Hanson and his long-suffering partner Dawn Holloway have compiled a peerless library of sighting reports, many that have not been made public before.

Other books include a look at the Berwyn Mountains UFO case by renowned Fortean Andy Roberts and a series of forthcoming books by transatlantic researcher Nick Redfern. CFZ Press are dedicated to maintaining the fine quality of their works with Fortean Words. New authors tackling new subjects will always be encouraged, and we hope that our books will continue to be as ground-breaking and popular as ever.

Haunted Skies Volume One 1940-1959 by John Hanson and Dawn Holloway
Haunted Skies Volume Two 1960-1965 by John Hanson and Dawn Holloway
Space Girl Dead on Spaghetti Junction - an anthology by Nick Redfern
Fort the Lore - an anthology by Paul Screeton
UFO Down - the Berwyn Mountains UFO Crash by Andy Roberts